CANADA: SYMBOLS OF SOVEREIGNTY

CONRAD SWAN
York Herald of Arms

Canada: Symbols of Sovereignty

An investigation of the arms and seals
borne and used from the earliest times
to the present in connection with
public authority in and over Canada,
along with consideration of
some connected flags

UNIVERSITY OF TORONTO PRESS
TORONTO AND BUFFALO

© University of Toronto Press 1977
Toronto and Buffalo
Printed in Canada

Library of Congress Cataloging in Publication Data

Swan, Conrad Marshall John Fisher, 1924 –
  Canada, symbols of sovereignty.
  Includes index.
  1. Heraldry – Canada. 2. Seals (Numismatics) –
  Canada. 3. Flags – Canada. 4. Canada – Seal.
  I. Title.
  CR212.S9   929.6'0971   76-20511
  ISBN 0-8020-5346-7

This book has been published during the
Sesquicentennial year of the University of Toronto.

Every reasonable precaution has been taken to trace the owners of copyright material and to make due
acknowledgment. Any omission will be gladly rectified in future editions.

This book is dedicated to

CONTENTS

PREFACE

The widespread use of arms and seals of public authority by almost every state in the world today is a fact so obvious as hardly to cause comment. Nevertheless, it is curious that while so much has been written upon such arms and seals as individual objects of study, they have attracted little attention as the expression of principles of constitutional as well as of international law.

Such late mediaeval treatises as *De Insigniis et Armis* by Bartolo di Sassoferrato and the eighteenth-century volume *A System of Heraldry* by Alexander Nisbet are among the very few works which treat of this aspect of arms. Indeed, since Nisbet little has been attempted save the repetition of his observations despite the immense developments which have taken place in this particular field of armory.

In a sense, seals of public authority have been better served. *Great Seals of England* by Alfred Benjamin and Allan Wyon (1887) and other learned monographs and articles attest to this fact. In more recent years, all of us have been placed under a further debt of gratitude by the work of other eminent scholars, such as the late Sir Hilary Jenkinson, the author of such studies as 'The Great Seal of England: Deputed or Departmental Seals' which appeared in *Archaeologia* in 1935/36; similarly, among French scholars we are indebted to Louis Rouvier for his *Chancellerie et Les Sceaux de France* (1950). Yet again, for those concerned with North America, and the colonial history of the United States in particular, the penetrating works of Peter Walne – starting with 'The Great Seal Deputed of Virginia' in 1958[1] – are of cardinal importance.

As far as Canada is concerned, 'The Insignia of New Brunswick' by the late W.F. Ganong in 1903[2] and 'The Great Seals and Arms of Ontario' by George W. Spragge in

1959[3] were the sole pioneer works until my 'Canadian Arms of Dominion and Sovereignty' appeared in 1960.[4]

The parallel relationship of arms of public authority to seals of public authority never appears to have been investigated either in Canada or elsewhere. Further, as Canada has developed from colony to sovereign state, its armorial and sigillographic experience affords a remarkable spectrum for investigation, not only as far as the actual arms and seals themselves are concerned as physical objects, but also as the expression of a basically organic evolution of constitutional concepts.

The purpose of this book is to study those arms and seals which have expressed in the past and do express now sovereign and public authority in relation to Canada; their rise, evolution, and development, along with their interrelationship and the constitutional arrangements of which they are functional, administrative symbols.

Some general principles and the armorial and sigillographic position of the federal authority are discussed in chapters 1 to 4. The remaining chapters are devoted to an investigation of the particular circumstances, both historical and contemporary, surrounding the arms and seals of the provinces and territories, in the order in which one notes the first continuous European settlement. This is an arbitrary division, but such are necessary in works of this nature.

Conrad Swan
York

College of Arms
London

.

1 *The Virginia Magazine of History and Biography* 66, 1, pp. 1-21
2 *Acadiensis* 3, pp. 135-42
3 *Ontario History* 51, 1, pp. 32-37
4 *Recueil du Ve Congrès International des Sciences Généalogique et Héraldique à Stockholm 1960* (Stockholm 1961) pp. 250-73

ACKNOWLEDGMENTS

In connection with the preparation of this work I wish to record my particular gratitude to the Canada Council for their grant in aid of research; to St Thomas More College in the University of Saskatchewan who invited me to deliver, as their Canadian Centennial Project, 1967, the paper entitled 'Arms for Canada' upon which a part of this book is based; to my colleague Sir Anthony R. Wagner, KCVO, DLitt, FSA, Garter Principal King of Arms, for permission to study the *Garter Papers;* to my other brother officers of the College of Arms for numerous kindnesses, much encouragement, and sympathetic assistance at all times; and to my publishers, University of Toronto Press, who despite many difficulties caused by the present inflation have, notwithstanding, persevered in the publication of this work. In this regard I am particularly indebted to R.I.K. Davidson, Editor (Social Sciences), and to Margaret Parker of the Editorial Department.

In addition to these I am indebted for help by many others who are mentioned at appropriate points in the course of this book and to those who have granted permission for the use of illustrations and other material (see pages 261-2).

Publication of this volume has been made possible by grants from the Social Science Research Council of Canada, using funds provided by the Canada Council, and from the Publications Fund of the University of Toronto Press, including grants to that press from the Andrew W. Mellon Foundation, the Ontario Arts Council, and the University of Toronto.

ABBREVIATIONS

PANS Public Archives of Nova Scotia
PAO Public Archives of Ontario
PRO Public Record Office, London
QSA Queensland State Archives
ROM Royal Ontario Museum, Toronto
SA Society of Antiquaries of London
Tonnochy Tonnochy, A.B. *Catalogue of British Seal Dies in the British Museum.* London, Trustees of the British Museum 1952
UKA Records of Ulster King of Arms
WCS Wyon Collection of Seals
14 and 15 Garter Volumes fourteen and fifteen of the bound *Garter Papers*

Numbers in the text between brackets refer to colour plates (e.g. [plate 1.1]), or figures (e.g. [2.1]). Notes may be found at the end of each chapter.

PLATES

The following Herald Painters, College of Arms, have prepared illustrations for this volume:

John Bainbridge plates 2.1, 2.2, 6, 17, 21.1, and 21.2 and figures 4.8, 4.9, 6.1, and C5

Frank Berry plates 15.1 and 18.1 and figure 11.3

F. Booth plate 14

Gerald Cobb, MVO plate 16.1

Dulcie Corner plate 20.1

Dennis Field all flags

Henry W. Gray, MVO plates 16.2 and 20.2 and the armorial dedication

Norman Manwaring, Hon. FHS plates 7 and 8

Geoffrey Mussett plate 18.2

Robert J. Parsons, BA, ATC plates 11.1, 15.2, and 19 and figure 10.10

1.1 'Englishmen in a skirmish with Eskimos' after John White, almost certainly during Frobisher's expedition to Baffin Island in 1577 (detail). This illustration, showing the banner of St George charged in the centre with the arms of Elizabeth I, is the earliest known contemporary example of the use of arms of dominion and sovereignty in Canada

BL

1.2 Biscuit-coloured dependent seal, typical of the colonial period prior to c. 1832: obverse of the second George III Great Seal Deputed of Upper Canada

ROM: 970.312.2

2.1 Armorial bearings of La Compagnie des Indes occidentales

2.2 Armorial bearings of La Compagnie d'occident

3 *Royal Arms of France surrounded by the collars of St Michael (nearer shield) and the Holy Ghost.*
Polychrome woodcarving taken from a gate at Quebec in 1759
PAC

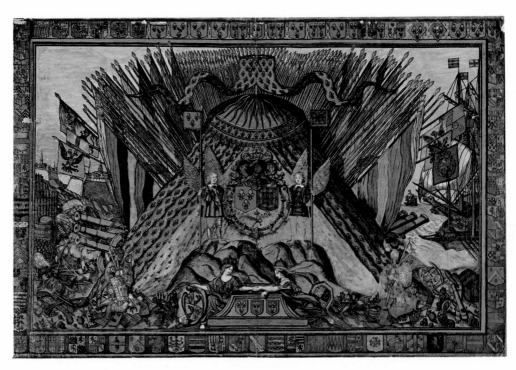

4 Full achievement of the Royal Arms of France (from 1589) without motto (see figure 3.9)
Bibl. nat., Paris

5 *Royal Arms (from 1603) of James VI and I as King of Scotland.*
Original study prepared under the supervision of Sir Thomas Innes of Learney, Lord Lyon King of Arms
Author's collection

6 *Armorial bearings of the Hudson's Bay Company*

7 *Armorial bearings of Spain*

8 Armorial bearings of Imperial Russia

9 Illuminated heading of indenture for Henry VII's Chapel,
Westminster Abbey, showing the Royal Arms of Henry VII (1485-1509)
PRO E33/2. Crown copyright

10 Royal Stuart arms showing those of James VI and I as King of England (1603-25).
Contemporary illumination on vellum
CA: M7. Kts: Bath & Gart: f. 46

11.1 Arms of Nassau for William III (1689-1701)

11.2 Royal arms as borne 1714-1801. Polychrome woodcarving in Trinity Church, St John, New Brunswick

HIS

MOST EXCELLENT MAJESTY

KING GEORGE

THE THIRD.

12 *Royal arms as borne 1801-16, from the vellum Bath Book prepared for George III in 1803 by George Nayler, Genealogist and Blanc-Coursier Herald of the Order of the Bath* CA: *Bath Book, p. 13*

13.1 Royal arms as borne 1816-37. Panel behind the justices' bench in the Supreme Court of New Brunswick, Fredericton (tempus George IV, 1820-30)

13.2 Royal arms of general purpose as borne from 1837, and up to 1931 for Canada, from Garter's Roll of the 4th Session of the 13th Parliament of the United Kingdom, 26 January 1841 House of Lords Record Office: Garter's Roll 176

14 Armorial bearings of dominion and sovereignty and of general purpose of Her Majesty the Queen in right of Canada, frequently referred to, for brevity's sake, as the arms of Canada

15.1 Arms of Prince Edward Island

15.2 Armorial bearings of Newfoundland

16.1 *Arms of New Brunswick*

16.2 *Arms of Quebec*

17 Armorial bearings of Nova Scotia

18.1 Arms of Manitoba

18.2 Arms of Saskatchewan

19 Armorial bearings of Ontario

20.1 *Arms of Alberta*

20.2 *Arms of British Columbia*

21.1   Armorial bearing of the Northwest Territories

21.2   Armorial bearings of the Yukon Territory

22.1 *National flag of Canada*

22.2 *The Queen's personal Canadian flag*

22.3 *Flag of the Governor General*

22.4 *Flag of the Lieutenant Governor of Manitoba*

22.5 *The Union Banner or Jack*

23.1 Flag of Nova Scotia

23.2 Flag of Prince Edward Island

23.3 Flag of New Brunswick

23.4 Flag of Quebec

23.5 Flag of Ontario

24.1 *Flag of Manitoba*

24.2 *Flag of Saskatchewan*

24.3 *Flag of Alberta*

24.4 *Flag of British Columbia*

24.5 *Flag of the Northwest Territories*

24.6 *Flag of the Yukon Territory*

CANADA: SYMBOLS OF SOVEREIGNTY

CHAPTER I

Arms of dominion and sovereignty and of public authority

The basic function of arms is identification.[1] The arms of sovereign authorities – known technically as arms of dominion and sovereignty – are borne in order to identify armorially their authority and jurisdiction.[2] While sovereignty is considered classically as, in the first instance, based on territory, nevertheless the arms of sovereign states identify not a given geographical area but rather that intangible supreme authority – sovereignty vested in one person, persons, or institutions of the state concerned, depending upon its particular constitution. Were this not so, and if the ensigns were intended to identify a precise geographical-political territory, then, logically, the slightest increase or decrease in its size would have to be reflected in a variation of the arms concerned. This would have resulted, by way of example, in some twenty-six changes, at least, in the Arms of the United States in order to accommodate the growth from the original thirteen to the present fifty states of the Union. In fact, the Arms of the United States, as established by Act of Congress in 1782,[3] which expressed sovereign authority exercised over an area comprising a narrow strip down the eastern seaboard of America, had in no way to be changed when mile after mile to the west was brought under that same sovereign authority in the course of the next one and a half centuries.[4]

Conversely, when the Netherlands was completely overrun by the armies of the Third Reich during World War II, Queen Wilhelmina and her government had to function from foreign soil,[5] yet this was done without any essential diminution of the basic authority of that sovereignty. The result was that the arms expressive of particular public authority needed in no way to be altered despite the complete loss of the geographical-political territory upon which, originally, the sovereign power had been based.

Such examples can be multiplied almost *ad infinitum,* but the two cited will, I feel, make the point abundantly clear that arms of sovereign authorities relate primarily to authority and not to territory.

It will, therefore, be appreciated that such arms are not in essence hereditary, but rather pass by succession, election, or conquest. Accordingly, from the moment Her present Majesty succeeded King George VI as sovereign she began to bear the identical royal arms that the previous sovereign had borne, not primarily by virtue of being the daughter of her father, but rather because she had become the Queen Regnant, and the armorial expression of that office happens to be certain royal arms which the previous sovereign had borne as sovereign and for no other reason.

Indeed, the *sui generis* character of such arms is well borne out by the armorial position of the royal children. Unlike those of other armigerous parents, the royal offspring have no hereditary rights to the parental arms *per se.* Other children have from the moment of birth an incipient right to the arms of their armigerous fathers while the royal children must wait until some particular moment when the regnant parent decides to assign arms for the prince or princess. Usually such arms follow the general design of the arms of the sovereign, but each element in the case of a royal child is always very carefully differenced by a label or other means.[6] Technically, as *differenced* arms they are different arms, and so escape the solecism of two or more persons bearing the symbol of supreme sovereignty which, constitutionally, may be borne by one person only.[7] No state can be indifferent to such acts.

When through succession two or more sovereignties come to be held by one person, as when James VI of Scotland succeeded to the throne of England in 1603, the armorial ensigns of the several sovereignties are usually marshalled together. Similarly, when George Louis of Hanover succeeded to the throne as George I of Great Britain, the arms of dominion and sovereignty of his German dominions were combined on one shield with those of Great Britain and of Ireland.

When election brings about exercise of sovereign authority, the arms which pertain to that authority are borne frequently, but not always, in combination with the personal arms of the elected ruler. Accordingly, when Prince William of Orange was elected by Parliament to be William III of England in 1689 he bore the same royal arms as had all sovereigns of that country since 1603, and to these he added his own personal Arms of Nassau.[8] A similar case is that of the elective kings of Poland between the sixteenth and eighteenth centuries.[9]

On the other hand, the Grand Masters of the Sovereign and Military Order of Malta have from very early days to the present quartered the arms of the order with their own.[10] In some cases, as with the popes, their personal arms alone are borne which, however, are marshalled with certain external insignia of sovereignty – the tiara and crossed keys. In other instances, for example, the presidents of the United States of America, personal arms are not combined with those borne *ex officio* as exercising the sovereign authority, whether they have been elected to that office or have succeeded, by virtue of the constitution, following the demise of a president in office. Similarly, with the election in 1905 of Prince Carl of Denmark to be King of Norway, as Haakon VII, he bore the arms of dominion and sovereignty of Norway alone,[11] as does his son, King Olaf V.

The third way mentioned by which such arms of authority may pass is by conquest, whether by invasion or internal revolution. Accordingly, when, following his victory at the Battle of Bosworth Field in 1485, Henry Tudor became Henry VII of England, he immediately bore the appropriate arms of sovereign authority to the exclusion of his own personal arms.[12] Similar instances in modern times in South America and Africa, where revolutionary victors have taken over the official arms of their predecessors in the supreme office of the state, are too numerous to mention, but will be familiar to all.

When conquest is achieved by a sovereign authority, then it is usual for the arms of the latter to replace the previous ensigns of dominion and sovereignty. Accordingly, when, as a result of Queen Anne's War, peninsular Nova Scotia was transferred from the French to the British Crown by the Treaty of Utrecht, in 1713, the arms of the former were replaced by those of the latter as the ensigns of public authority over that area; a similar case is that of New France following the French and Indian War and its conclusion by the Treaty of Paris, in 1763, as will be discussed in chapter 3.

The origin of arms of sovereign authority at times may be found in personal arms, as with the celebrated Scottish lion within a double tressure flory counter-flory, probably borne first by King William the Lion and certainly by his son Alexander II (1214-49). Soon they had become so identified with the Scottish Crown that they became the armorial expression of its jurisdiction and so ensigns of sovereign authority. As a consequence these arms were borne by all subsequent Scottish kings, whether of the original house or not, upon succeeding to the throne.[13]

A similar change from private use to official function appears to have taken place with the French fleur-de-lis which was already a badge under Louis VII (1137-80), although it was not placed on the Royal Seal of France until the time of Louis VIII (1223-6).

On the other hand, some arms have been arms of dominion and sovereignty from the outset, as with the harp of Ireland. This started as a Tudor badge,[14] but with the accession of James VI and I to the crowns of England and Ireland he constituted the third quarter of his royal arms as *azure a harp or, stringed argent,* in token of his sovereignty in and over Ireland.

When discussing arms of dominion and sovereignty it will be convenient to make a distinction between, on the one hand, those used for *general purposes,* which may, therefore, be described as *arms of general purpose,* and, on the other hand, those used for *particular purposes,* which, similarly, may be described as *arms of particular purpose.* Accordingly, it will be seen that the royal arms as borne by the Kings of France in token of their sovereign authority, whether in France or across the seas in New France, were one and the same and might therefore be described as the ensigns for the general purposes of government, that is to say in the administration of their realms wherever situated, as will be discussed in detail in chapter 3.

Similarly, what are frequently termed the English and then the British Royal Arms are ensigns for the general purposes of government and have been and are borne and used in all the sovereign's realms and territories, wherever they may be, for which particular arms have not been assigned. This follows from the nature of such arms, which, as we have already seen, refer essentially to authority, and not to geography.

However, we note that from an early date arms have been assigned for particular purposes, in other words to serve as ensigns of public authority, as ensigns expressing the sovereign authority, for particular departmental purposes and specific areas of administration. As a result, even within a unitary state, such as the United Kingdom, it will be noted that the royal authority expresses itself armorially in one way for general and supreme purposes and in others for specific, particular purposes. Thus we note the royal arms for use within Scotland,[15] which are ensigns of public authority, notwithstanding the many and real differences between them and that form of the royal arms used in other parts of the United Kingdom, for example.

Similarly, there was an historic development overseas, as with the arms for Nova Scotia (c. 1625), Newfoundland (1638), Jamaica (1661), Ontario, and the other three foundation provinces of Canada (1868), and subsequently for the other provinces. All of these arms are in fact arms of the sovereign *in right of* Nova Scotia, Newfoundland and so on, for the *particular purposes* of administration, in connection with the governing of certain areas.[16] For the sake of brevity and convenience, we frequently refer to such arms as the 'Arms of Nova Scotia' and the like, but it will be appreciated that they identify public authority and not a geographical area, let alone even the inhabitants subject to that public authority.

It is of interest to note that in the seventeenth century, when the arms of Nova Scotia and of Jamaica were assigned, the helm borne as part of the complete armorial achievement, certainly for the latter, was a royal helm.[17] In view of what has just been said, this would appear to be logical. Arms for Newfoundland were also assigned at about this time, but no contemporary examples of the helm borne in connection with them appear to have survived.

However, almost two centuries passed before further arms were assigned in connection with overseas authority. When they were, in 1868, for the four foundation provinces of Canada, arms only, without crests, were established, so that the question of what helm was appropriate did not arise. Nevertheless, by the turn of the nineteenth and twentieth centuries, with dominion status a new yet developing phenomenon within the British Empire, it was obviously felt that a royal helm was inappropriate for arms assigned for a dominion or its provinces as it had apparently come to be identified in the official mind as a token of supreme sovereignty when used in association with arms of public authority. Accordingly, when arms were established for the Commonwealth of Australia in 1908 and 1912[18] and again for the Union of South Africa in 1910,[19] while crests were provided in each case, in none was a helm laid down in the official records. Similarly, when a crest was added to the existing armorial achievement for Ontario in 1909, no particular helm was assigned. Indeed, it would seem that the first time a helm was established for a dominion was in the 1921 Royal Proclamation of Arms for Canada. The helm assigned on this occasion was a royal helm, but this was regarded then as a special exception. When the time finally came to decide upon a helm appropriate for provincial arms which had a crest, the form chosen was a tilting helm of steel, vizor closed facing the viewer's left.[20] This type of helm goes back to the earliest days of heraldry, when it was borne by both sovereign and knight. It will be appreciated that the variation in helms now used in order to indicate rank, degree, and status did not come into general use in armory until relatively modern times. The royal helm laid down for Nova Scotia upon the restoration of its ancient arms in 1929 is an exception based on seventeenth-century usage at the time when these ensigns were originally assigned.

Arms of public authority can, naturally, alter in their status depending upon the nature of the authority they signify. Accordingly, it has been known for arms of dominion and sovereignty of a completely independent state to become those of a province. An example of this would be the arms of Poland: *gules, an eagle displayed argent, crowned or*. Until the late eighteenth century these were the arms of a sovereign state. After the partitions of Poland they became, eventually, the arms of a province within the Russian Empire and were so marshalled on the dexter wing of the eagle supporter of the arms of dominion and sovereignty of that authority.[21] Following World War I, the Arms of Poland once again became those of a sovereign state.

Other changes in the significance and status of arms can take place, as with those of Canada. When assigned in 1921 they were the royal arms of the sovereign in right of Canada. That is to say, they were the armorial expression of supreme internal public authority throughout the whole of Canada and so expressed public authority in its federal aspect.

Vis-à-vis the royal arms for general purposes borne by the sovereign as exercising the supreme authority throughout the entire British Empire as then conceived and understood with all its legal and constitutional implications, the royal arms assigned for Canada in 1921 stood basically in much the same relationship as do the royal arms as borne in Scotland. In other words, they were royal arms for specific yet restricted and internal purposes, and could *not* at that date be regarded as arms of dominion and sovereignty of a sovereign and independent state; in short, they were arms of particular purpose.

However, during the next decade the constitutional position of Canada evolved steadily.[22] By 1931, with the Statute of Westminster,[23] formal recognition was given to equality of constitutional status as sovereign states between Great Britain and Canada and those other self-governing parts of the British Commonwealth then described as dominions.

For some time Canada had acted as a sovereign entity, not only internally, but also in her international relations, by making war and peace, concluding treaties, exchanging ambassadors, and the like. The Statute of Westminster simply accorded formal parliamentary recognition to a pre-existing situation – a familiar and recurring pattern often noted in those areas of history with which the British are concerned.

Indeed the statute, passed in December 1931, was anticipated heraldically by the introduction of a new official flag for the Governor General of Canada in February of that year.[24] Before this, his flag had consisted of the Union Banner or Flag, commonly called the Union Jack, debruised in the centre by a plate or white disc charged with the Arms of Canada ensigned by a royal crown and surrounded by a wreath of maple leaves. Thus was identified the representative of both the sovereign *and* the imperial government. By the time of the statute this dual role no longer obtained, and the Governor General had become the personal representative of the sovereign *alone*. Accordingly, when the Earl of Bessborough was about to take up his duties as Governor General it was decided to change the official flag to consist of an oblong, dark blue background on which was placed *upon a royal crown proper, a lion statant guardant royally crowned also proper,* and underneath a gold scroll inscribed CANADA in letters sable.[25] As the Crown was 'the symbol of the unity of the Empire,'[26] it was felt, apparently, that a part of those royal ensigns most anciently associated with the monarchy would be appropriate as the heraldic identification of the sovereign's personal representative. Accordingly, the crest from the royal armorial bearings of general purpose was chosen as the principal charge.

Other heraldic reflections of the changing constitutional position of Canada followed. Of these, possibly the most significant was the design of the Great Seal of Canada of King George VI.

The constitutional importance of the great seal, that *clavis regni* as it has been called,[27] will be appreciated. Further discussion follows in chapter 2, and it will suffice to recall here that from Confederation onwards, every great seal of Canada had displayed as its principal heraldic adjunct the royal arms *of general purpose,* with Canada represented by shields of arms of the four foundation provinces. With the Great Seal of George VI a radical change was made in that the traditional armorial elements were replaced entirely by the armorial bearings of Canada as assigned in 1921. From this great seal onwards, and so including that of Her present Majesty, the *sole* heraldic identification is in this form.[28]

Granted to identify federal public authority, the Arms of Canada assigned in 1921 evolved in their significance as the federal authority evolved with the gradual constitutional developments of the period. Following the Statute of Westminster and the formal recognition of Canada as a sovereign state, the arms became the expression of this characteristic and so arms of supreme rule, that is to say of dominion, and of self-determination, that is to say of sovereignty. In other words, they had become royal arms of dominion and sovereignty as borne by the sovereign in right of Canada and used in the federal administration and government, both for domestic and international purposes, in token of sovereign independence. In short, they had become arms of general purpose.

That arms can change in their significance follows essentially and logically from the fact that their very *raison d'être* is to signify, to identify in this instance, a particular authority. It seems almost too obvious to mention that that authority had a certain position both nationally and internationally in 1921 which was seminal compared with the position it holds at the time of writing (1975). However, when one is associated with a political entity which is organic in its constitutional development, as is Canada, one may, if one is not very careful, tend to see the past through the eyes of the present, a tendency which is fatal to a right appreciation of history and historical circumstances.

As has been touched upon already, provincial arms remain arms of particular purpose. They are the arms of the sovereign in right of Saskatchewan, Manitoba, and so on, in accordance with the federal constitution of Canada whereby certain powers are reserved exclusively for provincial exercise.

We note here a good example of how the phrase 'arms of particular purpose' can upon occasion signify somewhat different situations. It has been observed already that in the United Kingdom, the royal arms for use within Scotland are arms of particular purpose, but because of the unitary constitution of the state of which Scotland forms a part, they signify an authority somewhat different vis-à-vis the authority expressed by the Arms of Dominion and Sovereignty of the United Kingdom from, for example, the Arms of New Brunswick vis-à-vis the Arms of Dominion and Sovereignty of Canada. This follows from the fact that the constitutions of the two states concerned differ in fundamental respects.

Nevertheless, while there may be differences, all arms of particular purpose do have at least one essential characteristic in common, and that is that no matter how much of the sovereign power may constitutionally be reserved to the authority they represent – as in the case of Canadian provinces – arms of particular purpose identify an authority which is something less than the supreme sovereign authority of the state concerned.

From what has been said already, it follows from the Canadian constitution that the arms of the territories are arms of particular purpose.

It will be appreciated that arms of sovereignty are borne and displayed in all manner of ways when assertion of authority is required. They are to be found on great seals, letters patent, official publications, Crown property (movable and immovable), service uniforms, and official writing paper, and in a myriad other ways when authority is to be identified.

Indeed, it is of particular interest that the original claims laid to Canada by the explorers of the fifteenth and subsequent centuries were, as often as not, made in armorial form.

When John Cabot landed[29] on St John the Baptist's Day, 1497, he 'set up the royal banner (*bandera regia*)' (see figure 4.7) and took possession of the land in the name of King Henry VII of England,[30] and set up a large cross, 'una gran +'[31] This was in accordance with the letters patent issued on 5 March 1496 to Cabot and his sons, whereby they were empowered to sail on voyages of discovery under the 'banners, flags and ensigns' of the king, which they were to set up and so acquire 'the dominion, title and jurisdiction of the ... islands and mainlands so discovered' for Henry VII.[32] Such were the usual provisions for similar patents at this time.[33]

Some thirty-seven years later Jacques Cartier performed a similar heraldic ceremony at Gaspé Harbour on Friday, 24 July 1534. On this occasion, in the presence of a number of Indians, he records that he had 'a cross made thirty feet high ... unde the cross-bar of which we fixed a shield with three fleurs de lys in relief, and above it a wooden board, engraved in large Gothic characters, where was written VIVE LE ROY DE FRANCE'. He goes on to say, 'We erected this cross on the point in their presence and they watched it being put together and set up. And when it had been raised in the air, we all knelt down with our hands joined.'[34]

Impressive and indeed moving though these vignettes are, nevertheless possibly the fullest account we have of the assertion of sovereignty by means of heraldic ceremonial comes to us from *The Jesuit Relations*.[35] This took place at Sault Ste Marie at the instance of the Intendant Talon, who despatched Simon François Daumont sieur de Lusson 'to take possession, in his place and in his Majesty's name [Louis XIV], of the territories lying between the East and the West, from Montreal as far as the South sea, covering the utmost extent and range possible.'[36]

The place chosen for the ceremony was a hill overlooking the village of Sault Ste Marie, and the day was 4 June 1671. Here, in the presence of the 'Ambaffadeurs, au nombre de quatorze Nations'[37] of the Indians, de Lusson caused a cross to be planted 'and then the King's standard to be raised, with all the pomp that he could devise,' accompanied by the singing of the *Vexilla*.[38] 'Then the French Escutcheon, fixed to a Cedar pole, was also erected, above the Cross; while the *Exaudiat* was sung, and prayer for his Majesty's Sacred person was offered in that faraway corner of the world.'[39]

Whereupon de Lusson, in customary form for such occasions, took possession of those regions, while the air was filled with repeated shouts of 'Vive le Roy' and the discharge of musketry 'to the delight and astonishment of all those peoples, who had never seen anything of the kind.'[40] The significance and import of the ceremony was then explained to the assembled throng by de Lusson as well as a Jesuit missioner, Claude Allouez. 'The whole ceremony was closed with a fine bonfire, which was lighted toward evening, and around which the *Te Deum* was sung.'[41]

The marking of historic events and important occasions with heraldic ceremonial, at times more elaborate, at times less so, has continued on from the events just described down to the present day throughout the world and, indeed, beyond. The annexations of the colonial period, with the raising of an armorial banner or flag to mark the event, are well known. And more recently, upon a country's achieving independence, the lowering of one flag and the raising of another as the climax of elaborate ceremonies are fresh in our memories with the devolution of the British Empire, especially in Africa. This desire to mark off and make patent through symbolic, heraldic forms occasions which it is felt should be engraved on the memory of man appears to have become so strong that when the Union of Soviet Socialist Republics made its first soft landing on the moon with Luna IX in 1966,[42] it was not a copy of *Das Kapital* or some other work of cardinal importance to the Soviet system that was left there to mark Luna IX's arrival, but rather red pennants bearing the Arms of Soviet Russia.[43] Similarly, when the Americans placed the first men on the moon on 21 July 1969, this momentous occasion was proclaimed by unfurling an heraldic banner or flag: *gules, six barrulets argent, on a canton azure, fifty mullets also argent,* more commonly called the Stars and Stripes.

Nearer home, when in 1970 it became obvious that a serious attempt was about to be mounted, under American auspices, to see if the Northwest Passage could be used commercially for the transportation of Alaskan oil, Ottawa quickly despatched the CGS *Labrador* to accompany the SS *Manhattan* in this undertaking. The CSS *Hudson* was also ordered to proceed independently, so that, as the *Globe and Mail* (Toronto) put it, Canada would 'have shown the flag in an area many Canadians consider vital to their future,'[44] thus reasserting and reconfirming Canadian sovereignty there.

In the preparation of this chapter I am especially indebted to my colleagues, George Drewry Squibb, QC, MA, FSA, Norfolk Herald Extraordinary, for the benefit of his opinion on many of the legal intricacies involved, and Lt. Col. Rodney Onslow Dennys, MVO, OBE, FSA, Somerset Herald of Arms, for his knowledge of certain medieval heraldic texts.

NOTES

1 'ad cognoscendum' as Johannes de Bado Aureo put it succinctly in his *Tractatus de Armis* (c.1394), the text of which appears in E.J. Jones, *Medieval Heraldry: Some Fourteenth Century Heraldic Works* (Cardiff, Wm Lewis (Printers) 1943) p. 142.

2 A. Nisbet, *A System of Heraldry* (Edinburgh 1742) part 3, chapter 2, p. 89. One notes in the earliest known heraldic treatise *De Heraudie* (Cambridge University Library, MS EE. 4. 20 ff. 160ᵛ - 161ᵛ, a late fourteenth-century copy of an almost certainly late thirteenth-century work) arms borne by virtue of authority and jurisdiction: 'Le Roy d'Alemaigne porte l'escu d'or a un egle de sable ove double bek. Et ove double bek pur le graunt seignourie, quar touz les roys de christientee deveroient par droit estre en sa subjectione, c'est assavoir s'il soit emperoure'; f. 161ᵛ appears in Ruth J. Dean, 'An Early Treatise on Heraldry in Anglo-Norman' in U.T. Holmes, ed., *Romance Studies in Memory of Edward Billings Ham* California State College Publications 2 (1967) p. 27; and see Rodney Dennys, Somerset Herald of Arms, *The Heraldic Imagination* (London, Barrie and Jenkins Ltd. 1975) pp. 60-1.

3 20 June 1782, see *Journals of the Continental Congress* 22, pp. 339-40

4 The widely held belief that a new mullet or star was added to the Arms of the United States upon the entry of each new state to the Union is erroneous: this applied to the flag but not to the arms.

5 From the United Kingdom, London in particular

6 For example, the Prince of Wales bears a *label of three points argent* charged on the arms, crest, and supporters, among other differences, see CA: 182.197; Princess Anne, a *label of three points argent, the centre point charged with a heart and the other points with a St George Cross gules* on her arms and supporters, see ibid. 266, and so on.

7 cf. Bartolo di Sassoferrato, *De Insigniis et Armis* (published 1358, possibly written before 1354) chapter 2: 'Insignia singularia dignitatis, puta regis, nemo defert, nec rebus suis depingere facit principaliter, accessorie sic,' see Jones, *Medieval Heraldry*, appendix 1, where the *De Insigniis* is printed, p. 224 ff.

8 *Azure, billety and a lion rampant or* marshalled, in this instance, on an inescutcheon

9 Nisbet, *A System of Heraldry*, part 3, chapter 2, p. 90, and see CA: 134.11.

10 This is an example of a sovereign entity which has no territory, and so is somewhat analogous to the United Nations in that, from the point of view of international law, both are regarded as having international personalities – exhanging diplomatic representatives, issuing passports, entering into international agreements and the like.

11 *Gules, a lion rampant crowned or, holding a long handled axe argent:* see Order of the Garter stall plate of this sovereign, St George's Chapel, Windsor Castle.

12 *Quarterly France Modern and England within a bordure azure, charged alternately with fleurs-de-lis and martlets or*

13 J.H. Stevenson, *Heralrdy in Scotland* 2 (Glasgow, James Maclehose and Sons 1914) pp. 390-1

14 Obverse of the Chancery Seal for Ireland, Edward VI, see Hilary Jenkinson, 'The Great Seal of England: Deputed or Departmental Seals,' *Archaeologia* 85, plate 91, no. 5.

15 The Union with Scotland Act, 1706, is certainly not as explicit as it might have been on this matter. However, there is no doubt as to the *practice,* as, for example, on the seal for use in Scotland under article 24 of the Articles of Union in place of the former Great Seal of Scotland, on the writing paper of Holyrood Palace as well as of government departments in Scotland, in official publications such as the *Edinburgh Gazette,* on tabards of the Scottish Officers of Arms, and the like, *Scotland* is marshalled in the 1st and 4th quarters, *England* in the 2nd, and *Ireland* in the 3rd; the Scottish crest is used and the unicorn becomes the dexter supporter. It is interesting to note, however, that the Royal Banner (often mistakenly referred to as the Royal Standard) flown in the Queen's presence in Scotland, and the royal armorial car flags flown from Her Majesty's automobile, are in the other form: 1st and 4th *England*, 2nd *Scotland*, and 3rd *Ireland*. There is, nevertheless, no real inconsistency here, as for certain purposes royal authority is indicated in one heraldic form, and for others in another. For further discussions on this subject see Stevenson, *Heraldry in Scotland,* chapter 15 and Sir Thomas Innes of Learney, *Scots Heraldry* (Edinburgh, Oliver & Boyd 1956) chapter 16.

16 Since 1962 when Jamaica was granted independence, her arms have, naturally, been arms of dominion and sovereignty and not arms of *particular purpose.*

17 CA: Walker's Grants 11.5

18 CA: I 75.186 and I 76.270 respectively

19 CA: I 76.58

20 The well-known 'Brocas helm' of c.1500 preserved in the armory of the Tower of London is a favourite archetype for this form of helm.

21 See Order of the Garter stall plate of Nicholas II of Russia, St George's Chapel, Windsor Castle.

22 For a discussion of the gradual development of the constitutional position of Canada see Maurice Ollivier (KC, Joint Law Clerk of the House of Commons of Canada), *Problems of Canadian Sovereignty* (Toronto, Canada Law Book Company, Ltd. 1945).

23 22 Geo. V, c. 4; text in ibid. appendix 2

24 CA: Standards 11.2: the Lord Chamberlain to Garter King of Arms, 25 February 1931

25 For further details see chapter 4.

26 CA: 15 Garter, Flags f. 51: memorandum dated February 1930 on Governors General prepared by the Lord Chamberlain, sent to Sir Henry Farnham Burke, Garter King of Arms, 17 March 1930

27 Lord Campbell, *Lives of the Lord Chancellors* (London, John Murray 1848) 1, p. 23

28 For detailed descpriptions of these two great seals see chapter 4.

29 The exact site of the landfall is the subject of much discussion. The most scholarly opinion seems to be that it was in the Bay of Fundy area — Southern Nova Scotia or even Maine.

30 'et havendo asai errato in fine capitoe a terra ferma, dove posto la bandera regia et tolto la possessione per questo Alteza, et preco certi segnali, se ne retornato': second despatch of Raimondo di Soncino, in London, to the Duke of Milan, 18 December 1497, in H.P. Biggar, ed., *The Precursors of Jacques Cartier 1497-1534: A Collection of Documents Relating to the Early History of the Dominion of Canada* (Ottawa,

Government Printing Bureau 1911) p. 17

31 Lorenzo Pasqualigo to his brothers Alvise and Francesco Pasqualigo, 23 August 1497, in ibid. p. 13

32 The text of the letters patent appears in ibid. pp. 7-8: 'plenum ac liberam auctoritatem, facultatem et potestatem navigandi ad omnes partes ... sub banneris, vexillis et insigniis nostris ... ac licenciam dedimus affigendi predictas banneras nostras et insignia in quocumque ... insula seu terra firma a se noviter inventis ... dominum, titulum et jurisdiccionem eorundem ... insularum ac terre firme sic inventorum nobis acquirendo.'

33 For example, to Richard Warde and others, 19 March 1501, and to Hugh Eliot and others, 9 December 1502, texts in ibid. pp. 41-51 and 70-80 respectively

34 'Comment les nostres planterent vne grande croix sur la poincte de l'entrée dudit hable ... Le xxiiime jour dudict moys, nous fismes faire vne croix, de trente piedz de hault, qui fut faicte devant plusieurs d'eulx, sur la poincte de l'entrée dudit hable, soubz le croysillon de laquelle mismes vng escusson en bosse, à troys fleur de lys, et dessus, vng escripteau en boys, engravé en grosse lettre de forme, où il y avoit, VIVE LE ROY DE FRANCE. Et icelle croix plantasmes sur ladicte poincte devant eulx, lesquels la regardoyent faire le planter. Et après qu'elle fut eslevé en l'air, nous mismes tous à genoulx, les mains joinctes, en adorant icelle devant eulx': H.P. Biggar, *The Voyages of Jacques Cartier* (Ottawa, King's Printer 1924) pp. 64-5

35 Reuban Gold Thwaites, ed., *The Jesuit Relations and Allied Documents* 55 (New York, Pageant Book Company 1959) pp. 104-15

36 Ibid. p. 106: 'pour en fa place & au nom de fa Majesté, prendre poffeffion des terres qui fe trouvent entre l'Est & l'Ouest, depuis Montreal jufqu' à la mer du Sud, autant & fi avant, qu'il fe pourroit.'

37 Ibid.

38 Ibid. p. 107

39 Ibid. p. 108: 'Enfinte l'Escuffon de France ayant été attaché à un poteau de Cedre, fut auffi élevé de deffus de la Croix, pendant qu'on chantoit l'*Exaudiat,* & qu'on prioit en ce bout du monde pour la personne Sacrée de fa Majesté.'

40 Ibid. p. 109

41 Ibid. p. 115

42 The date of take-off of the spacecraft was 31 January.

43 For a photograph see the *Daily Telegraph,* 5 February 1966.

44 29 September and 17 October 1970

CHAPTER 2

Seals of public authority

When France and then Britain each in turn came to provide for the administration of Canada, both powers were heirs to a long tradition of authentication and indication in sigillographic form of decisions and decrees made in virtue of sovereign authority, whether at the instance of the sovereign himself or those acting in his name. In fact the development of this official use of seals in both France and Britain had sprung from common roots and can be traced back certainly to the reigns of Edgar the Pacific, 959-75,[1] Louis Le Débonnaire, 814-40,[2] and Charles Le Simple, 898-929,[3] who used antique gem portrait busts to which new and appropriate inscriptions were added.

By the eleventh century one finds in France the rise of the large state seals as under Henry I, 1031-60, and then under St Edward the Confessor of England, 1042-66. With the accession shortly afterwards of Duke William of Normandy to the throne of England as William I, we arrive at the basic form of the great seal, as it came to be called, which all English and British kings were to follow thereafter.

From about this time the general form of such great seals was more or less established in France as well as in England. In France, the sovereign was shown as enthroned in robes of peace, and into the other side of the great seal was impressed a small counter seal, armorial in nature. Basically, this was the form of the Great Seal of France when the French Crown first established its authority in New France and it was this form which continued down to the Treaty of Paris, 1763, by which this area was transferred to the British Crown.

While this work does not intend to concern itself primarily with the great seals of France or of Great Britain – respectively the *Grand Sceau* and the Great Seal of the

Realm – nevertheless, it may not be out of place to discuss some examples of particular relevance to Canada in order to appreciate the roots from which official sigillography in this country stems.

Let us begin with the Great Seal of France. In view of the highly centralized form of government centred on Versailles which the French provided for New France, especially from the moment it became a royal province in 1663, the *Grand Sceau* had a direct significance for that area to a degree which one could never attribute to the British Great Seal of the Realm for reasons which will become obvious later.

GRANDS SCEAUX

FRANCIS I 1515-47

The great seals of the kings of France which had immediate relevance to their realm of New France began with that of Francis I, in whose name the voyages of discovery and the explorations of Jacques Cartier laid the foundations for the subsequent exercise of French authority in this vast area.

In the great seal of this monarch one notes almost all the principal elements which occur on those to follow right down to the last, that of Louis XV, which were to signify the word and deed of the French king for this part of North America. Eight of the nine basic elements to be found on these seals occur in that of Francis I [2.1].

One notes, first of all, the figure of the seated king on a throne. Second, he wears the royal mantle. This was, in reality, usually blue – often velvet – and covered with a semy of gold fleurs-de-lis. Slit up the right side it allows that arm to protrude, while the hem on the other side is caught up and draped over the left arm. An ermine cape covers the shoulders and falls from the throat to about mid-chest. Third, in his right hand the king holds the symbol of authority, or sceptre, which consisted of a long rod tipped with a fleur-de-lis, all gold; in his left hand is the *main de justice* – a further sceptre, also gold, the finial of which was formed, usually, by a right hand in the position of taking an oath, that is to say with the index and second finger extended and upright while the third and little fingers are bent downwards towards the palm, the thumb extended to the viewer's right. Fourth, the king is crowned. In the case of Francis I, the crown consists of a jewelled circlet from which rise five fleurs-de-lis: a large one in the centre flanked on either side by two smaller, and then two half fleurs-de-lis, of the same size as the centre one, at the left and right hand extremities of the crown. Fifth, two lions, symbols of power and majesty, lie at the monarch's feet. Sixth, above the throne is a canopy down from which hang curtains forming a pavilion; it is decorated with semy of fleurs-de-lis. Seventh, two winged angels support and hold back the curtains of the pavilion; on the seal of Francis I they are almost lost behind the canopy. The eighth and final element of this seal consists of the legend round the circumference, which is contained within two concentric circles: FRĀCISCVS ·DEI · GRACIA · FRANCORVM · REX · PRIMVS. (The extended form and translation of this inscription and of the other royal styles and titles which occur upon seals mentioned in the course of this work will be found in appendix A, pp. 225-8. The positioning of stops in legends is indicated throughout by raised dots, as above; the actual form of the stop in each case will be seen in the relevant illustration.) With a diameter of 3⅞ inches (98 millimetres), the impression of the Great Seal of

2.1 Great Seal and counter seal of Francis I, 1515-47
AN: D 93 and D 93 bis

Francis I was made of wax and depended from the document by means of a piece of vellum or silk cords.

It was a characteristic administrative practice of France that in addition to the great seal impressed onto one side of the wax used, on the other side would be impressed a relatively small counter seal. That of Francis I, like all the others which related to New France, is essentially heraldic and comprised three basic elements: a shield of arms of *France Modern,* a royal crown, and winged angels as supporters. It has an open royal crown as worn by the king on the great seal and a broadly based yet pointed shield. Each of the supporting angels, on either side of the shield, kneels on one knee. The whole design is contained within a plain circle.[4]

The concept and treatment of both the great seal and the counter seal are late Gothic. This is somewhat singular when one recalls that probably the last role in which His Most Christian Majesty saw himself was that of a gothic king.

HENRY IV 1589-1610

It was not, in fact, until 1608 that the French really established themselves permanently in New France with the founding of Quebec. We must, therefore, pass from the Valois-Angoulême dynasty to that of the House of Bourbon, from the Gothic manner of seal engraving under Francis I, to the Renaissance inspiration as evinced under Henry IV (1589-1610), in order to continue our investigations.

The great seal of the latter king [2.2] contains all eight elements discussed before, although their expression is in accordance with the artistic taste of the time. A ninth

2.2 Great Seal and counter seal of Henry IV, 1589-1610
AN: 106 and 106 bis

element is to be noted on this seal, in that the king wears round his shoulders, over the ermine cape, the collars of the Orders of St Michael and of the Holy Ghost. The royal crown is now arched and has a fleur-de-lis rising from the point where the arches meet. This type of crown is worn by the monarchs on all the subsequent great seals of which we shall treat. The winged angel supporters are now much more prominent and figure beside the king on either side. As with the Great Seal of Francis I, the upper part of the canopy and the lower part of the design beneath the lions at the sovereign's feet spill over, as it were, onto the legend band which reads, starting at the upper right, HENRICVS QUARTUS DEI GRATIA FRANCORUM REX. The diameter of the seal is approximately 4 1/4 inches (108 millimetres).

The counter seal has the usual three elements, but in this instance and from now on the royal crown which ensigns the shield is arched and is similar to that worn by the sovereign on the great seal. The attitude of the winged angel supporters on the counter seal of Henry IV is a further development in that they are in a somewhat seated position and support the shield on their knees.[5]

LOUIS XIII 1610-43

The great seals of Louis XIII contain the same basic nine elements as that of his father, Henry IV. Once again the artistic interpretation is in accordance with the manner of the time and with certain concessions to the sartorial demands of the period, such as, for example, the ruff about the sovereign's neck. On the third and fourth great seals for Louis XIII [2.3], an innovation is introduced whereby the legend is lengthened and

2.3 *Great Seal and counter seal (post 1616) of Louis XIII, 1610-43*
AN: 110 and 110 bis

2.4 *Great Seal and counter seal of Louis XIV, 1643-1715*
AN: 116 and 116 bis

rendered in French instead of Latin. Starting at the lower left it reads LOUIS XIII PAR LA GRACE D DIEV ROY D FRANCE ET D NAVARRE. The diameter of the seal is approximately 4¼ inches (108 millimetres).

The counter seal contains the basic three elements noted so far, but in this instance the supporter angels stand on either side of the shield.[6]

LOUIS XIV 1643-1715

The Great Seal of Louis XIV [2.4] shows the boy-king who ascended the throne at the age of five years. Basically, the nine elements found in the last two great seals discussed are present here too, but the general interpretation is in accordance with the artistic taste of the period, and one notes that the ruff of Louis XIII is replaced by a broad, turned-down collar as fashion required by this time. The angel supporters who hold back the pavilion curtains appear to be almost as large as the king himself. In a cartouche beneath his feet the year of engraving, 1643, is inscribed.

The legend starts at the lower left and runs around the top of the seal: LOVIS · XIIII · PAR · LA · GRACE · DE · DIEV · ROY · DE · FRANCE · ET · DE · NAVARRE. The diameter is 4¼ inches (108 millimetres).

The counter seal is almost completely identical with that of Louis XIII.[7]

LOUIS XV 1715-74

The last Great Seal of the French Crown which applied to New France was that of Louis XV [2.5]. All nine elements to be found since the Great Seal of Henry IV are to be found in this seal. The angels on either side, however, uphold purely vestigial pavilion curtains. The royal mantle is arranged in such a way as to show the breeches and stockings of the king, and a long wig helps to complete the artistic feeling of the period. *La main de justice* on this occasion shows an open hand, and the king sits on a high-backed throne.

The legend, which starts at the lower left, reads LOVIS · XV · PAR · LA · GRACE · DE · DIEV · ROY · DE · FRANCE · ET · DE · NAVARRE. The diameter is 3½ inches (89 millimetres).

The counter seal shows a considerable change both in content and interpretation. An oval shield of *France Modern,* hatched in part, is surrounded by the collars of the Orders of St Michael and of the Holy Ghost. All are placed on a cartouche which is ensigned by an arched royal crown. The whole treatment is strongly reminiscent of that representation of the royal arms, executed in wood and polychrome, which was taken from a gate at Quebec in 1759 and is now preserved at the Public Archives in Ottawa (see plate 3). The angel supporters, mounted on clouds, are placed somewhat behind the cartouche upon which they rest their exterior arms. With their other arms and hands they uphold an arched royal crown above the shield in a way unlike any of the other counter seals we have discussed. The whole treatment is a most interesting example of rococo.[8]

GREAT SEALS OF THE REALM

Like the French, the British consider the great seal 'the emblem of sovereignty, the *clavis regni,* the only instrument by which on solemn occasions the will of the sovereign can be

2.5 *Great Seal and counter seal of Louis XV, 1715-74*
AN: 127 and 127 bis

expressed. Absolute faith is universally given to every document purporting to be under the Great Seal, as having been duly sealed with it by the authority of the Sovereign.'[9] However, one finds, as one would expect, that the English and British seals have developed from their French and Anglo-Norman roots in different ways than those of the kings of France.

Let us, therefore, examine a selected few of these highly important instruments of government which have particular historical as well as archetypal relevance for Canada, their counterparts here to-day being their lineal descendants.

HENRY VII 1485-1509

It was by virtue of letters patent issued under the Great Seal of Henry VII that John Cabot and his colleagues undertook, in 1497, their voyage across the Atlantic to the west during which they discovered Canada and claimed it in the name of their royal patron.

The obverse of the seal of Henry VII [2.6] shows the king in his robes of estate, crowned and holding the orb and sceptre – the symbols of authority. In a compartment are the royal arms of *France Modern* and *England* quarterly. On either side of the footboard is a rose, possibly symbolic of the two houses he had brought together – York and Lancaster. The reverse shows the king mounted and wearing elaborate armour and a tabard of the royal arms. The horse bardings are enriched with armorials, and the background has a diaper of the royal badges of France and England. The foreground is dotted with flowers and rabbit holes.

The legend reads HENRICUS · DEI · G'RA · REX · ANGLIE · & FRANCIE · & DOMINUS ·

2.6 Obverse and reverse of the Great Seal of Henry VII, 1485-1509

SA: A 25

2.7 Obverse and reverse of the Great Seal of James VI and I, 1567 (1603)-1625, as King of Scotland

SA: A 28

HIBERNIE ·. On the reverse G'RA is extended to GRACIA. The diameter is 4½ inches (115 millimetres).[10]

The dual capacity of the sovereign, in robes of peace on one side of the seal and leading his nation in war on the other side, is a typical arrangement for almost all great seals from the reign of William of Normandy onwards. It is significant that it was the portrayal of the sovereign in robes of peace which was chosen to be the theme for the first permanent great seal deputed of Canada, in 1869, and has been used for this purpose ever since by all its successors, as will be discussed in greater detail subsequently.

JAMES VI AND I 1567 (1603)-1625

It was James VI of Scotland and I of England who issued letters patent in 1621 to Sir William Alexander investing him with Nova Scotia. The patent was passed under the Great Seal of Scotland [2.7].

The obverse of this seal shows the king mounted and wearing armour and a crown. His left hand holds the reins and his right brandishes a sword. The horse bardings show large Tudor rose and thistle badges. Between the legs of the galloping horse is a view, possibly of Edinburgh. In the upper part of the seal, on either side of the king, are further royal badges, a fleur-de-lis to the right, and a portcullis to the left. Within two concentric circles following the greater part of the circumference is the motto, starting at the lower left, DEVS · IVDICIVM · TVVM · REGI · DA (Give to the King, O God, Thy faculty of judgement – Psalm 72:8).

The reverse shows the Royal Arms of Scotland, as described in chapter 3, and includes the shield, crown, supporters, and wreath of thistles and St Andrew's badge as well as the Garter. Between two concentric circles which follow the greater part of the circumference are the royal titles, starting at the lower left, IACOBVS · D · G · MAG · BRIT · FRAN · ET · HIB · REX. The diameter is 5⁹/10 inches (150 millimetres).[11]

This seal is of particular interest as it contains most of the elements which were soon to characterize the deputed great seals of seventeenth- and eighteenth-century British America: an armorial side, comprising shield of arms, crown, supporters, Garter, and royal titles, and the other side containing an effigy of the sovereign combined with and at times superseded by a direct reference – at times allegorical, at others pictorial – to the area concerned together with a motto or allusive phrase (see also pp. 27-8 below).

CHARLES II 1660-85

Charles II had four great seals in all, and it was with the third [2.8] that the letters patent were sealed, in 1670, establishing and investing with their territorial and other rights the Company of Gentlemen Adventurers trading into 'Hudsons Bay,' more commonly called the Hudson's Bay Company.

This great seal, engraved by Thomas Simon, is extremely ornate and armorial badges constitute an important part of the design. On the obverse, the king, in robes of estate, is seated on a throne with a shell-shaped back. Two couched lions are at the base. Behind each are three badge banners: to the left they display St George and the dragon, a rose, and a crowned thistle – alluding to England and Scotland. To the right the badge banners show the Union (as established in 1606), a crowned fleur-de-lis, and a crowned harp – alluding to Great Britain, the ancient but by this time purely historical claim to France, and finally Ireland. Above the canopy over the king are the royal arms as borne by Charles II and described in detail in chapter 3. The arms are supported by winged *amorini*. The legend reads CAROLVS · II · DEI · GRA · MAG · BRITAN · FRAN · ET · HIB · REX · FID · DEFENSOR.

The reverse shows the king mounted and in classical armour, his head wreathed with laurel. In the background is to be seen a view of London. The legend on this side is the same as for the obverse save that it is given in a fully extended form but for the word MAGNAE which is contracted to MAG. The diameter is 5²/₅ inches (137 millimetres).[12]

ANNE 1702-14

It was with the third Great Seal of Queen Anne [2.10], used from 1707 to 1714, that the Treaty of Utrecht was ratified which confirmed to the British Crown undisputed possession of Acadia (Nova Scotia),[13] the Hudson Bay country, and Newfoundland.

The great seal showed the queen in robes of estate seated on a carved throne, holding sceptre and orb. On the left-hand side is a lion sejant reguardant crowned, supporting an oval shield bearing the Cross of St George; and to the right is a unicorn sejant, gorged with a crown and chained, supporting a similar shield bearing the Cross of St Andrew. Allegorical figures of Piety, holding a model of a church, and Justice, holding scales and a bundle of Roman fasces, accompany the queen to the right and left respectively. On the canopy is an ornamental shield of the first and fourth quarters of the royal arms as established in 1707 (described in detail in chapter 3) ensigned by a royal crown and supported by two angels blowing trumpets. Badges of rose and thistle are used freely in the general design. The legend band reads ANNA · DEI · GRATIA · MAGNAE · BRITANNIAE · FRANCIAE · ET · HIBERNIAE · REGINA · FIDEI · DEFENSOR · ETC with a rose and a thistle used alternately as stops.

The reverse consists of a figure of Britannia seated at the foot of a rocky cliff. In her right hand she holds a lance, and with her left supports an oval shield bearing the Royal Arms of England impaling Scotland. On the left-hand side grow, from one plant, a rose and a thistle ensigned by a royal crown, in allusion to the union of England and Scotland just concluded prior to the making of this seal. The legend, with similar stops as on the obverse, reads BRITANNIA · ANNO · REGNI · ANNAE · REGINAE · SEXTO (Britain in the sixth year of the reign of Queen Anne). The diameter is 6 inches (152 millimetres).[14]

EDWARD VII 1901-10

The Great Seal of the Realm of Edward VII [2.11] has been chosen for discussion for two reasons. First, it was one of the very last to be applicable to Canada, and second, it is the sole example of such a great seal upon which Canada is referred to specifically.

The obverse shows the king seated on a throne, wearing a royal crown and holding the sceptre and orb. He wears robes of estate and the collar of the Order of the Garter. The whole treatment of this part of the seal is almost identical with that to be found on the Great Seal Deputed of Canada for this reign. Behind the king, on the upper part of the throne, stand figures of St Michael and St George, to the left and right respectively. On

2.8 Obverse and reverse of the third Great Seal of Charles II, 1660-85
SA: A 34

2.9 Contemporary illustrations by the engraver of the great seal,
from Vertue's **Works of Thomas Simon,** *2nd edition*

2.10 Obverse and reverse of the third Great Seal of Anne, 1702-14
SA: A 37

2.11 Obverse and reverse of the Great Seal of Edward VII, 1901-10
PAC: PDP

either side of the king are placed, to the left, Britannia holding a ship, and, to the right, Justice with scales and sword. The legend, starting at the upper right, runs round the circumference: EDWARDVS VII · D · G · BRITT · ET TERRARVM TRANSMAR · QVAE IN DIT · SVNT BRIT · REX F · D · IND · IMP ·.

The reverse shows the king generally dressed and crowned as before, except that as he is mounted he wears high military riding boots. In the lower background are ships, while in the left upper background is a shield of the royal arms accompanied by an unusual arrangement of the Garter. Above the king's head is the motto DIEV ET MON DROIT, which is placed over a wreath of roses, thistles, and shamrocks. Rising up from the bottom of the seal, and following the circumference on either side, are branches of oak around which a ribbon is entwined and inscribed CANADA WEST INDIES NEWFOVNDLAND BRITISH AFRICA GIBRALTAR MALTA EASTERN COLONIES AVSTRALIA NEW ZEALAND. The diameter is 6¼ inches (159 millimetres).[15]

DEPUTED GREAT SEALS

In addition to great seals of the realm, other official seals have existed from an early date. As government became more and more complex, so it was found necessary to have departmental seals to indicate the sovereign will as far as the particular department was concerned. This was especially so when the administration of large areas was carried on in the monarch's name, but at great distances from the central seat of government. Accordingly, one notes the rise for this purpose of what are termed deputed great seals. The parallel here between, on the one hand, great seals of the realm and arms of dominion and sovereignty for general purposes, and on the other hand, deputed great seals and arms of public authority for particular purposes will be obvious.

Henry III's seal for Gascony of about 1242 – described in royal letters as *sigillum quo utimur in Vasconia* (the seal we use in the land of the Basques)[16] – and the Irish great seal of about 1227 are among the earliest examples of such deputed seals.[17] By the reign of Edward IV (1461-83), we have the legend round the circumference of a seal declaring it to be the seal of the king *terre sue Hibernie* (for his land of Ireland), and we find that on at least one document to which an impression is attached it is described as *magnum sigillum suum regni sui Hibernie usitatum* (his great seal for use in his Kingdom of Ireland).[18] Earlier still, in 1342, we note in Wales a reference made to 'the King's seal for the Government of North Wales.'[19] These few among many examples will suffice to show the steady development of the use of deputed great seals under the authority of the English Crown.

Accordingly, when plantations and provinces were established under its authority in America, precedents were well settled for issuing deputed great seals so that the sovereign will could be indicated and authenticated locally. The decentralized form of government, typical of British colonies, whereby considerable local and internal responsibility was placed upon local governors, executive councils, and later legislative assemblies, made the existence of great seals deputed for local purposes both desirable and possible. All offices were bestowed by the governor, with the result that the necessary commission or letters patent required passage under the great seal, as did writs summoning an assembly of the legislature, and others directing the sheriffs to arrange for elections of local representatives to attend the legislature. All causes in Chancery were decided by the governor, and as all land held in the colonies was for a long period held of the Crown technically, 'as of' a royal manor, all this meant an ever increasing amount of business in the seventeenth century and beyond which would normally require grants and other documents passed under the Great Seal of the Realm. The result was that authentication of such documents was provided for by great seals deputed for use on the spot.[20]

Thus, by the time it was decided to provide a great seal deputed for Nova Scotia in 1730 (see figure 7.2), which thus became the first such instrument of its kind which I have so far discovered for Canada, we have a well-established process of administration in this matter within the British colonies.

Further, we can say that from the reign of George II until that of William IV the deputed great seals in Canada were double-sided. The reverse contained the royal arms of dominion and sovereignty, that is to say the royal arms of general purpose, appropriate to the time of engraving, while round the circumference was placed a recitation of the royal titles in Latin – technically referred to as the legend – abbreviated in form so as to fit conveniently in the space available on what is usually referred to as the legend band.

On the obverse the engraving referred more particularly to the colony concerned, and usually contained three main elements: first, an allegorical or symbolic motif or scene or a panoramic view; second, a motto or allusive sentence in the exergue; and finally, a legend band round the circumference which contained a direct reference to the area concerned.

There were three exceptions to these conventions: the first Great Seal Deputed of Quebec (1763) and the only two of Cape Breton Island (1785 and 1816). As was general at the time with two-sided seals in other British American colonies, the 1763 seal for Quebec had for its obverse a symbolic composition which includes a representation of the sovereign. Despite this being a widely followed custom at the time in the administration of the Crown throughout its American provinces, the 1763 Quebec seal is, apparently, the only Canadian example to include an effigy of the sovereign. Indeed, the only other occasion upon which the sovereign's effigy appeared on a Canadian deputed great seal of the colonial period occurred with that provided for British Columbia following its creation in 1858. By this time all such seals were single-sided. The other exceptions concern the two great seals deputed of Cape Breton Island. Unlike the other colonial seals prior to the reign of William IV, those of Cape Breton were single-sided and intended for impression directly onto the surface of the documents concerned. A wafer of wax (shellac), sometimes covered with paper, was usually employed to receive the impression. Although unusual, such deputed great seals were not unknown in colonial administration, as one notes, for example, with those of New Jersey from the reign of Queen Anne onwards.[21]

The impressions of the dependent double-sided seals were usually made upon natural coloured beeswax through paper which covered both sides. The use of paper-covered wax appears to have been almost without exception and went back to the earliest colonial days in North America. The reason for this has never been fully explained, especially as such was not the custom with the other deputed great seals, such as, for example, those for Ireland. It is possible that the custom arose in North America

2.12 *Great Seal Deputed of Nova Scotia*
covered with printed form
PANS: *box marked 'Seals,' document*
4 November 1812

2.13 *'Double exposure' of the Great Seal*
Deputed of Nova Scotia
PANS: *box marked 'Seals,' document*
24 April 1812

following the earliest deputed great seal there, that of Virginia during the reign of James I, which was applied over a wafer of paper-covered wax.[22]

Almost without exception in Canada these seals were appended from documents by means of tapes of material, although there are a few instances where tags of vellum were used, as with an impression of the 1792 George III Great Seal Deputed of Upper Canada preserved in the Royal Ontario Museum.[23] The use of laces of cord, silk ribbon, and the like has so far not come to my notice for the colonial period.

As the matrices were generally engraved in a relatively low relief the resultant impression through paper was not always as sharp and clear as one might desire. Nevertheless, the use of a paper covering in this way has probably helped greatly to preserve the seals in a better condition than if they had not been so protected. The paper used appears to have been ordinary office paper of no special variety and was generally quite plain. However, either inadvertence or an over-zealous regard for economy on the part of the clerk who actually attached the great seal must explain the use of a printed form, doubtless spare about the office, as the paper covering for the impression of the Great Seal Deputed of Nova Scotia upon a land grant to John Gschwindt of Halifax, Surgeon, and Isabella Ellis of Halifax, of a thousand acres in Sydney County, dated 4 November 1812 [2.12].[24] Other curiosities are not unknown, as with the Great Seal Deputed, also of the same province, which was impressed onto paper-covered wax in the usual way and then, as if for good measure, turned over and allowed to receive the impress of the matrices once again so that one has what might be termed a 'double exposure' with both the obverse and reverse appearing on each side of the impressed seal [2.13].[25]

By and large the double-sided Canadian deputed great seals of the colonial period were large and approached nearly, if they did not quite equal, the size of the great seals of the realm[26] for the corresponding period. On an average the diameters of the latter varied between about 5⁴/₅ and 6¹/₁₀ inches (148 and 155 millimetres respectively)[27] and the former measured about 4¹/₂ inches (115 millimetres).

Starting in the early nineteenth century, one notes a return to the earlier precedent of single-sided deputed great seals. At about the same time a single-sided Great Seal of the Realm was taken into use for certain categories of documents.[28] With these it was possible to impress the seal directly onto the surface of the document concerned with or without a wax and/or paper wafer. Great administrative convenience follows from such a practice, in that ordinary paper can be used for the documents which pass under the seal rather than vellum which is really the only satisfactory material when a dependent seal of wax is employed. There are, on the other hand, obvious drawbacks to direct impression of a seal onto the surface of a document – often referred to technically as *en placard* – and these include the poorer lasting quality of paper as compared with vellum. Competent application of a seal upon any sort of materials – wax, paper, or a combination – is an art which, alas, is not always achieved, or at least not always practised, by the clerks usually charged with the actual sealing of documents. Consequently, while the results achieved with wax are generally better, those *en placard* where paper alone is involved are all too frequently poor.[29] If, then, the functional purpose of a seal is to be the *clavis regni,* to be taken as the visible token of the very act and deed of the sovereign power authenticating and validating an act, and if the details of this symbol, this sign, are indistinct, it would seem that one is justified in feeling that such forms of impression leave much to be desired.

On the other hand, dependent seals are capable of great aesthetic qualities. In the first place, double and large surfaces are available which allow the engraver full scope for the exercise of his art, so that the seal impression can become a thing of great beauty in itself. Wax and cellulose[30] can be used and both are capable of accepting a fine rendering from the matrices. Wax is certainly less durable, but when protected by a metal seal box, or skippet as it is called, it can be preserved with great sharpness of detail. Cellulose, however, is a modern invention, exceptionally hard and durable, which takes a fine impression from the seal dies. This material is now used for the dependent Great Seal of the Realm in the United Kingdom.[31] Finally, the dependent seal has a certain dignity about it which can never really be achieved by any other manner of sealing. Such alone is fully worthy to be the token of supreme authority, the insignia of sovereignty. It would seem that it was for this reason that the Great Seal of Canada, which is usually impressed *en placard,* when attached to the proclamation of 28 January 1965 bringing into being the national flag of Canada, was made to depend by means of red and white corded silk ribbon.[32]

It may therefore be said that from about 1832/33 during the reign of William IV, Canadian great seals and deputed great seals have been applied *en placard* with a few notable exceptions.[33] This is so to the present day.

The process by which deputed great seals were brought into being for British North America was well developed by the time of George II when what appears to be the first such Canadian seal was required for Nova Scotia. Indeed, so well did it serve its purpose that the process continued down to Confederation and somewhat beyond. As will be seen from the following chapters, it was the Board of Trade and Plantations (and its successors exercising colonial responsibility)[34] who decided when a seal was needed for a particular overseas territory.[35] Following their formal representation to the Crown, the Sovereign in Council issued a royal warrant authorizing the Board of Trade and Plantations to have the seal made. A further such warrant was issued to the chief engraver of seals ordering him to make the seal and sanctioning the payment of his fees and reimbursement for the materials. The chief engraver received through the Board detailed instructions towards the preparation of the seal such as the design, inscriptions, and the like which were contained in an order in council. The contraction of the royal titles in the legend was left to his discretion.

Upon completion, the seal, along with a proof impression in wax, was submitted for approval to the King in Council. With this given, a royal warrant was issued transmitting the seal to the Board of Trade and Plantations and ultimately another warrant was issued to the governor of the colony authorizing its use. Once the latter had been signed by the king, the board arranged for a covering letter of transmittal to the governor concerned who, in due time, received the seal and took it into official use in the colony.

At the same time, in obedience to the royal warrant authorizing the use of the new seal, the governor was required to return the matrices of the old deputed great seal for formal defacement by the Sovereign in Council. Up to the reign of Edward VII (1901-10) such seals were almost invariably made of sterling silver and following defacement they were usually melted down in order to provide the metal for new seals. However, some of them have fortunately been preserved – for example, all matrices of all the deputed great seals and subsequently the great seals of Canada from Queen Victoria (1869) down to the present, which are lodged at the Public Archives of Canada in Ottawa. The brass female matrices of the temporary great seals deputed of Ontario and Quebec for use immediately following Confederation have also been preserved and are now housed in the British Museum. The defaced Great Seal Deputed of the Province of Canada was given to the Honble William McDougall, CB, as its last provincial secretary, and the temporary Great Seal Deputed of Canada following Confederation was directed to Mr (later Sir) Hector Louis Langevin, Secretary of State of Canada. The vast majority, however, of earlier Canadian seals would seem to have been destroyed in 1843 when 'a number of Old Silver Seals returned from the Colonies after the accessions to the Throne of Their Late Majesties King George the Third and George the Fourth, and King William the Fourth; and Her present Majesty [Queen Victoria]'[36] were melted down.

After the chief engraver had handed the silver matrices of a new seal to the Board of Trade, frequently, at least in the colonial period, in a shagreen box for protection, he presented his account for his work and materials to the Treasury. The latter would send the account to the Master and other officials of the Royal Mint and ask them to check it and say whether or not the charges were reasonable. The Mint officials gave their findings to the Treasury who accordingly issued a warrant to the engraver for his payment. The colony concerned would then meet these costs unless it were fortunate enough to have another ordered to pay, as Nova Scotia appears to have been following the supply of her first deputed great seal in 1730. On this occasion a royal warrant was directed to the Receiver of the Revenues in Virginia to pay 'John Rolls, Chief Engraver of Seals, for the making and engraving of several seals ... used on the Plantations in America.'[37] Some will probably feel that there was an element of advance poetic justice in all this.

Usually, new seals were required only at the beginning of a reign unless changes in the royal arms took place, as, for example, in 1801 upon the Union of Great Britain and Ireland, and in 1816 when the king's German Dominions had become a kingdom.

When a sovereign died, a royal warrant was sent to each colonial governor authorizing the continued use of the deputed great seal of the deceased monarch until a seal could be prepared in accordance with the Act of Succession.[38] As a consequence, it is quite common to come across documents dated well into a new reign but bearing the seal prepared for the late sovereign. Quite apart from the period taken in deciding what the designs were to be, the actual process involved in seal engraving required a considerable amount of time. When a large number of seals were needed, as would be the case at the outset of a reign, it was but natural that the Great Seal of the Realm and others of a metropolitan character would have to be completed first, with the various deputed great seals of the overseas territories taking their turn thereafter. As a consequence, one finds that frequently a considerable period elapsed before the Canadian seals were completed. The average delay was about three years, and the greatest eight years – this latter under George IV. The shortest time taken was the five months within which the deputed great seal was prepared for New Brunswick in 1785. This followed the erection of the area into a province, and the engraving could proceed untrammelled since this was in the middle of a reign and no other seals were required at the same time.

In general, the provision of great seals deputed for Canada was accomplished in this way up to Confederation, when first temporary and then in 1869 permanent seals were assigned for both the federal and the four foundation provincial authorities.

Subsequent to that, and especially following the Federal Act, 40 Victoria, c.3 of 1877, the provinces have been responsible for bringing into use and altering their own deputed great seals, usually by provincial Orders in Council. The actual matrices were made locally or by private contract in the United Kingdom, as with the 1911 British Columbia seal.

Since Confederation the tradition within the provinces generally has been to have a permanent deputed great seal rather than a new one following the beginning of each new reign. Newfoundland, however, appears to be the exception to this provincial custom.

On the other hand, for federal purposes first the great seals deputed and then the Great Seal of Canada have followed the tradition whereby a new one is engraved for each succeeding reign. In the early twentieth century these were made at the Royal Mint in London and forwarded at the instance of and through the Colonial Office. However, the last one to be made there, for King George VI, was ordered at the instance of the Privy Council of Canada, reflecting the development of the Canadian constitution following the Statute of Westminster in 1931. The Great Seal of Canada of Her present Majesty was not only brought into being by the Canadian Privy Council, but was also the first to be made in the country at the Royal Canadian Mint at Ottawa.

What has been said previously concerning the metamorphosis, as it were, of the Arms of Canada from being arms of particular authority to ones of general authority, that is to say their becoming arms of dominion and sovereignty following the Statute of Westminster, applies, *mutatis mutandis,* to the Great Seal of Canada.

In 1867 the Great Seal of Canada, as well as those of the four foundation provinces, assigned following Confederation, were all deputed great seals in that while supreme each within its own sphere of competence, the Great Seal of the Realm (of the United Kingdom) continued to be the supreme token of the sovereign authority. However, as the years passed, and the Canadian constitution gradually evolved, one comes to the point following the Statute of Westminster when this ceased to be the situation and the Great Seal of Canada became the supreme token of the sovereign authority for Canada, that is to say it became the great seal of the monarch in right of Canada – as sovereign of Canada and *not* by virtue of being sovereign of any other realm or territory. Accordingly, today the Great Seal of Canada, being the supreme token of the will of a sovereign state, is to Canada what the Great Seal of the Realm is to the United Kingdom. As a logical result one notes that from 1 October 1947 even the very office of Governor General is constituted by letters patent under 'Our Great Seal of Canada,' while the commission of appointment of each bears the Royal Sign Manual, the signature of the Prime Minister of Canada, and the Great Seal of Canada. [39]

On the other hand, the provincial great seals remain technically deputed great seals, as following Confederation they derive their authority from the federal authority of the Crown, a principle enunciated by Sir John A. Macdonald in 1869. [40] However, such provincial great seals are *sui generis* among deputed great seals in that they are tokens of the will of an authority many of whose powers are specified and guaranteed exclusively to them as reserved powers, [41] which powers in a unitary state would be exercised by the central administration.

PRIVY SEALS

Following the royal practice in such matters, it has long been the custom in administration derived from the British tradition for certain pre-eminent senior officials, such as governors, to use seals which, while incorporating their own personal arms, are, nevertheless, used in an official capacity. Such are called privy seals.

Accordingly, we find governors throughout the British period making use of privy seals. As the colonial secretary explained to the Earl of Mulgrave, Lieutenant Governor of Nova Scotia, in 1858, the great seal deputed of the province was to be used for 'all things that shall pass (or ought to pass) the Seal of the Province; that is to say – Acts of the Legislature, Proclamations, Grants, and all formal Instruments'; on the other hand certain other categories of acts including 'official appointments made by your Lordship, in pursuance of authority vested in you ... should properly be authenticated under your Lordship's Seal of Arms.'[42] The convenience of having two such seals of the highest authority for the conduct of affairs is obvious, and we find that this tradition has been maintained down to the present day with the privy seals of the Governors General. Yet again, at the provincial level, the Lieutenant Governors of Newfoundland, Nova Scotia, Quebec, Ontario, and Manitoba[43] continue to make use of such seals; those of New Brunswick, Prince Edward Island, British Columbia, and Saskatchewan have not for some years now; the Lieutenant Governor of Alberta appears never to have done so.

In connection with this chapter and others where seals are concerned, I am most grateful for all the help so generously given by R.H. Ellis, FSA, Secretary of the Royal Commission on Historical Manuscripts; Patricia Malley, The Crown Office, House of Lords; Graham Pollard, Keeper, Department of Coins and Medals, Fitzwilliam Museum, Cambridge; J.E. Lucas, Secretary of the Royal Mint; M.A.F. Borrie, Assistant Keeper, Department of Manuscripts, and J. Cherry, Assistant Keeper, Department of Medieval and Later Antiquities, both of the British Museum; Peter Walne, FSA, County Archivist of Hertfordshire; and Joan Gibbs, Paleography Room, University of London Library.

NOTES

1 BM Catalogue 3

2 Ibid. 18061

3 Ibid. 18068

4 AN: D 93 and D 93 bis, and see also Louis Rouvier, *La Chancellerie et les sceaux de France,* second edition (Marseille, Impr. Marseillaise 1950), under the heading *Francis I.*

5 AN: D 106 and D 106 bis, and see also Rouvier, *Chancellerie* under the heading *Henry IV.*

6 AN: D 110 and D 110 bis, and see also Rouvier, *Chancellerie* under the heading *Louis XIII.*

7 ANQ: Grands Formats: 'Lettres patentes pour un amortissement au Jésuites du Canada, 12 mai 1678' (legend almost completely effaced); PRO: SP 108/73: ratification of the Treaty of Utrecht, 18 April 1713 (counter seal in good condition), and see also AN: D 116 and D 116 bis and Rouvier, *Chancellerie* under the heading *Louis XIV.*

8 ANQ: Papiers de Léry, AP-C-23-3, no. 12: 'Commission de capitaine d'infanterie en Canada pour Gaspard Joseph Chaussegros de Léry, 1er mai 1757' (legend effaced) and see also AN: D 127 and D 127 bis, and Rouvier, *Chancellerie* under the heading *Louis XV.*

9 Lord Campbell, *Lives of the Lord Chancellors (London, John Murray* 1848) 1, p. 23

10 SA: A 25

11 Hilary Jenkinson, 'The Great Seal of England: Deputed or Departmental Seals,' *Archaeologia* 85, pp. 323-5

12 SA: A 34

13 Cape Breton Island remained French.

14 SA: A 37

15 PAC: PDP: letters patent creating Richard William Scott, Secretary of State of Canada, a Knight Bachelor, 1909

16 Jenkinson, 'The Great Seal of England,' p. 308

17 Ibid. p. 314

18 Ibid. p. 319

19 Ibid. p. 326

20 Ibid. p. 335 and see also Beamish Murdoch, *Epitome of the Laws of Nova Scotia* 1 (Halifax, Nova Scotia 1832) pp. 55-61 and 131.

21 For details see Peter Walne, 'The Great Seal Deputed of New Jersey,' *Proceedings of the New Jersey Historical Society* 79 (October 1961) pp. 223-31

22 PRO: SP 9/198, and for articles and notes on the Virginia Seals see E.S. Evans, 'The Seals of Virginia' published as part of the *Seventh Annual Report of the Library Board of the Virginia State Library* 1909-10; E.K. Timings, 'A Collector's Piece,' *Archives* Michaelmas 1951; Sir Hilary Jenkinson, *Guide to Seals in the Public Record Office* (London, HMSO 1954) p. 45; and Peter Walne, 'The Great Seal Deputed of Virginia,' *The Virginia Magazine of History and Biography* 66, 1, pp. 1-21.

23 ROM: 970.312.2. A notation indicates that it came from a document dated 16 June 1804.

24 PANS: box marked 'Seals'

25 Ibid. unattached seal removed from the land grant to Patrick Fenner of 300 acres at East River, Picton, 24 April 1812

26 I.e. of England, Scotland, the United Kingdom of Great Britain, and the United Kingdom of Great Britain and Ireland

27 Under Victoria the diameter of the Great Seal of the Realm expanded to $6^{1}/_{4}$ inches (158 millimetres).

28 Sir Henry Churchill Maxwell-Lyte, *Historical Notes on the Use of The Great Seal of England* (London, HMSO 1926) pp. 326-7

29 Good results can be had with seal impressions directly onto vellum, if done carefully, as is the current practice in the Court of the Lord Lyon at Edinburgh.

30 Dexel cellulose acetate moulding granules are used.

31 And for some other official seals, such as, for example, those of the Order of the Garter

32 Preserved in the Library of Parliament, Ottawa

33 In addition to the National Flag Proclamation of 1965, I have come across two dependent impressions of deputed great seals intended to be used *en placard*. These are both preserved in the Provincial Archives of New Brunswick (PANB Provincial Secretary): a patent appointing John Campbell Allen to be an Assistant Judge of the Supreme Court of Judicature of the Province of New Brunswick, 21 September 1865, where the great seal deputed of the province is impressed onto two pieces of square white paper with a wax wafer between and

depended from the patent by red tape; and another patent to James A. Harding, Sheriff of the City and County of St John 'to enquire whether Alexander Ballock be a lunatic or not,' 19 April 1865, where the dependent seal impression is as on the Allen patent save that the paper used in this case is blue.

34 Such as the Department of War and Colonies and the Department of Colonies

35 There is a good summary of the whole process by which deputed great seals came into being in PRO: PC 2/85 Privy Council August 1714-February 1716/17, p. 227: order of the Privy Council, 17 June 1715.

36 Royal Mint, London: Royal Mint Record Book (1843-5), 1/39, p. 4: C.E. Trevelyan, Treasury Chambers, to the Master of the Mint, 4 April 1843, and again p. 142 (7 December 1843) and p. 160 (20 December 1843)

37 *Calendar of Treasury Books and Papers, 1729-1730*, p. 235: royal warrant to John Grymes, Receiver of the Revenues in Virginia, 15 December 1729

38 6 Anne, c. 7, s. 9

39 *Letters Patent Constituting the Office of Governor General of Canada effective October 1, 1947* (Ottawa, King's Printer 1947)

40 PRO: CO 42/676, ffs. 322-7r: memorandum by Sir John A. Macdonald concerning the dominion and provincial great seals, 25 June 1869

41 From the British North America Act, 1867 (30 and 31 Vic., c. 3, s. 92 and 93)

42 PANS: vol. 102, Secretary of State to governors 1858, doc. 35, ffs. 186-92: Lord Stanley, Colonial Secretary, to the Earl of Mulgrave, Lieutenant Governor of Nova Scotia, 7 May 1858 (no. 16)

43 The privy seals of the lieutenant governors of Newfoundland, Ontario and Manitoba have for some years now tended to be of an official design rather than of their own arms.

CHAPTER 3

Arms of dominion and sovereignty for Canada

Were we to start this investigation with the first arms of dominion and sovereignty which pertained to Canada, then we would consider those of King Henry VII of England. It was in his name that John Cabot discovered and claimed certain parts of this country in 1497.

However, it fell to the French to establish the earliest continuous responsibility for and development of Canada, so let us begin with an examination of their armorial tokens of supreme power, of sovereign authority in and over what they termed New France, consequent upon the voyages of discovery by Jacques Cartier in 1534. As we have already seen in chapter 1, the accession of these vast areas to the Crown of France was proclaimed in armorial form by Jacques Cartier on the shores of Gaspé Bay on 24 July 1534, during the reign of Francis I.

FRANCIS I 1515-47

At this time, the arms *azure, three fleurs-de-lis-or,* comprised the royal ensigns of that kingdom [3.1].[1] In English this design is termed *France Modern* in contradistinction to *France Ancient* – *azure, semy-de-lis or* – which consisted of a blue background upon which were scattered an indeterminate number of gold fleurs-de-lis. This was done in such a way that a shield or banner of these arms appeared as if the design had been cut from a larger design so that some of the fleurs-de-lis near the edges were cut into and therefore only partly visible. In this form the arms of France date from the reign of Louis VIII (1223-26). In about 1375, however, Charles V changed the powdered lilies to three in honour of the Blessed Trinity, and so we have *France Modern*.

*3.1 Royal Arms of Francis I, 1515-47, surrounded by the collar of
the Order of St Michael, with cypher and salamander badge
Olivier and Hermal,* Reliures 25, *pl. 2487, no. 12 (see note 1)*

There is much discussion among scholars as to the origin of the charge known as the fleur-de-lis. It is to be found in East Indian, Egyptian, and Etruscan decorations, and in Roman and early Gothic architecture. It is difficult to decide whether the conventional fleur-de-lis was originally meant to represent the lily or the white iris (the flower-de-luce of Shakespeare), or an arrow or spear head.

The fleur-de-lis was first definitely connected with the French monarchy in an *ordonnance* of Louis le Jeune in about 1147 and first figured on the seal of Philip Augustus in 1180. Tradition soon attributed the origin of the fleur-de-lis to Clovis, founder of the Frankish monarchy. For this the explanation was that the fleur-de-lis represented the lily given to him by an angel at his baptism. According to a more rationalistic explanation, it was the figure used on a sceptre at the proclamation of the Frankish kings.

Be that as it may, there is little doubt that this charge, which is capable of an almost infinite variety of interpretations, is possibly one of the most beautiful of all armorial forms. It soon became symbolic of France, and of her authority, remaining as such throughout the entire period of her sovereignty over Canada.

At the time of Francis I, the royal crown most usually displayed in conjunction with the arms comprised a jewelled circlet from which rose four large and four small fleurs-de-lis placed alternately. In representations, as on the counter seal, only a large central fleur-de-lis flanked by two small ones and then two half fleurs-de-lis at either edge of the circlet complete the visible composition.

The other type of royal crown used in conjunction with the royal arms, as on the Counter Seal of Henry IV, consists of a jewelled gold circlet. Upon this are set eight

3.2 *Royal arms comprising*
France Modern *and* Navarre *accollé*
BN: *Réserve Fol. Lm³ 121: La Roque,* Blasons,
frontispiece (see note 2)

3.3 *Reverse of the* Kebeca Liberata *medal, 1690*
PAC: PDP

fleurs-de-lis (five only usually visible in representations) from which rise as many arches (sometimes only six). These meet over the centre and are topped by a fleur-de-lis. The spine of each arch is decorated with gold crockets. Possibly because of the Old Alliance between France and Scotland one finds the same type of characteristic decoration on the arches of the Royal Crown of Scotland, guarded in Edinburgh Castle.

Two angels frequently act as supporters for the arms.

Basically, the royal arms remained in this form during the entire duration of the French authority in New France. Indeed, it was in this form that they most frequently seem to have appeared. Such additions as did occur, especially as the period wore on, comprised grand collars of royal orders which surrounded the shield of arms. Usually these were the Orders of St Michael and of the Holy Ghost, as in a superb example, carved in wood and fully coloured, preserved in the Provincial Museum at Quebec.

The Order of St Michael was founded in 1469 by Louis XI. The badge of the order consisted of a gold, oval medallion upon which was a representation of St Michael the Archangel in combat with the Devil. This was suspended from a collar which consisted of shells linked together by twisted coils, all of gold; through the centre of the collar passed a black cord.

The Order of the Holy Ghost was founded by Henry III in 1578. What the Garter is to the English, the Holy Ghost was to the French. The badge was a gold, eight-pointed Maltese Cross, edged in green and white. Each point was blunted with a small ball, fleurs-de-lis were placed between the interstices, and in the centre of the cross there was a white dove, head downwards and with wings extended, symbolic of the Holy Ghost. This badge was suspended from a collar which consisted of three repeated devices; first, a helm in profile resting against a trophy of six flags; second, an enflamed fleur-de-lis; and third, four royal crowns placed with the under part of their circlets in such a way as to form a hollow square, in the centre of which was at times the letter H and at others the letter L.

HENRY IV 1589-1610

It should be noted that from the reign of Henry IV, under whom Quebec City was founded (in 1608), the official royal arms [3.2] comprised not only *France Modern,* but also *Navarre* placed accollé, that is to say side by side. The latter were: *gules, a cross and a saltire of chains affixed to an annulet in the fesse-point and a double orle of the same all or.* [2] These most distinctive arms, with a red background, a cross and saltire of gold chains all connected together and to a double line of similar surrounding chains, were brought by the King of Navarre to the royal achievement upon his becoming the first King of France of the House of Bourbon as Henry IV, in 1589.

Nevertheless, as mentioned before, the most usual form the royal arms took in connection with Canada was *France Modern* alone. The celebrated *Kebeca Liberata* medal struck in 1690 to commemorate the siege of Quebec by Sir William Phips and his defeat by the Count de Frontenac, is a case in point [3.3]. The medal is of silvered bronze and has a diameter of 1⅝ inches (41 millimetres). On the reverse, France, represented as a female figure, holds an oval shield bearing the three fleurs-de-lis alone. A beaver, representing Canada, is placed at her feet. In the background are various banners, trophies of war. On the one most clearly visible, royal arms for England are em-

*3.4 Beauséjour-Memramcook chalice and paten (c. 1736)
with royal arms engraved on the foot and the rim respectively
Musée acadien de l'Université de Moncton*

3.5 Detail of royal arms on the rim of the paten

blazoned. However, instead of the first quarter containing the Grand Quartering of *France Modern* and *England* quarterly – as actually occurred in the royal arms of the time – on this banner *England* only is depicted.[3] Obviously His Most Christian Majesty was in no mood to humour the pretensions of his brother monarch and cousin by blood, William III of Orange, so recently on the English throne.[4]

A further example of the use of *France Modern* alone in Canada is to be found in the engraving of the royal arms on the Beauséjour-Memramcook chalice and paten of about 1736 now preserved in the Musée Acadien at Moncton, New Brunswick [3.4 and 3.5]. Two branches of palm are also included outside the shield, but these are purely decorative embellishments and not an intrinsic part of the arms, just as with the *main de justice* and sceptre with the fleur-de-lis which were occasionally placed in saltire behind the shield [3.6].

LOUIS XIII 1610-43, LOUIS XIV 1643-1715, LOUIS XV 1715-74

For Louis XIII, Louis XIV, and Louis XV, indeed right up to the end of the French regime in New France, the position concerning the royal arms continued along the lines just discussed [3.7 and 3.8, and plate 3].

It possibly ought to be mentioned that upon occasion, although not to the author's knowledge in Canada, the royal armorial bearings of France included: a shield of *France Modern,* royal helm, crown, mantling; collars of the Orders of St Michael and of the Holy Ghost; the *main de justice* and sceptre with the fleur-de-lis, in saltire; angel supporters wearing dalmatics – at times tabards [3.9 and plate 4] – of *France Modern* supporting banners of those same arms; with a crowned pavilion *azure, semy of fleurs-de-lis or, lined ermine,* above which flies an oriflamme, *gules, semy of fleurs-de-lis or:* accompanied by a *cri de guerre,* MONTJOYE SAINT DENIS (a call to victory addressed to the Patron of France),[5] and the motto, LILIA NON LABORANT NEQUE NENT (The lilies neither do they labour nor spin [St Matthew 6:28] – an obvious pun on the arms) [3.10].[6]

HENRY VII 1485-1509

While there is no doubt that the French were the first to express their authority in Canada continuously in heraldic form, nevertheless it is probable, indeed almost certain, that heraldry was first introduced to this country as an expression of English authority. This took the form of the banner of St George flown from the ship of John Cabot when, sailing under the authority of Henry VII of England, he crossed the North Atlantic and explored the coasts of Labrador, Newfoundland, and possibly Cape Breton Island. Further, Cabot claimed these territories for his patron by the heraldic ceremony described in chapter 1, with the result that the first arms of dominion and sovereignty applicable to Canada were those as borne by the Tudors. Further, as all this took place in 1497, if one accepts that three years later began the Modern Period, as many historians are wont to do, one might claim as a result that Canada and heraldry began their association in the Middle Ages.

Henry VII bore:

Arms: *quarterly, France Modern and England;* the shield was usually encircled with the Garter and ensigned by a royal crown

*3.6 Royal Arms of Louis XV, 1715-74,
with* main de justice *and sceptre placed in saltire
Olivier and Hermal,* Reliures 25, *pl. 2495, no. 21 (see note 1)*

*3.7 Obverse of jeton of 1645 (diameter 1 ¹/₂₀″, 27 mm)
National Currency Collection,
Bank of Canada, Ottawa*

*3.8 Reverse of silver 15 sols of New France
(Canada) of 1670 (diameter ⅞″, 22 mm)
National Currency Collection,
Bank of Canada, Ottawa*

3.9 *Full achievement of the Royal Arms of France (from 1589) without motto (see plate 4)*

BN: *Réserve: Vélins 25 PC 10: Chevillard*, Grand Armorial, *f. 1*

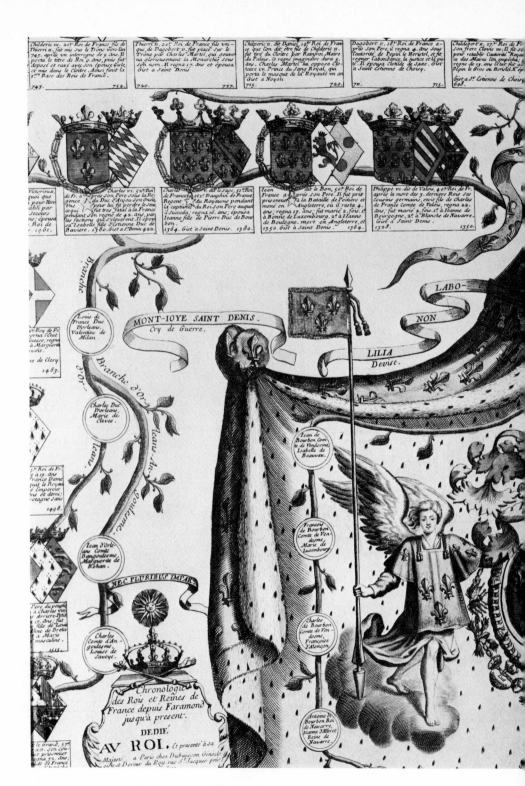

3.10 *Full achievement of the Royal Arms of France (from 1589) with motto*

BN: *Réserve: Vélins 25 PC 10: Chevillard*, Grand Armorial

Crest: *on a chapeau encircled by a coronet a lion statant guardant crowned or; mantling gules, lined ermine*

Supporters: *a dragon gules, and a greyhound argent*[7]

Motto: DIEU ET MON DROIT (God and my right) [plate 9]

We have already discussed the composition of *France Modern*. *England*, on the other hand, signifies: *gules, three lions passant guardant in pale or*, that is to say, on a red background three gold lions, heads turned towards the viewer, with the right foreleg of each beast raised. It will be appreciated that *England* in this context is an heraldic term, rather than a geographical entity. Indeed, when first created in the reign of Richard I (Richard Cœur de Lion, 1189-99),[8] and for the following century and a half, this design was intended to be the armorial expression of a sovereignty which was exercised on both sides of the English Channel – almost as much in France as in England.

The French quartering entered the English arms in 1340 when Edward III asserted his succession to the throne of France *de jure matris*. Accordingly, he employed the then new practice of quartering the arms of his two sovereignties, yielding first place to the more ancient of the two, and so placing the French arms in the 1st and 4th quarters, with *England* in the 2nd and 3rd.

Thus for about the next half-millennium until 1801, the golden lilies of France on an azure field remained in what we might term first the English and then the British royal arms. We shall note their return in connection with Canada on a later occasion.

When Edward III quartered *England* and the arms of France, the latter were at that time *azure, semy of fleurs-de-lis or*, or *France Ancient*, which have already been discussed earlier in this chapter. It will be recalled that in about 1375, Charles V of France reduced the number of fleurs-de-lis to three and, accordingly, in 1405 Henry IV of England followed suit, with the result that by the time the Tudors came to the throne eighty years later the royal arms were well established as, quarterly, *France Modern* and *England*.

The Garter was frequently placed round the Tudor shield. This is the most characteristic part of the insignia of this order of which the monarch is sovereign. Founded in about 1348 by Edward III, it is the oldest secular order of chivalry in the world (orders such as the Sovereign and Military Order of Malta, founded in 1099, are essentially religious). The Garter is shown in emblazonments coloured blue and inscribed in gold letters in old French HONI SOIT QUI MAL Y PENSE (Shame to him who evil thinks). A gold buckle and guard at the threading end of the Garter completes this part of the insignia of the order.[9]

A royal crown frequently ensigned the shield. Rising from a jewelled rim were fleurs-de-lis and crosses paty placed alternately with the former in the centre. From these rose arches, usually four in number, embellished with crochets. Where they meet is placed an orb and cross, symbolic of the triumph of Christ over the world. When on a crown it recalls the classical Christian position that no matter the mechanics, form, or manner of exercise, all legitimate authority comes ultimately from God.

The crest of Henry VII consisted of a red velvet chapeau or cap turned up with ermine and surrounded by a coronet. Upon the top of the chapeau stands a gold lion, its head crowned and in the same position as in the arms: *a lion statant guardant or, regally crowned proper*. The mantling or material which hangs down from beneath the crest on either side of the helm is red, lined with ermine. The construction of the sovereign's helm at this time appears to have varied considerably. At times it had an open vizor and bars,[10] sometimes shown in profile,[11] and at other times what would now be termed an esquire's helm was used.[12]

On either side stand the supporters. At times, as in plate 9, a red dragon is to the dexter (left hand to the viewer) and a silver greyhound to the sinister (right hand to the viewer). The dragon had long been the device of the Anglo-Saxon kings. It will be recalled that a dragon standard, constructed along lines similar to an airfield wind-sock, was flown by Harold at the battle of Hastings. Yet again, Henry Tudor at the Battle of Bosworth Field fought under the standard of the Red Dragon of Cadwallader. Upon his victory, Henry introduced a red dragon as one of the supporters to the royal arms. The greyhound is an ancient and popular heraldic charge, and was especially so with the Tudors. Indeed, at times Henry vii had greyhounds alone as supporters. Upon other occasions under this monarch the red dragon forms the sinister supporter, and a gold lion is placed on the dexter side. This king of beasts, renowned for its ferocity, appears to have been introduced into the royal arms by the saintly Henry vi.

The supporters stand on a green compartment or grassy hillock. Upon this is placed the royal motto scroll inscribed DIEU ET MON DROIT. This motto was first used by Henry v (1413-22), the victor of Agincourt, and in addition to some others has been retained down to Her present Majesty.[13]

However, following Cabot's explorations and claim of the country for his patron, little was done to assert the authority symbolized by these arms. This situation continued until 1584, when Sir Humphrey Gilbert proclaimed English sovereignty in Newfoundland. From then on the Royal Arms of the English, subsequently the British, Crown came more and more to the fore with the assertion and consolidation of authority and sovereignty in Canada.

JAMES I 1603-25

The royal arms borne by James I of England by virtue of the sovereignty to which he succeeded upon the death of the last of the Tudors, Elizabeth I, in 1603, were as follows:

Arms: *quarterly, 1 and 4, grand quarters, France Modern and England quarterly; 2, Scotland; 3, Ireland;* the shield was usually encircled with the Garter
Crest: *on a royal crown proper, a lion statant guardant or, regally crowned proper; mantling or, doubled ermine*
Supporters: *dexter, a lion rampant guardant or, regally crowned proper* (for England); *sinister, a unicorn argent, armed, unguled and crined or, gorged with a coronet composed of crosses paty and fleurs-de-lis gold, a chain affixed thereto of the last passing between the forelegs and reflexed over the back* (for Scotland)
Motto: DIEU ET MON DROIT [plate 10]

When James ascended the throne of England as first of that name as well as first of the House of Stuart, he had already been James vi of Scotland since 1567. Uniting two sovereignties in himself, he quartered the royal arms of each, placing those of England in the first quarter, with those of Scotland in the second: *or, a lion rampant within a double tressure flory counter-flory gules.* These had been the Arms of the Scottish Crown since Alexander II (1214-49), and are usually referred to in heraldry simply as *Scotland.* On a gold background is placed a red lion rampant which, in turn, is surrounded by two narrow parallel red stripes which follow the shape of the shield, banner, quarter, or the like upon which it is placed. Red fleurs-de-lis, facing outwards and inwards alternately, are placed across the red stripes, but with those parts of the fleurs-de-lis between the stripes cut away.

For the first time the arms of Ireland – *azure, a harp or, stringed argent,* more simply referred to as *Ireland* – were incorporated into the royal arms under the Stuarts.

From Henry VIII to the present the crest has been the same; similarly, the mantling – gold, lined ermine – has been the same since Elizabeth I. By the reign of James, a barred helm affronté was usual for a sovereign – often silver with gold embellishments. Ultimately, this became gold throughout and has been so used ever since.

A gold lion supporter has already been noted under Henry VII. The unicorn, which had already occurred in royal Scottish heraldry, was introduced by James I.[14] This mythical beast of armory is coloured silver with gold horn, mane, and hooves. Round its neck is a gold coronet, from which depends a gold chain which passes between the forelegs and over the back.

It will be recalled that, as King of Scotland, James had decided upon the plantation of Nova Scotia in connection with the colonisation plans of Sir William Alexander, later Earl of Stirling and Viscount of Canada. This will be discussed in further detail in chapter 7. At this juncture it will suffice to note the armorial expression of dominion and sovereignty under which the scheme was launched. As the plantation was a Scottish venture, the appropriate ensigns of public authority were those borne by James as King of Scotland, which were as follows:

Arms: *quarterly, 1 and 4, Scotland; 2, grand quarters, France Modern and England quarterly; 3, Ireland;* the shield was usually encircled with a collar of thistles from which depended a badge of St Andrew

Crest: *on a royal crown proper a lion affronté sejant gules, armed and langued azure, royally crowned proper holding in the dexter paw a sword and in the sinister paw a sceptre both proper, and in an escrol over the same the motto* IN DEFENS; *a royal helm with mantling or, doubled ermine*

Supporters: *dexter, a unicorn argent, armed, crined and unguled or, royally crowned proper gorged with a coronet composed of crosses paty and fleurs-de-lis gold, a chain affixed thereto of the last passing between the forelegs and reflexed over the back supporting a lance proper from which flies to the dexter a banner azure, charged with a saltire argent* (for Scotland). *Sinister, a lion rampant guardant or, royally crowned proper supporting a like lance from which flies to the sinister a banner argent, charged with a cross gules* (for England)

Motto: NEMO ME IMPUNE LACESSIT (No one provokes me with impunity) [plate 5]

As will be seen, the armorial bearings are similar to those which appertained to the English Crown but with a rearrangement. *Scotland* is placed in the first and fourth quarters, *England* in the second, and *Ireland* in the third. The crest ante-dates the personal union of 1603 and is the final form evolved over many years in Scotland from the time of Robert II (1370-1)[15]

The supporters have opposite places to those they occupy for his other sovereignty, and for the Scottish Crown they support banners of national flags. The general influence of these Royal Arms of James VI and I for Scotland upon those of Canada, as assigned in 1921, will be appreciated immediately.

CHARLES I 1625-48

The Royal Arms of England under Charles I were as for his father, James I.

OLIVER CROMWELL, Lord Protector 1653-58

Under Oliver Cromwell, the royal arms were superseded by:

Arms: *quarterly, 1 and 4, argent, the Cross of St George gules* (for England); *2, azure, the saltire of St Andrew argent* (for Scotland); *3, azure, a harp or, stringed argent* (for Ireland); *and on an inescutcheon in pretence sable, a lion rampant argent* (the personal arms of Oliver Cromwell)
Crest: *the royal crest of England* (as borne by Charles I) *and a royal helm with mantling sable and ermine*
Supporters: *dexter, a lion rampant guardant royally crowned or; sinister, a dragon with wings elevated gules, purfled or*[16]
Motto: PAX QUAERITUR BELLO (Peace is sought by war – adapted from Cornelius Nepos, *Epaminondas* 5.4)

The origin or inspiration of each official charge, as it were, is obvious. It may not be out of place to draw attention, however, to the fact that crowns, as used in this Republican achievement, do not themselves necessarily indicate monarchy but rather sovereignty. Another much longer-lived example of the use of the crown by a republic will be found in the complete armorial achievement of the oldest republic in the world, San Marino. The Arms of the Polish Republic between the two world wars would be another case in point.

CHARLES II 1660-85, JAMES II 1685-8

Upon the Restoration of the Monarchy in 1660, Charles II bore the royal arms as borne by his father, Charles I, and similarly with James II when he succeeded to the throne in 1685.

WILLIAM III AND MARY II 1689-1702

William III, as an elective sovereign, marshalled his paternal Arms of Nassau, *azure billety and a lion rampant or*[17] with the royal arms as borne since 1603 [plate 11.1]. He placed *Nassau* on an inescutcheon, and this is the usual form in which the royal arms were borne throughout his reign. A good example of these arms in carved and painted wood will be found in that Loyalist foundation, All Saints Anglican Church at St Andrew's, New Brunswick. It was brought there by the Reverend Samuel Andrews, formerly Rector of St Paul's in Wallingford, Connecticut, when he came in 1786. At times, however, the royal arms as borne by William III were impaled with the royal arms as borne by his wife, Mary II – which were those of all Stuart sovereigns since 1603 – in order to emphasize the joint nature of the reign when both sovereigns were regnant.

ANNE 1702-14

Upon the accession of the last of the Stuarts to the throne, Queen Anne bore the royal arms as had her father, James II, and her uncle, Charles II, before her. The arms remained the same until the Union of England and Scotland to form the United Kingdom of Great Britain in 1707, when the royal arms were remarshalled as follows:

Arms: *1 and 4, grand quarters, England impaling Scotland; 2, France Modern; 3, Ireland;* the shield usually encircled with the Garter
Crest and Supporters: as described under James I[18]
Motto: SEMPER EADEM (Always the same)

It will be noted here that in these arms *England* is marshalled *impaling Scotland,* as with a matrimonial achievement for the arms of a husband and his wife. *France Modern* is placed in the second quarter, and *Ireland* remains constant in the third. The contemporary and very fine communion flagon and alms basin of St Paul's Church, Halifax, engraved with these second Royal Arms of Queen Anne will be recalled [3.11].[19]

GEORGE I 1714-27

The next reign brought a change in the royal arms when George I of the House of Guelph or Hanover succeeded to the throne upon the death of his cousin Queen Anne. With the advent of a new house the royal arms were marshalled as follows:

Arms: *quarterly, 1, England impaling Scotland; 2, France Modern; 3, Ireland; 4, Hanover;* the shield usually encircled by the Garter[20]
Crest, supporters, and motto: as since the Stuart monarchs [3.12]

The Arms of Hanover, to be found in the fourth quarter of the royal arms, comprised: *tierced in pairle reversed: 1, gules, two lions passant guardant in pale or* (for Brunswick); *2, or, semy of hearts gules, a lion rampant azure* (for Luneburg); *3, gules, a horse courant argent* (for Westphalia); *and over all an inescutcheon gules, charged with the golden crown of Charlemagne* (the augmentation or badge of the Arch Treasurer of the Holy Roman Empire, an office held by the Electors of Hanover). That is to say, the arms are divided down the middle to the centre point, after which the line of division curves to the left and to the right until the edges of the shield, quarter, banner, and the like are met. In the first, or upper left, division are placed two gold lions passant guardant against red (for Brunswick). In the upper right division a blue lion rampant stands against a gold background scattered with red hearts (for Luneburg); the third and lower division is red with a silver horse in full gallop (for Westphalia). At the centre of the total design is placed a small red shield upon which is emblazoned a representation of the crown of the Emperor Charlemagne.

The arms will be found engraved on the Georgian Communion flagon and chalice among the Communion plate of St Paul's Church, Halifax.[21] There is a further example, this time carved in wood and coloured, of about 1714. Originally erected in Boston, it was brought after the American Revolution to Saint John, New Brunswick, where it is now in Trinity Church in that city [plate 11.2].

3.11 Royal Arms of Queen Anne as borne 1707-14 on the communion flagon of St Paul's Church, Halifax, Nova Scotia, and detail showing the letter A for Anne beneath the re-engraved G for George I

3.12 Indian Chief silver medal with
royal arms as borne 1714-1801 (George I, II, and III)
Royal Ontario Museum, Toronto: 949.69.3

3.13 Indian Chief silver medal with
royal arms as borne 1801-16 (see plate 12)
Royal Ontario Museum, Toronto: 950.112

GEORGE II 1727-60

George II bore the same royal arms, crest, supporters, and motto as did his father George I. Apparently the first known occurrence of these arms in Canada for this second sovereign of the House of Hanover is to be noted on the 1730 Seal of Nova Scotia, which will be discussed in chapter 7.

GEORGE III 1760-1820

Until 1801 George III bore the same royal arms as had obtained since 1714. Upon the Union of Great Britain with Ireland in 1801 to form the United Kingdom of Great Britain and Ireland, the royal arms were marshalled as follows:

Arms: *quarterly, 1 and 4, England; 2, Scotland; 3, Ireland; and over all an escutcheon of Hanover ensigned with an electoral bonnet;* the shield usually encircled by the Garter[22] Crest, supporters, and motto: as since the Stuart monarchs [3.13 and plate 12]

The opportunity was taken to remove the quartering of France since the Crown of England had not exercised any sovereignty in France since the loss of Calais under Mary Tudor (1558). The return of *France Modern* to the Arms of Canada will, however, be discussed subsequently in this chapter.

The electoral bonnet was a species of cap of maintenance in that it was made of red velvet and turned up with ermine. The latter was finished with an indented upper edge which showed against the red velvet. A gold tassel at the centre of its velvet crown completed the bonnet.

3.14 Wood carving on the back of the throne in the Legislative Assembly Chamber, Fredericton, showing the royal arms as borne 1801-16

Few examples of the royal arms as marshalled in 1801 are to be found in Canada. One occurs on the upper part of the back of the throne in the Legislative Chamber in Fredericton, New Brunswick [3.14]. Here the supporters have been placed in a *couchant* position on either side of the shield, so reminiscent of the late eighteenth and early nineteenth centuries. Another example occurs on the mace of the Senate of Canada [3.15]. Highly embossed in silver-gilt on the arms plate, it is located inside the circlet of the crown and forms the top and cover to the head or bowl of the mace. As the royal arms were slightly altered again in 1816, these two examples are of extreme interest because of their rarity in Canada.

1816

In the year 1814, Hanover became a kingdom and accordingly the electoral bonnet was replaced by a royal crown two years later. This particular crown consisted of a jewelled circlet upon which were set a central cross paty and four strawberry leaves, visible in representations. From these rose five pearl- and jewel-encrusted arches, also visible in representations, which met under an orb and cross.[23]

GEORGE IV 1820-30

George IV bore the royal arms as marshalled in 1816. Behind the bench of the Supreme Court of New Brunswick the arms of this sovereign are emblazoned in full colour as the central motif in a typical late eighteenth- and early nineteenth-century classical compos-

3.15 Royal arms as borne 1801-16 on the arms plate of the mace of the Senate of Canada
Office of the Gentleman Usher of the Black Rod, Ottawa

ition [plate 13.1]. Three arches, each supported by Corinthian columns, create as many niches. The central one is filled with the Royal Arms of George IV complete with shield, crest, helm, mantling, supporters, and motto, as well as a wreath of roses, shamrocks, and thistles placed beneath the arms and supporters. In the niche to the viewer's left stands a female figure in classical attire, personifying Mercy with her looking glass, book of the law, and clarity of intellect (suggested by the rays of light about her head). In the opposite niche stands a similar figure holding the sword and scales of Justice. Above each of the central columns is the cypher $G.R \atop IV$. Painted on canvas and surrounded by a suitable gilt frame, this armorial piece is probably one of the finest of its kind in Canada which relates to the short reign of this sovereign.[24]

WILLIAM IV 1830-37

The royal arms as borne by William IV were the same as for his brother and predecessor, George IV. Their occurrence on the deputed great seals in Canada, issued during the reign of William IV for Upper Canada and other provinces will be discussed in subsequent chapters.

VICTORIA 1837-1901

As a result of the Salic Law, Queen Victoria did not succeed to the Kingdom of Hanover and accordingly the shield of that kingdom ensigned by its particular crown was removed from the royal shield, with the result that royal arms became as follows:

Arms: *quarterly, 1 and 4, England; 2, Scotland and 3, Ireland;* the shield surrounded by the Garter[25]
Crest, supporters, and motto: as for William IV [plate 13.2]

In other words, we have now arrived at that form of the royal arms of the British Crown which since the accession of Queen Victoria down to the present are borne by virtue of sovereignty in all places and at all times where no other arms have been specifically assigned. That is to say, they are royal arms of general purpose. Commonly, but inaccurately, this form of the royal arms is referred to as the arms of the United Kingdom, although, as indicated already, royal arms refer to authority and jurisdiction rather than a geographical area.

Possibly the most dramatic representation of these arms in Canada occurs at Government House, Ottawa, where they are carved in stone in the tympanum above the principal entrance. Not to be compared with the work of Soucy and MacCarthy about the main entrance to Parliament at the base of the Peace Tower on Parliament Hill, from the point of view of sophisticated armorial carving, nevertheless those over Government House have that ingenuous charm of work by local craftsmen interpreting ensigns of such great authority and dignity that they rendered them in size, it is believed, second to none in existence.[26]

EDWARD VII 1901-10

The royal arms as borne by Edward VII were those as borne by his mother, Queen Victoria (see figure 2.11). The interpretation, however, especially concerning the form of royal crown, was that favoured from about 1880 onwards when what is termed the imperial crown came into use. Instead of being depressed under the cross and orb, as on the mace of the Senate of Canada [3.16], the four arches of the crown were raised into semi-circular arches as, for example, upon the head of the mace of the Legislative Assembly of New Brunswick [3.17].[27] This type of crown continued in use until the beginning of Her present Majesty's reign.

Although the adoption of this form of heraldic crown was inspired very largely by the assumption of the title of Empress of India by Queen Victoria (1877), it will be recalled that such a crown predated the existence of a British Empire by many years. The Tudors had used such a form – the stone carvings of Henry VII's crown in King's College Chapel, Cambridge, are an excellent example.[28]

GEORGE V 1910-36

Upon the death of King Edward VII in 1910, his son succeeded as King George V and continued to bear the same royal arms as had his father as sovereign of Canada. In fact, between Confederation in 1867 and 1921 there were no official and particular ensigns of federal authority for the sovereign in right of Canada distinct from the royal arms just referred to. A royal warrant was issued on 26 May 1868[29] for the design of a great seal for the Dominion of Canada, which was to consist of a shield bearing quarterly the arms of the four original provinces, Ontario, Quebec, New Brunswick, and Nova Scotia, as assigned to each individually by the same warrant. Details of these arms will be discussed subsequently in the chapter on each province concerned.

It should be noted that this design was specifically assigned as that for the 'Great Seal of Canada which said Seal shall be composed of the Arms of the said Four Provinces Quarterly'[30] and not as arms of federal authority, which fact is further borne out by the customary summary inscribed at the foot of the warrant in which it is described as a 'Warrant granting Armorial Bearings for the Provinces of Ontario, Quebec, Nova Scotia, New Brunswick, and a Great Seal for the Dominion of Canada.'[31]

However, from the outset, as it proved, the seal design as laid down in the warrant was regarded as the 'Armorial Bearings for the Dominion,' to quote the Secretary of State for the Colonies when forwarding the royal warrant to the Governor General.[32] Little wonder, then, that at length they were to be found carved on the supporting wall of the canopy over the main door of the viceregal residence at Ottawa. This, coupled with a natural patriotic desire for a symbol of identification, not to mention the convenience, if not requirement, of such a symbol for governmental purposes, led to the widespread use of the design as the Arms of Canada. Even Sir Joseph Pope, Under Secretary of State for External Affairs, who took a great interest in these matters, as we shall see, had accepted, for some time at least, this widely held view.[33] By 1915, however, he was moved to ask his friend and collaborator, Ambrose Lee, then York Herald of Arms, 'if any armorial bearings have ever been assigned to the Dominion of Canada.'[34] Pope had concerned himself with the matter of provincial and federal arms since 1897.[35] Indeed, there can be no doubt that it was due to his efforts, in collaboration with Lee, who was successively Bluemantle Pursuivant, York Herald, Norroy King of Arms, and ultimately Clarenceux King of Arms, that by 1906 every province had received a royal warrant of arms.

*3.16 Head of the mace of the Senate of Canada showing the arches of the crown
depressed under the cross and orb in the form known as St Edward's crown
Office of the Gentleman Usher of the Black Rod, Ottawa*

3.17 Head of the mace of the Legislative Assembly of New Brunswick showing the crown in the form known as an imperial crown, with the arches domed Fredericton

3.18 *Seal of the Deputy to the Governor General, made between 1871 and 1906 (probably during the 1890s before 1896), showing the many-quartered shield often used as the Arms of Canada before 1921*
PAC: PDP

Although Pope had once been in favour of an aggregation of provincial arms in order to form those of federal authority [3.18], by 1907 he had come to hold the view that they ought to be a distinct and separate device.[36] Accordingly, he and Lee started to discuss possible designs,[37] but Pope had to admit that no one in authority in Canada wanted to concern himself, at that time, with these tokens of federal identity. Nevertheless, he never lost sight of the need for such a device, and he continued to discuss the matter with Lee: even during World War I, in 1915, he found time to write to York Herald and say that he thought Canada ought to have arms of her own and that he was 'not without hope when this terrible war is over, this may be brought about.'[38]

And so it was. With the war ended, the most catastrophic the world had known up to that time, Canada emerged with a greater awareness of her own identity, doubtless owing, in part at least, to the conspicuous and independent part she had played both in the fighting and in the subsequent peacemaking.

As a consequence of this, as Pope explained to Lee, 'there is a feeling here among those who have given any consideration to the subject, that the time has arrived when Canada should have Arms of her own, distinct from the provinces of which the Dominion is composed.'[39] This led to the government of Canada obtaining an Order of the Governor General in Council[40] for the appointment of a committee to investigate not only the matter in its broader aspects but also the desirability of requesting the king to institute ensigns armorial of federal public authority for Canada. The committee was a distinguished group: Thomas Mulvey, KC, Under Secretary of State, was chairman, with Sir Joseph Pope, KCMG, CVO, ISO, Under Secretary of State for External Affairs, A.G. Doughty, CMG, Litt. D, Dominion Archivist, and Major-General W.G. Gwatkin, CB,

CMG, of the Department of Militia and Defence, as members.[41]

The committee addressed itself to its task with a will, and on the College of Arms side it had the enthusiastic and sympathetic assistance of Ambrose Lee, York Herald. York's attitude, and indeed that of the college as a whole, was expressed succinctly when he told Pope in June 1919, 'We should be very glad to meet the wishes of the Dominion authorities in any way possible';[42] as to the details of the design the arms might take, York felt that 'it would help us very much if suggestions could be put forward from your side.'[43]

By January 1920, the Canadian committee had arrived at a design which included many of the basic elements ultimately to be assigned by the king in the following year. This they forwarded to the Officers of Arms, being those members of the royal household whose duty it is to assist the sovereign in matters armorial. York passed the design to Sir Henry Farnham Burke, KCVO, CB, FSA, a celebrated master of the art and science of heraldry, who, as Garter King of Arms, bore the principal responsibility for advising the monarch concerning arms.[44]

Garter was not enamoured of what he saw, for two basic reasons. The first was a purely personal reaction; he felt that 'the Arms for Canada should be as simple and distinctive as possible, such as a maple leaf within a tressure flory.'[45] The second was much more serious; he felt that as 'the suggested Arms for Canada are ... a variation of the Royal Arms, [this is] a matter in which we must walk very warily,'[46] for the very good reason that the royal arms are governed by the Union with Ireland Act (1800)[47] as declared by the proclamation of 1 January 1801. As a result the arms for Canada could not be dealt with in the normal manner, that is by means of a royal warrant. Basically, the question as Garter saw it was whether the proposed arms were in contravention of an Act of Parliament. As the principal adviser to the sovereign in matters armorial, and faced with a stated decision of the sovereign in Parliament, Garter was in duty bound to investigate this difficult constitutional situation.

His position was made all the more difficult coming, as it did, at one of those junctures of history when practice was outrunning constitutional theory. The Statute of Westminster was still a decade away, and in theory the British Parliament was the supreme authority as far as Canada was concerned. However, as so often happens in the history of British institutions, certain practices and customs, of which subsequent statutes are but formal statements, were well on the way to full development by the early 1920s. Nevertheless, while it is not difficult to trace historical developments with the benefit of hindsight, their ultimate shape is rarely so obvious to those immediately concerned, especially in human affairs when the possible courses to be taken are often several and by no means pre-ordained. In other words, there are none so aware of the importance of the human element in affairs of state as those at the very heart of such developments.

Garter had to make sure that whatever was done in this situation was not done unconstitutionally or illegally and so to the dishonour of the Crown and of Canada, and he was in honour bound to take all reasonable action to clarify the position. Accordingly, in order to obtain the best advice available, he consulted the Deputy Earl Marshal, Lord Fitzalan of Derwent; the Secretary of State for the Colonies, Winston Churchill; the Private Secretary to King George V, Lord Stamfordham; and the Law Officers of the Crown, among others.

On the other hand, York Herald, possibly because of his long association with Sir Joseph Pope, clearly sensed the changing circumstances of the time and early in 1920 told Garter frankly, 'My *private* opinion is that the Canadian Government's position is strong enough to ensure their getting what they may decide to ask for.'[48]

In the meantime the Canadian authorities were anything but inactive and, probably becoming aware of Garter's reticence over their design, decided to press on all fronts for its acceptance. Towards the end of the year, the Colonial Office was pressing Garter for a decision,[49] and before the year was ended Lord Stamfordham confirmed to him that 'endless attempts have been made to get round the corner to the King with regard to the proposed Arms of Canada';[50] these attempts were obviously not without effect, for by mid-November the Secretary of State for the Colonies informed the Governor General that he was 'given to understand that the King will gladly give his consent to the proposed incorporation of portions of the Royal Arms.'[51]

In the spring of the following year, the Canadian authorities decided to move up their heavy artillery, as it were, and so on 30 April 1921 the Privy Council of Canada ordered that the 'necessary steps be taken to submit the report of the Committee to His Majesty the King for confirmation, with a request that His Majesty might be pleased to direct the College of Arms to record the device which accompanied it as the Arms of the Dominion of Canada.'[52] Ten days later Mr Churchill informed the Governor General that the king had approved the design of the arms and that a warrant would be issued when the necessary Canadian Order in Council and new design were received by mail.[53] Then, in order to try and hasten the matter forward, Churchill wrote in his own hand to the Deputy Earl Marshal, observing that as the king had approved the design, and the Canadian government was so informed, there was really no alternative but to accept the situation.[54] Thus spoke the politician, but if Churchill thought that through the Deputy Earl Marshal he could move Garter to change his stand, he must have overlooked, for the moment at least, the fact that the incumbent of that office was Irish, one of a race which tends to become more stubborn, or more firm, depending upon one's point of view, the more it senses opposition. Garter remained unshaken; he could see no adequate reason to alter his opinion, and further the Law Officers had not yet given their opinion.

Spring gave way to summer, during which, in answer to what he obviously considered an importunate enquiry from the Colonial Office, Garter growled, 'I am not yet in a position to say when the Warrant will be ready for submission to His Majesty.'[55] It was early winter when, at last, Garter was vindicated and 'the Colonial Office ... properly strafed,' as he put it,[56] for, on 24 October, the Attorney General gave as his opinion that the king might properly be advised to proceed to the matter of the Canadian arms by a royal proclamation.[57] Now that a method had been arrived at whereby the arms could be assigned without infringing the Union with Ireland Act of 1800, Garter was free to arrange matters accordingly, which he did with speed. The result was that within four weeks, that is to say on 21 November 1921, King George V assigned by royal proclamation the following armorial bearings for Canada [plate 14]:

Arms: *tierced in fesse the first and second divisions containing the quarterly coat following namely, 1st, gules, three lions passant guardant in pale or; 2nd, or, a lion rampant within a double tressure flory counter-flory gules; 3rd, azure, a harp or, stringed argent; 4th, azure, three*

fleurs-de-lis or, and the third division argent, three maple leaves conjoined on one stem proper
Crest: *upon a royal helmet mantled argent, doubled gules the crest, that is to say, on a wreath of the colours argent and gules, a lion passant guardant or, imperially crowned proper and holding in the dexter paw a maple leaf gules; the whole ensigned with the imperial crown proper*
Supporters: *on the dexter a lion rampant or, holding a lance argent, point or, flying therefrom to the dexter the Union Flag; on the sinister a unicorn argent, armed crined and unguled or, gorged with a coronet composed of crosses patty and fleurs-de-lis a chain affixed thereto reflexed of the last, and holding a like lance flying therefrom to the sinister a banner azure, charged with three fleurs-de-lis or*
Motto: *below the shield upon a wreath of roses, thistles, shamrocks and lilies a scroll azure, inscribed with the motto* A MARI USQUE AD MARE in letters gold on the exemplification which accompanied the proclamation[58]

The design is traditional, and its inspiration patent. As the great majority of Canadians are of English, Scottish, Irish, and French descent, the arms long associated with those four countries are included in the first four divisions of the shield (these arms have already been discussed at some length in this chapter.) The final division – the three maple leaves on a silver field – represents the nation created by the endeavours of all her peoples, whether of French, British, or other origins. The 1921 emblazonment of these armorial bearings showed the maple leaves as vert or green. In 1957, however, as the blazon calls for 'three maple leaves conjoined on one stem *proper*,' it was decided officially to follow a legitimate interpretation and emblazon the leaves and stem as gules or red 'in order to accord with Canada's national colours as exemplified by the mantling and its wreath.'[59]

Upon a gold royal helmet, facing the viewer and with five bars, is placed the crest. This is a royally crowned gold lion passant guardant holding a red maple leaf. The crest stands upon what is termed a wreath – a twisted piece of silk – of the colours of Canada, argent and gules, or silver and red. Mantling of this metal and colour falls down from beneath the wreath on either side of the helm. Above the crest is placed a royal crown in virtue of the monarchical quality of the Canadian constitution.[60] Originally, the particular form used was that known as the Imperial Crown, with its characteristic dome-like arches. Since 1957, however, for all government purposes the design of the crown has followed the preference of Her present Majesty for arches depressed at the centre, which are somewhat closer to St Edward's Crown used in the coronation.[61]

The assignment of a royal helm in connection with arms of public authority, other than the Royal Arms of the Sovereign as borne in virtue of supreme overall sovereignty, was unusual, although there were precedents, as witness the Arms of Nova Scotia (c. 1625), which will be discussed in chapter 7, and the Armorial Seal of Jamaica (1661).[62] The inclusion of a royal crown in such armorial bearings was up to this time, it would seem, unprecedented, with the exception of those for Scotland.

The supporter on the viewer's left is a gold lion which holds a silver lance with a gold head. From this flies, to the left, a banner of the Union, commonly called the Union Jack. The other supporter holds a similar lance from which flies, to the right, a banner of *France Modern*. This latter supporter is a silver unicorn with horn, mane, and other tufts of long hair as well as hooves all coloured gold. A coronet of alternate crosses patty and fleurs-de-lis forms his collar, and from this falls a chain, reflexed over the back, once again all gold.

The strong Scottish influence with regard to the supporters will be apparent when one recalls the armorial bearings as borne by the Stuarts as sovereigns of Scotland following the accession of James VI and I to the English throne in 1603.

The inclusion of the lilies of France in ensigns of public authority for Canada is of particular interest, as it marks a return to a tradition which had endured, in one form and another, from 1497 until 1801, as already noted in this chapter.

The motto, usually in letters of gold on a blue scroll, A MARI USQUE AD MARE, is an obvious allusion to the geographical position of the country. It is taken from the *Psalmus lxxi Salomonis, Et dominabitur a mari usque ad mare, et a flumine usque ad terminos terrae,* which is rendered in the Douay Version (71:8) as, 'And he shall rule from sea to sea, and from the river unto the ends of the earth'; and in the Authorised Version (72:8) 'He shall have dominion also from sea to sea, and from the river unto the ends of the earth'. It would appear that we owe this motto to the Reverend George Munro Grant, Principal of Queen's University, who for many years had travelled the country 'preaching powerful Presbyterian sermons' on this text which he advocated as Canada's motto.[63] If the grain fell upon stony ground in the east, not so on the prairies, for the text A MARI USQUE AD MARE had been used in an official connection since 1906, being inscribed on the head of the mace of the Legislative Assembly of Saskatchewan, which was first used in that year.

The wreath placed about the motto scroll is composed of lilies, roses, thistles, and shamrocks, which echo the general theme of the arms.

The evolution to the present constitutional significance of these arms has already been discussed in chapter 1.

In the preparation of the French section of this chapter I am gratified for the help received from and good offices of Molly Walker, Assistant Education Officer, The British Council, Paris.

NOTES

1 In this discussion the details of the arms are based, in the main, upon Louis Rouvier, *La Chancellerie et les sceaux de France,* second edition (Marseille, Impr. Marseillaise 1950) and E. Olivier and G. Hermal, *Reliures armoiriées françaises* 25 (Paris, Ch. Bosse Libraire 1938).

2 Sometimes shown as a single orle, and see BN: Réserve Fol.Lm³ 121: G.A. La Roque, *Les Blasons des armes de la royale maison de Bourbon* (Paris, Chez Pierre Firens 1626) frontispiece.

3 *Gules, three lions passant guardant in pale or,* that is to say, on a red background three gold lions one above the other, with the right foreleg raised and with the head facing the viewer.

4 Archives de la Grande Seminaire à Québec: for a description and illustrations see *A Pageant of Canada* (Ottawa, Queen's Printer 1967) pp. 100-1.

5 In return for victory a cairn (Monjoye/Montjoye) will be raised; see Baron Meurgey de Tupigny (Président, Société française d'héraldique et de sigillog-raphie), 'Cris de guerre et devises héraldiques,' *Vie et langage,* Larousse no. 203 (February 1969) pp. 62-73.

6 BN: Réserve: Vélins 25 PC.10, *Grand Armorial* des Sr. Chevillard, Père et Fils, ff.[10 and 11] and 55 (noted at bottom right hand) where the sinister supporter wears a dalmatic of the Arms of Navarre and supports a like banner.

7 Others borne by Henry VII were: *A lion or* and *a dragon gules; two greyhounds argent.*

8 On the obverse of the second Great Seal of Richard I

9 It is of interest to note that Henry IV of France, under whom Quebec was founded, was a Knight of the Garter. His stall plate (*tempus* Elizabeth I) in St George's Chapel, Windsor Castle, shows the Arms of France surrounded by the Garter.

10 CA: Rous (Warwick) Roll

11 CA: Prince Arthur's Book, Vincent MS 152, p. 73

12 Ibid. p. 54

13 Examples of other royal mottos are: *Semper eadem* (Queen Elizabeth I and Queen Anne) and *Veritas temporis filia* (a personal motto of Queen Mary I).

14 Two lions guardant appear to have been the original Scottish supporters.

15 J.H. Stevenson, *Heraldry in Scotland* 2 (Glasgow, James Maclehose & Sons 1914) p. 396

16 A.R. Wagner (Richmond Herald), *Historic Heraldry of Britain* (London, Oxford University Press 1948) pp. 74-5 and plate 18

17 That is to say: a blue background scattered with gold brick-like charges placed vertically; over this design is placed a gold rampant lion

18 CA: I 27.11 ff: text of Order of the Privy Council, 17 April 1707, and emblazon-ments of arms, etc.

19 C.E. Thomas, 'St. Paul's Church, Halifax, Revisited,' *Collections of the Nova Scotia Historical Society* 33 (1961) pp. 41-3

20 CA: I 27.43-4: text of order in council, 6 December 1714, and emblazonment

21 Thomas, 'St. Paul's Church ... Revisited'

22 CA: I 36.73-5: text of proclamation declaring the details of the royal arms, 1 January 1801

23 CA:141.204 and ibid. pp. 205-7 for proclamation ordering the change, 8 June 1816

24 The Spanish and Russian arms applicable in the late eighteenth and early nineteenth centuries to part of what we now know as British Columbia are discussed in appendix C.

25 CA:151.131 and ibid. pp. 132-4 for proclamation stipulating these arms, 26 July 1837

26 Department of Public Works *Report, 1914*. It is not known with certainty who carved the arms – possibly James M. Scott, who modelled them, for which he was paid $384.00 (see Auditor General's report for the year ending 31 March 1914).

27 Presented on 15 February 1937 to the Legislative Assembly of New Brunswick by Col. the Honble Murray MacLaren, PC, CMG, MD, CM, LLD, FRCS, Lieutenant Governor; see *The Synoptic Report of the Proceedings of the Legislative Assembly of the Province of New Brunswick*, Session of 1937 (2nd Session of the 38th Legislature) p. 9.

28 For further examples see CA Box 40, no. 42: Vellum Roll of Arms of Peers present at Parliament, 1514; no. 41: ibid. for 1523; no. 40: ibid. for 1540, each headed with the arms of Henry VIII.

29 CA:163.124b-e

30 Ibid. 124d

31 Ibid. 124b

32 PAC: RG, 2, series 5, vol. 1, file 2641A: Privy Council Despatches, A 1868, vol. 2, no. 2641A: the Duke of Buckingham and Chandos, Secretary of State for the Colonies, to Viscount Monck, Governor General of Canada, 14 October 1868

33 As late as the 1964 edition of *The Arms of Canada* (Department of the Secretary of State of Canada) (Ottawa, Queen's Printer 1964, p. 4), one notes the observation, 'the Arms originally assigned to Canada after Confederation by the Royal Warrant of Queen Victoria dated May 26, 1868, were composed of the Arms of the four Provinces arranged quarterly on one shield.'

34 CA:14 Garter, f. 61: Sir Joseph Pope, Under Secretary of State for External Affairs, to Ambrose Lee, York Herald of Arms, 10 June 1915

35 Ibid. f. 300: same to same, 9 March 1907

36 Ibid. f. 21: same to same, 13 September 1907

37 Ibid. f. 22: same to same, 10 September 1907

38 Ibid. f. 64: same to same, 29 July 1915

39 Ibid. f. 85: same to same, 4 April 1919

40 PC: 668, 26 March 1919

41 For informative observations on the *personae* involved in, and the general background to, the design of the armorial bearings of Canada see Judge John R.L. Matheson's address given at the Annual General Meeting of the Heraldry Society of Canada, 9 November 1968, in *Heraldry in Canada* 2 (December 1968) pp. 10-27.

42 CA:14 Garter, between ff. 89 and 90: Ambrose Lee, York Herald of Arms, to Sir Joseph Pope, Under Secretary of State for External Affairs, 25 June 1919

43 Ibid. f. 87v; same to same, 13 June 1919 (copy)

44 Ibid. f. 90: Ambrose Lee, York Herald of Arms, to Sir Henry Burke, Garter Principal King of Arms, 15 January 1920

45 Ibid. f. 98: unsent letter from Ambrose Lee, York Herald, to Sir Joseph Pope, Under Secretary of State for External Affairs, in which Garter's opinion is specifically quoted, 22 March 1920

46 Ibid. f. 91: Sir Henry Burke, Garter Principal King of Arms, to Ambrose Lee, York Herald of Arms, 16 January 1920

47 Article I of the Union with Ireland Act 1800 (39 and 40 Geo. III, c. 67)

48 CA: 14 Garter, f. 97: Ambrose Lee, York Herald of Arms, to Sir Henry Burke, Garter Principal King of Arms, 24 January 1920

49 Ibid. f. 111: Under Secretary of State, Colonial Office, to same, 26 October 1920

50 Ibid. ff. 116-17: Lord Stamfordham, Private Secretary to the King, to same, 4 November 1920

51 PRO: CO 523/57/54784: Lord Milner, Secretary of State for the Colonies, to the Duke of Devonshire, Governor General of Canada, 19 November 1920

52 PC: 1496

53 CA: 14 Garter, f. 147: Winston S. Churchill, Secretary of State for the Colonies, to the Governor General of Canada, sent 4.30 PM, 10 May 1921 (copy)

54 Ibid. f. 145: same to Lord Fitzalan of Derwent, Deputy Earl Marshal, 21 May 1921

55 Ibid. f. 153: Sir Henry Farnham Burke, Garter Principal King of Arms, to the Under Secretary of State for the Colonies, 3 August 1921

56 Ibid. f. 190: same to Sir Almeric FitzRoy, KCB, KCVO, Clerk of the Privy Council, 16 November 1921 (copy)

57 Ibid. f. 188: opinion of the Attorney General, 24 October 1921

58 CA: I 78.285-6. Text printed in *The Arms of Canada*, p. 3

59 *The Arms of Canada*, p. 6

60 CA: 14 Garter, f. 87: Sir Joseph Pope, Under Secretary of State for External Affairs, to Ambrose Lee, York Herald of Arms, 4 April 1919

61 CA: I 81.317 as approved by Her Majesty, May 1952

62 CA: Walker's Grants II. 5

63 Address by Matheson, *Heraldry in Canada*, p. 28

CHAPTER 4

Seals and flags of Canada

SEALS

Great Seal Deputed of Canada

VICTORIA 1867-1901

With the creation of the new federal state of Canada in 1867, a seal was required immediately for the general purposes of government.[1] Accordingly, by 1 June of that year a temporary Great Seal Deputed of Canada was apparently ready in anticipation of Confederation one month later.[2] The design comprised a shield of the royal arms of general purpose as borne from 1837 surrounded by the Garter [4.1]. Above the shield is placed a royal helm and mantling with the royal crest flanked on either side by the cypher V, to the viewer's left, and R, to the viewer's right. The lion and unicorn supporters, in their accustomed places, stand upon the motto scroll which is inscribed DIEU ET MON DROIT. This design is mostly contained within a circle of pellets which passes behind the crest and motto scroll, both of which go over into the legend band. The latter is inscribed, starting at the left and going round over the top of the seal, VICTORIA D · G · BRITT · REG · F · D ·[3] (Victoria by the Grace of God Queen of the Britains, Defender of the Faith); and starting once again at the left hand side of the seal and going down round the bottom of the legend band, SIGILLUM CANADAE (The Seal of Canada). Rising up from the centre base of the legend band and extending over the motto scroll are a rose, a thistle, and a shamrock growing from one stem. The outer edge of the seal consists of a rope design as well as a plain circle. The diameter is 3⅛ inches (79

4.1 Impression of the temporary
Great Seal Deputed of Canada, 1867-9
PAC (see note 4)

4.2 Proof impression of the Great Seal
Deputed of Canada, 1869-1904
BL: Detached Seals XLIV.222

millimetres).[4] The seal was impressed directly onto the face of the document concerned over a wafer of wax, which in turn was covered by a square of paper (at times white, at others blue) usually placed in diamond.

It is a seal of great vigour and clearness of line, and an example of the renaissance of heraldry and sigillography which had already begun at that period of Victoria's reign.

By November 1868 the Governor General had received a copy of the royal warrant assigning arms for the four provinces and designating what the design of the permanent great seal was to be.[5] However, as no actual deputed great seal was forwarded at the same time, he refrained from publishing the text of the royal warrant in the Gazette for the time being, lest by doing so documents issued in future under the temporary deputed great seal in use were rendered invalid.[6]

The delay in sending the permanent deputed great seal had been caused by a change of mind, apparently, on the part of the British Cabinet over the design it should incorporate. By May 1867 this had been agreed and settled,[7] but a little over a year later, in July 1868, alterations were decided upon so the seal would be consistent with the arms it was proposed to grant.[8]

The work was entrusted to the Wyon brothers, Joseph Shepard and Alfred Benjamin, the celebrated engravers, in August 1868.[9] The intricate work of engraving having been completed, probably by February 1869,[10] the deputed great seal was forwarded to the Governor General and, in accordance with his instructions from the Colonial Office, he had returned the temporary deputed great seal for its official defacement by December of that year.[11]

Following a precedent set on behalf of the Honble William McDougall, CB, to whom the defaced matrices of the Great Seal Deputed of the Province of Canada had been given 'as a memorial of his having been the last Provincial Secretary,'[12] a similar arrangement was ordered for Sir (then Mr) Hector-Louis Langevin, Secretary of State of Canada.[13]

The permanent Great Seal Deputed of Canada sent to Ottawa in 1869[14] was single-sided and showed Queen Victoria seated beneath a triple gothic canopy [4.2]. She wears robes of estate, a crown, and the collar of the Order of the Garter; in her right hand she holds a sceptre and in her left an orb. In the niche to her left is an oak tree from which depend two shields; the upper bears the Arms of the Province of Quebec and the lower the Arms of New Brunswick. To the queen's right, a similar oak tree bears in the upper shield the Arms of the Province of Ontario and in the lower the Arms of the Province of Nova Scotia, all of which arms are as granted by the royal warrant of 26 May 1868. The background beneath the three arches is semy of lions passant guardant. On either side of the central arch is a scroll inscribed DIEV ET (to the left) and MON DROIT (to the right). The background outside the gothic canopy is filled with a diaper of trellis and stylized flowers. At the centre point against the diaper is engraved the year of Confederation: 18 (to the left) and 67 (to the right). This whole design is contained in a deeply cut frame decorated with small and large quadrilobate stylized flowers. The legend, starting on the left and going round the top of the seal, reads VICTORIA DEI GRATIA BRITANNIAR · REGINA F · D · and, starting once again at the lower left and going round the bottom of the seal, IN CANADA SIGILLVM (The Seal in Canada). Placed over the legend band and inner frame, beneath the queen's feet, is a shield of the royal arms of general purpose as borne since 1837, which, like the other four armorial shields on this seal, is hatched in part. A circular frame deeply engraved and containing trefoils and leaves arranged alternately completes the outer edge of the seal, of which the diameter is 4³/₄ inches (121 millimetres). It was to be impressed directly onto the surface of the document concerned, frequently over a square of paper and wafer of wax.[15] A proof impression in red wax in excellent condition is preserved at the British Library.[16]

This deputed great seal was, for Canada, a radical development in design. By the British North America Act of 1867, a completely new experiment in imperial government was brought into being. In view of this it was doubtless felt that a new type of seal was required unlike all those so far brought into being for British North America during the reign of Victoria. Seen in its wider context of the seals of the Empire of this period it was, in fact, a development of the seals engraved by the Wyons at about this time for the colonies of Lagos[17] and Queensland,[18] although it was a much grander conception, being almost twice their size. The sigillographic concept later to be described in this work as the Newfoundland pattern, with its royal arms above a frame containing an allegorical scene, which by the 1860s had been produced with profusion for a global empire, was completely eschewed for the new seal for Canada, with the result that an instrument of government fully worthy of this precursory occasion was produced.

It will not, however, have escaped attention that this truly regal seal produced for the new state was not, in fact, in accord with the royal warrant of 1868, which laid down the principle that the Great Seal Deputed of Canada was to 'be composed of the Arms of the ... Four Provinces Quarterly,'[19] that is to say of the arms of Ontario, Quebec, New Brunswick, and Nova Scotia marshalled on one shield. How the change came about is not, as yet, apparent. Some thought appears to have been given to the design of a seal to include such a quarterly shield,[20] but this must have been before May 1868 when a request for the substitution of maple leaves for the proposed wheat sheaf on the Arms of Ontario was made.[21] In fact, the only seals of federal authority which did have quarterly shields as stipulated in the royal warrant of 1868 appear to have been those of the Secretary of State of Canada,[22] and the Canadian government agencies abroad[23] – those seminal beginnings of the Canadian High Commissions and Embassies of today.

EDWARD VII 1901-10

Upon the death of Queen Victoria in 1901, following the usual custom, a royal warrant was forwarded through the Colonial Office to Ottawa authorizing the continued use of her seal until a new one could be prepared for her son and successor, King Edward VII.[24]

The design of the new monarch's Great Seal Deputed of Canada was similar to that of Queen Victoria's [4.3], but the gothic triple canopy and niches are generally spread out laterally. The king is dressed in robes of estate and seated on a throne, on the left arm of which he rests the orb. His crowned head faces slightly to his left, and beneath his left knee he wears the Garter. In contrast to the previous great seal, that of Edward VII has a plain circle as its extreme outer border in place of stylized flowers, and the inner frame has large quatrefoil flowers alternated with small octofoil flowers. The legend is very much longer than that of the previous seal and reads, starting at the bottom of the seal and going right round the circumference, EDWARDVS VII D · G · BRITT · ET TERRARVM TRANSMAR · QVAE IN DIT · SVNT BRIT · REX F · D · IND · IMP,[25] and, starting once again at the lower left on a separate scroll placed inside the legend band and over the inner frame, IN CANADA SIGILLVM 1904 (The Seal in Canada 1904).[26] A shield of the royal arms of general purpose as borne since 1837 is placed covering both the outer legend band and the inner legend scroll. The diameter is 5⅕ inches (132 millimetres). The seal was to be impressed onto the surface of the document concerned.

GEORGE V 1910-36

Upon the death of King Edward VII in 1910, he was succeeded by his second and only-surviving son, King George V. Again, following the usual procedure, a royal warrant was issued through the Colonial Office authorizing the continued use of the deputed great seal of the late sovereign until a new one could be prepared.[27]

The design of the seal of George V [4.4] is almost identical with that for his father except for certain details: the position of the head is now full face; the robes of estate are not kept back so as to expose the chest, lap, knees, and legs, but are drawn round the body and over the knees and legs; and the feet are resting on a platform instead of on a cushion. The inscription on the legend bands, both outer and inner, is exactly the same as for the previous monarch except that it commences, naturally, GEORGIVS V and ends 1912. The diameter is 5½ inches (140 millimetres).[28]

The gradual change in the status of George V's seal of Canada from being that of a deputed great seal to that of the Great Seal of the Sovereign of a Sovereign state has been referred to earlier in this work (pp. 32-3).

4.3 *Copper counterpart of the Great Seal*
Deputed of Canada of Edward VII, in use 1904-12
Royal Mint, London. Crown copyright

4.4 *Copper counterpart of the Great Seal*
Deputed of Canada, subsequently Great Seal
of Canada, of George V, in use 1912-40
Royal Mint, London. Crown copyright

EDWARD VIII 1936

With the death of King George V in 1936, the Privy Council of Canada requested that a royal warrant be issued by the king authorizing the continued use of the present Great Seal until a new one could be prepared,[29] but as the new sovereign had abdicated within less than a year, no great seal for King Edward VIII was taken into official use.

GEORGE VI 1936-52

As a consequence of the abdication, a further request by the Privy Council sought the continued use of the Great Seal of George V until one could be engraved for the new monarch, King George VI.[30] When this appeared, it proved to be a complete break in design from the three previous great seals [4.5]. An almost stark simplicity is the key note and the general treatment of the portrait of the sovereign is strongly reminiscent of some of the earliest Anglo-Norman great seals. The king sits on a high-backed throne against a plain background, wearing robes of estate, which are arranged over his knees, a royal crown, and the collar of the Order of the Garter. In his left hand he carries the sceptre, the sign of rule, while in his right he holds the sword of Justice. Before his footrest stands a panel upon which is placed the complete armorial achievement of the Royal Arms of Canada of general purpose, as established in 1921. A double legend band contains the inscription, starting at the outside upper right, GEORGIUS · VI · D · G · MAG · BRIT · HIB · ET · TERR · TRANSMAR · and then, starting again at the upper right, this time on the inner legend band, QUAE · IN · DIT · SUNT · BRIT · REX · F · D · IND · IMP ·; and

4.5 Copper counterpart of the
Great Seal of Canada
of George VI, in use 1940-55
Royal Mint, London. Crown copyright

4.6 Model of the counterpart of the
Great Seal of Canada
of Elizabeth II, in use from 1955
Royal Canadian Mint

finally, on a scroll which almost forms a canopy above the King's head, IN · CANADA ·
SIGILLUM (The Seal in Canada). Plain concentric circles form the edges of both legend
bands as well as a somewhat thicker one for the outer edge. The diameter is $5^2/5$ inches
(137 millimetres).[31]

Because of the dropping of the title Emperor of India from the royal style and titles, a
royal warrant dated 5 July 1950 was issued by King George VI calling for a new great seal
to be prepared. Unlike all previous and similar royal warrants, which were usually
issued from 'Our Court of St James,' this 1950 warrant gives the place of issue as
'Ottawa,' as has been the practice since. In fact, no second great seal was brought into
use for King George VI, as he died within two years of the warrant.

ELIZABETH II from 1952

Possibly it was because of the 1950 warrant that no royal warrant appears to have been
issued upon the death of the king in 1952 to authorize the continued use of his great seal
until one could be prepared for his successor, Queen Elizabeth II.

Whereas all previous great seals deputed as well as great seals of Canada had been
engraved at the Royal Mint in London, that for the new Queen was made at the Royal
Canadian Mint in Ottawa. It was designed by the Canadian artist Eric Aldwinckle, and
shows Her Majesty seated on the Coronation Throne [4.6]. She wears a long dress, robes
of estate, the collar of the Order of the Garter, and a representation of St Edward's
Crown, with which she was crowned; in the right hand is held the sceptre and in the left
the orb. Before the Queen, rising up from over the legend band to about the height of

the knees, are the royal armorial bearings of general purpose of Canada without the helm and mantling that were included on the previous great seal. Between two plain concentric circles, the inner one cut by the armorial bearings and the finial of the throne, is the legend band which is engraved, starting at the left bottom of the seal, REINE · DU · CANADA · ELIZABETH · II · QUEEN · OF · CANADA. The diameter is 5⁵/₁₆ inches (134 millimetres).

The seal was authorized for use by Her Majesty by a royal warrant dated 14 November 1955,[32] and on 25 February 1956 it was entrusted to the Governor General, who is the official keeper of the great seal, although the Registrar General has the day-to-day custody and responsibility for the security of the matrices. The various categories of instruments which issue under the great seal are regulated by the Public Officers Act and the Seals Act as stipulated in the Order of the Governor General in Council of 29 September 1966.[33]

The great seal is almost invariably impressed directly onto the surface of the document concerned over a paper wafer. However, a notable exception occurred with the proclamation bringing into existence the Flag of Canada on 28 January 1965. On this occasion the seal was impressed onto a separate piece of paper and depended from the proclamation by means of a white and red ribbon.[34] It was probably decided that, in view of the solemnity of the occasion and the importance of the instrument, a return to the former custom of depending a great seal would give added dignity.

Privy seals of the Governors General

All governors general since Confederation in 1867 have used privy seals in the execution of their duties. These include the personal arms of the incumbent of the office at the time. Details of the privy seals of the twenty-one governors general of Canada up to and including His present Excellency will be found in appendix B. There are, in fact, two privy seals. One comprises the arms of the governor general, without a legend, and is kept near the person of His Excellency, usually at Government House, Ottawa, and applied there. The other has arms and legend and is in the custody of the Registrar General.[35] The various categories of documents to which the privy seals are applied are governed by the same acts and regulations as for the great seal referred to above. As is customary with the use of privy seals, they are applied to the surface of the document concerned in the upper left-hand corner.

FLAGS

As we have already seen, it is probable that the royal banner, *quarterly, France Modern and England* [4.7], was the first flag to fly over what is now Canadian soil when John Cabot first reached North America in 1497 in the service of Henry VII of England. On the other hand, the first flags to fly over permanent settlements in Canada were those of Royal France.[36]

The Queen's personal Canadian flag

The Queen's personal Canadian flag [plate 22.2] consists of the Royal Arms of Canada

4.7 Banner of royal arms, 1405-1603
Author's collection

as assigned in 1921 – that is to say the details which usually appear on the shield – arranged in banner form. The centre of the design is charged with a dark blue roundel which bears in the centre a crowned E and is surrounded by a wreath of roses, all of which details are rendered in gold.[37] This flag is flown at times when the sovereign is personally present in Canada.

The establishment under Her present Majesty of a personal flag for use by the sovereign when present in Canada attests the fact that of all our monarchs so far she is the most peripatetic. The development of rapid inter-continental air travel coincided with her reign, and this has enabled her to make frequent visits to her realms and territories scattered over the face of the globe. As a result, a personal flag for use by the Queen in almost every one of them has been established.

All this is a far cry from former practice – prior to the jet age – under which the sovereign rarely left the British Isles, save for occasional visits to the Continent. The three major exceptions to this practice prior to those of Her Majesty are the visits of her grandfather, King George V, to India in 1911 for the Delhi Durbar and of her father, King George VI, to Canada in 1939 and to South Africa in 1947. On each of these occasions the sovereign's flag flown comprised a banner of the royal arms of general purpose of the British Crown as flown in the United Kingdom – frequently, but erroneously, referred to in that state as the royal standard.

Flag of the Governor General

By an order in council of 31 July 1869, Queen Victoria authorized an official flag for the

4.8 *Flag of the Governor General, 1869-1921*

Governor General, following a memorial on the subject by the Lords of the Admiralty. The flag was to comprise the Union Jack with, in the centre, a shield containing the arms of the four foundation provinces surrounded by a wreath of maple leaves ensigned by a royal crown [4.8].[38] Originally this flag was for use when the Governor General embarked in boats and other vessels, although in time its use became extended.

In 1931 the official flag of the Governor General was altered to its present pattern [plate 22.3]: dark blue, rectangular in shape, and longer in the fly than in the hoist. In the centre is a representation of the royal crest: *upon a royal crown proper a lion statant guardant or, royally crowned also proper.* Beneath this is a gold scroll inscribed in black letters: CANADA.[39] It appears that King George v personally suggested this design as early as 1928.[40]

Union Jack

The Union Flag [plate 22.5] or Union Jack, as it is commonly called, came into being in its original form in 1606 by the combination of the St George's Cross with that of St Andrew by a proclamation of King James vi and i, and came to Canada shortly thereafter, probably first in Newfoundland. Proclamations of Queen Anne in 1707, upon the union of England and Scotland to form the United Kingdom of Great Britain, and of George iii in 1801, upon the union of Great Britain and Ireland, further regulated its use. The latter also brought the flag to its present form, as a combination of the crosses of Sts George, Andrew, and Patrick – the patrons of the English, Scots, and Irish.

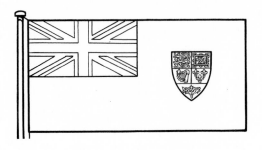

4.9 Canadian Red Ensign, 1921-65

While essentially a royal badge in banner form, and of a military nature, nevertheless the Union Jack soon enjoyed a wider, if unofficial, display when patriotic occasions and circumstances demanded: This situation obtained in the United Kingdom and almost to a greater extent in the Empire and the Commonwealth, with the result that on 18 December 1964 the federal Parliament approved resolutions recognizing the continued use of this flag as a symbol of Canada's membership of the Commonwealth of Nations and of her allegiance to the Crown. As practice has worked out subsequently, the federal government is extremely sparing in its display of the Union Flag. On the other hand, the provincial governments, except that of Quebec, and municipal authorities have continued to fly this flag in a widespread manner. In addition, as will be seen later, the Union Jack occurs in the provincial flags of Newfoundland, Ontario, Manitoba, and British Columbia, in one manner or another.

Canadian Red Ensign

The Red Ensign [4.9] was assigned in 1707 by a proclamation of Queen Anne to merchantmen. By a British Admiralty warrant of 1892 this flag, with a shield for Canada[41] in the fly, was authorized 'to be used on board vessels registered in the Dominion.'[42] In 1924 a Canadian order in council provided that the Canadian Red Ensign might be displayed abroad upon Canadian government buildings. A further such order of 1945 authorized its use[43] on federal buildings, inside Canada as well as abroad, until Parliament should adopt a national flag.

National Flag of Canada

It can be said that up to 1965 Canada had no official national flag, but flew several which were regulated by custom, Parliamentary Act, and orders in council.[44] This situation probably continued in Canada for as long as it did because it was, and indeed still is, rather more of a composite state than a single, homogeneous nation. As a consequence many efforts over the years to decide upon a design acceptable to all parts of the country met with obstacles which proved insurmountable. The inclusion of certain devices, revered by some, proved anathema to others. The suggestion of a design attractive to one group was quite meaningless to another. Much heat was engendered by discussions over what flag ought to be adopted: indeed, designing flags became something of a recurrent national pastime. In 1946, by way of example, a select committee of the House of Commons at Ottawa examined no less than fifteen hundred designs sent in from all over the country.

However, as the centenary of Confederation approached, the federal government decided to grasp firmly what had proved in the past to be such a very difficult nettle. After much discussion and debate, which was not without heat, both in Parliament and throughout the country, consultations with those interested or concerned, and the consideration of a positive Niagara of designs, Parliament recommended as the National Flag of Canada, *gules, on a Canadian pale argent, a maple leaf of the first*,[45] which was so proclaimed by Her Majesty The Queen on 15 February 1965 [plate 22.1].[46]

The flag is white and red, or argent and gules, being the colours of Canada as appointed by King George V in his proclamation of Canada's armorial bearings in 1921, discussed previously. The official proportions of the flag are two by length and one by width. The central white pale, or stripe, is rendered in such a way as to form a white square, the width of the flag, which is charged with a stylized red maple leaf.

Public opinion was divided over the design upon its inception as the National Flag of Canada. Some welcomed it enthusiastically, others were equally vocal in an opposite direction. Some, while unenamoured with the design, nevertheless out of respect for constitutional processes accepted it once it was proclaimed as the official flag of the state. Yet again, others were quite indifferent. As will be fully appreciated, such a combination of attitudes is not unknown at important turning points in a nation's history.

From impressions gained from conversations held with all manner of people during journeys made every year since 1965 throughout the country between Halifax and Vancouver, this still appears to be the position some ten years later. Without a doubt, the one aspect of heraldry in Canada which seems guaranteed to raise heat under collars in the shortest possible time is the National Flag, and it appears to be too soon, even yet, to be able to discuss the flag dispassionately in most general circles throughout the country.

It must, therefore, suffice to say that its official status cannot be gainsaid in view of the due constitutional manner in which it was brought into being and, further, that from the point of view of technical armory the flag cannot be faulted.

Unsatisfactory as this situation may be, from several points of view, there can be little doubt that Canada's lack of an official flag as late as the 1960s was, in view of the position she had achieved in world affairs by then, a matter of considerable embarrassment externally as well as internally. With the approach of the centenary of Confederation, it behooved the federal government to resolve the matter in one way or another in proper constitutional form.

That the final outcome would not be acceptable to all was almost inevitable bearing in mind the composition of this state — the vast geographical extent of which, coupled with a relatively small population, seems to militate in an inverse ratio against homogeneity.

Now that a particular flag has been established officially, with the passage of time it may well be that our grandchildren will be amazed that passions were so deeply stirred over a symbol of patriotic and national identity which they take for granted. Given the right combination of circumstances, that is how history so often comes about.

I am especially indebted to the following in connection with this and, in many instances, other chapters: His Excellency The Right Honourable Roland Michener, cc, when Governor General of Canada; Esmond Butler, cvo, Secretary to the Governor General; Brigadier General Louis-Fremont Trudeau, dso, obe, cd, Assistant Secretary to the Governor General; W.I. Smith, phd, Dominion Archivist; W. Kaye Lamb, phd, sometime Dominion Archivist; M. Bernard Weilbrenner, Director, Historical Branch, M. George De Lisle, Picture Division, M. Auguste Vachon, Historical Research Officer, Picture Division, A.E.H. Petrie, Extensions Officer and Curator, National Medal Collection, all of the Public Archives of Canada; Major C.R. Lamoureux, dso, Gentleman Usher of the Black Rod, the Senate; Lt Col D.V. Currie, Sergeant at Arms, House of Commons; Erik J. Spicer, Parliamentary Librarian, Ottawa; Mrs C.R. Vincent, for much research in Ottawa; Mrs J.M. White, Chief of the London Office, Public Archives of Canada; and Robert Mackworth-Young, cvo, fsa, Librarian, Windsor Castle, and Assistant Keeper of the Queen's Archives.

NOTES

1 The British North America Act, 1867, does not contain any specific article calling for the creation of a great seal of Canada. However, many official instruments require the use of one, and so we must conclude that the framers of the act did intend that such should exist.

2 PRO: CO 42/664, ff. 52-3r: Lord Monck, Governor General of Canada, to the Duke of Buckingham and Chandos, no. 86, 16 November 1867

3 For an extended version see appendix A.

4 PAC: RG 68 vol. 981 (chronological arrangement); affixed to a proclamation declaring the royal assent to an act for the relief of Joseph Frederic Whiteaves, 8 September 1868

5 26 May 1868

6 PRO: CO 42/671, ff. 251r-v: Lord Monck, Governor General of Canada, to the Duke of Buckingham and Chandos, Secretary of State for the Colonies, no. 202, 10 November 1868

7 Order in council, 22 May 1867

8 PRO: CO 324, vol. 170, pp. 279-80: Duke of Buckingham and Chandos, Secretary of State for the Colonies, to the Lord President of the Council, 27 July 1868

9 19 August 1868, see PRO: CO 42/671, ff. 252-3r: letter on behalf of the Duke of Buckingham and Chandos, Secretary of State for the Colonies, to Messrs Wyon, 2 December 1868 (draft)

10 PRO: CO 324, vol. 170, ff. 371-2: Sir F[rederic] Rogers, Downing Street, to Sir George Cartier, Bt., 11 January 1869

11 PRO: CO 42/678, ff. 101-2v: minute paper by G[ordon] G[airdner, Chief Clerk] for Sir Frederic Rogers, 31 December [1869]

12 PRO: CO 42/664, ff. 52-3r: Lord Monck, Governor General of Canada, to the Duke of Buckingham and Chandos, Secretary of State for Colonial Affairs, no. 83, 16 November 1867: and ibid. ff. 59 r and v: draft from Downing Street to Lord Monck, 7 May 1868: PAC: RG6, A1, vol. 156, file 531: note of Mr (later Sir) Joseph Pope, 14 June 1905

13 PRO: CO 42/678, ff. 101-2v: minute paper by G[ordon] G[airdner, Chief Clerk] for Sir Frederic Rogers, 31 December [1869], and latter's note subscribed

14 PAC: RG7, G21, vol. 157, file 282A: royal warrant authorizing the use of the Great Seal, dated 7 May 1869

15 ANQ: Grands Formats: 'Commission nommant à l'Hôtel du Gouvernement à Ottawa, Sir Adolphe Philippe Caron, Ministre des Postes du Canada, 25 janvier 1892'

16 BL: Detached Seals XLIV.222. The seal matrix (sterling silver with an ivory handle) is preserved in the Public Archives of Canada, Picture Division.

17 CA, WCS: 72.2

18 Tonnochy: 307 and QSA: GOV/1, despatch no. 5: Duke of Newcastle, Secretary of State for the Colonies, to Sir George F. Brown, KCMG, Governor of Queensland, 3 October 1859

19 CA: 163.124d

20 PAC: Picture Division: design of a great seal for Canada, ink drawing

21 PRO: CO 324, vol. 170, pp. 229-31 F[rederic] Rogers, to Sir Charles Young, Garter King of Arms, 29 April 1868

22 PAC: Picture Division: seal of the Secretary of State of Canada; bronze female, alloy male dies, 3 inches (76 millimetres) diameter; date unknown

23 Conrad M.J.F. Swan (York Herald of Arms), 'Some Canadian Seals by the Wyons, 1839-1912,' *Heraldry in Canada* 8 (June 1974) pp. 23-5

24 PAC: RG 68, vol. 956: royal warrant dated 29 January 1901

25 For the Latin in full and English translation, see appendix A.

26 Royal Mint, London: copper counterpart. The royal warrant for the taking into use of this seal was dated 30 September 1904; see PAC: RG 68, vol. 956.

27 PAC: RG 68, vol. 956: royal warrant dated 26 May 1910

28 Royal Mint, London: copper counterpart. The royal warrant was dated 7 October 1912: see PAC: RG 68, vol. 956.

29 PC: 1264, dated 29 May 1936. The royal warrant was dated 14 July 1936; see PAC: RG 68, vol. 956.

30 PC: 3184, dated 16 December 1936. The royal warrant was dated 5 March 1937; see PAC: RG 68, vol. 956.

31 Royal Mint, London: copper counterpart. The royal warrant was dated 19 January 1940; see PAC: RG 68, vol. 956.

32 PAC: RG 68, vol. 956

33 Order in council PC 1966-1887 of 29 September 1966 printed in *The Canada Gazette,* part 2, vol. 100, 12 October 1966, no. 19

34 The original is in the custody of the Public Archives of Canada.

35 There is also an *ad interim* privy seal for use by the Governor General while matrices bearing his own arms are being engraved. This *ad interim* seal consists of a shield of the Arms of Canada ensigned by a royal crown; the legend band consists of a circle of pellets on the inner edge and a rope design on the outer, and is inscribed, starting at the bottom left, GOVERNOR GENERAL · GOUVERNEUR GENERAL and then in base, · CANADA ·.

36 Many and varied, of which the white banner semy of gold fleurs-de-lis (*drapeau blanc fleurdelisé*) was possibly the most widely used; see Arthur G. Doughty, 'Le Drapeau de la Nouvelle France,' *Mémoire de la Société royale du Canada,* 3rd series (Ottawa 1926) 20, pp. 43-6

37 CA: I 82.217

38 The design was authorized by a despatch, no. 191, of Lord Kimberley, Secretary of State for the Colonies, to Sir John Young, Bt., Governor General of Canada, 16 July 1870; see PRO: CO 43/157.

39 CA: Standards II.2. In some representations in use the letters are shown as light blue.

40 CA: 15 Garter, Flags f. 43: Lord Stanfordham, Private Secretary to the King, to Sir Henry Farnham Burke, Garter King of Arms, 24 September 1928

41 The Arms of the four foundation provinces as assigned by royal warrant, 1868, marshalled on one shield

42 2 February 1892

43 By this date the arms in the fly were as assigned for Canada in 1921.

44 See Orders of the Privy Council of Canada nos. 843 (26 April 1922), 134 (26 January 1924), and 5888 (5 September 1945); *Statutes of Canada* 1934, Shipping Act, c. 44, s. 91 (1) (as amended); *Revised Statutes of Canada* 1952, 2, c. 33, s. 21.

45 CA: I 83.46-8

46 The original royal proclamation is preserved in the Library of Parliament, Ottawa.

CHAPTER 5

Newfoundland

ENSIGNS ARMORIAL

Following the grant by letters patent dated 13 November 1637 of King Charles I to James, Marquis of Hamilton, Philip, Earl of Pembroke and Montgomery, Henry, Earl of Holland, and Sir David Kirk of 'that whole Continent Island or Region commonly called NEWFOUNDLAND,' arms were assigned by letters patent dated 1 January 1637/38. This was accomplished under the hand and seal of Sir John Borough, Garter Principal King of Arms, 'for the greater honor and splendor of that Countrey and the people therein inhabiting ... [to be the] ... ppr[1] and peculiar Armes thereunto belonging to be used in all such cases as Armes are wont to be by other nations and countries.'[2]

The blazon of the ensigns granted on this occasion is:

Arms: *gules a cross argent, between in the 1st and 4th quarters a lion passant guardant crowned or, and in the 2nd and 3rd quarters a unicorn passant also argent, armed crined and unguled gold, gorged with a coronet a chain affixed thereto passing between his forelegs and reflexed over the back also gold*
Crest: *upon a wreath or and gules, an elk passant proper; mantled gules, doubled argent*
Supporters: *on each side a savage of the area armed and habited as for war*
Motto: QUAERITE PRIME REGNUM DEI [plate 15.2]

The silver cross on a red field immediately brings to mind the Arms of the Knights of St John, on whose patronal feast in 1497 Newfoundland was, by tradition, discovered by John Cabot. One might conjecture, therefore, that this fact influenced the choice of this basic design. Be that as it may, it is obvious that the crowned lions and the unicorns were

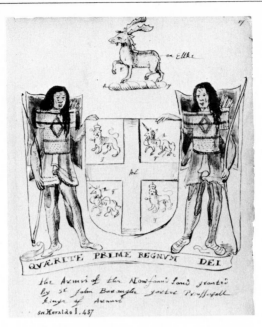

5.1 *Early seventeenth-century representation of the armorial bearings of Newfoundland with tinctures tricked*
CA: Misc, Gts. 4.7

inspired by the supporters of the royal arms as borne since 1603. Indeed these New-foundland arms, along with those for Nova Scotia, are the only ensigns of public authority of Stuart origin in Canada.

The crest calls for an elk in its natural colours. Presumably this was a seventeenth-century attempt to include what was thought to be an example of the fauna of New-foundland. In fact elk have never existed there. One can only conclude, therefore, that this was a misnomer for caribou, which has long been found on that island.

In the earliest (seventeenth century) depiction of these armorial bearings in the Records of the College of Arms, the supporters are stylized versions of indigenous Indians – the Beothuks – dressed and armed as for war [5.1]. They are, in fact, particu-larly interesting from the heraldic point of view as even their oldest representations[3] reflect a complete departure from the conventionalized Indians almost universal in armory during the seventeenth and eighteenth centuries. At that time heraldic Indians were usually portrayed wearing something akin to ostrich feather head-dresses and kilts.[4] On the other hand the Newfoundland supporters reflect an effort to follow the patent of 1638, which required that they be 'of the Clyme proper armed and apparaled according to their guise when they goe to Warre,'[5] that is to say, they should be a representation of actual local Indians, clothed and armed as they would be in reality.

The motto, taken from St Matthew's Gospel,[6] might be rendered 'Seek first the Kingdom of God.'

Despite the magnificent way in which the Garter of the day served the noble petition-ers with these arms, it is a curious irony of history that it took almost three hundred years before they were actually borne for Newfoundland.

It appears that soon after World War I, no one in that then dominion suspected the existence of these arms. Indeed, it was the desire of the Imperial War Graves Commission to include them on memorials in some thirty-five French cathedrals which apparently caused Newfoundland to make official enquiries into the matter. Late in 1924 the College of Arms was asked if the arms were, indeed, granted in 1638 and also if they were still applicable to Newfoundland.[7] Three months later, on 18 February 1925, Garter King of Arms confirmed and certified that it was so on both counts.[8]

SEALS

Great seals deputed of Newfoundland

Until the early nineteenth century it appears that no great seal deputed for the general government of Newfoundland was used or, in fact, even existed. So far no examples have come to light, either of seal dies or of impressions of seals particular to Newfoundland. Further, the voluminous state papers (colonial) preserved at the Public Record Office, London, which treat extensively with administration and other matters relating to Newfoundland, do not seem to contain any reference to the deputed great seals for that colony until the early nineteenth century.

However, on 31 December 1819 the Prince Regent authorized by warrant 'Thomas Wyon Esquire, Chief Engraver of Our Seals, to engrave a Great Seal to be made use of within our Island of Newfoundland according to the draft hereunto annexed,'[9] a copy of which is, alas, missing from these state papers. Whether or not such a seal was, in fact, prepared is not revealed. In any case within a month of the order the King was dead and a new inscription would have been required.

From 1820 onwards further references to a seal occur. On 1 May of the year following, a warrant was issued directing the Governor to pass letters patent under the Seal of the Island of Newfoundland in order to appoint an Attorney General.[10]

In 1827 a new seal was despatched to the governor along with a warrant signed by King George IV and dated 1 September of that year authorizing its use.[11] This followed the usual procedure when a new seal was sent for use in a colony. As 1827 did not coincide with or follow immediately the demise of a sovereign, and as no changes of constitutional importance took place about that time, one can only conclude that the seal despatched this year was the George IV Great Seal Deputed of Newfoundland, as most of the other British North American colonies received their seals for this monarch during this same year.

An example of an impression of this deputed great seal is preserved in the Provincial Archives [5.2].[12] The obverse contains an allegorical group symbolizing the historic and vitally important fishing industry of Newfoundland. Mercury stands in the centre and is portrayed in the classical manner with a winged cap but otherwise nude save for a cloak, which falls in graceful folds. In his left hand and crook of his arm he holds a caduceus, often used as a symbol of commerce in modern times. His other hand extends towards a fisherman whom he presents to Britannia standing on the right of the composition.

5.2 Obverse and reverse of the Great Seal Deputed of Newfoundland of George IV
PANL

The fisherman, who kneels on one knee and holds up his net, complete with floats, is rendered in the romantic manner strongly reminiscent of Byron. The shirt, the trousers, and the hair-style could well all have belonged to that idol of the romantic-liberal movement only recently dead when the matrices of this seal were engraved.

The interpretation of Britannia is strongly classical, with loose-flowing dress, cloak, and Grecian helmet. With her left hand she supports an oval shield which displays the Union Badge (or Jack) surrounded by a border charged with shamrocks, roses, and thistles placed alternately.

On the extreme left of the composition, near the fisherman, the prow of a vessel protrudes, possibly a large rowing boat or fishing smack.

In the exergue is the motto HAEC TIBI DONA FERO (I bring you these gifts). It is extremely doubtful if this is a quotation from the classics although it is cast into dactylic form – probably to gratify the classical ear and at the same time suit the device on the seal.

All is contained within a plain circle forming the inner edge of the legend band, which, starting at the lower left, is inscribed SIGILLUM TERRÆ NOVÆ INSULÆ · (The Seal of Newfoundland, or literally 'of the Island of the New Land'). The outer edge of the legend band is made up of a bead and reel pattern. The conception, treatment, and execution are Regency at its most elegant.

The reverse consists of the royal arms of the period 1816-37, as already discussed. In part they are hatched, that is to say the tinctures are indicated by a series of lines and dots. The arms are placed on a circular shield and surrounded by the Garter. These are ensigned by a royal crown of which the arches are deeply depressed beneath the orb and cross. The lion and unicorn supporters stand upon the motto scroll, which bears the inscription DIEU ET MON DROIT. A wreath of roses, shamrocks, and thistles is placed about this scroll.

The whole armorial design is contained within a plain circle which forms the inner edge of the legend band. The latter is inscribed, starting at the upper right, GEORGIUS · QUARTUS · DEI · GRATIA · BRITANNIARUM · REX · FIDEI · DEFENSOR ·. The outer edge of the legend band consists of a bead and reel pattern as for the obverse. The diameter is 4³/₁₀ inches (109 millimetres).

The impression we have been discussing is somewhat unusual in that it is one of the few examples of two-sided colonial seals of British North America which is not impressed through paper on either side and consists simply of hard red wax. Complete with two red tapes (now almost completely faded) doubled over into four as the laces for suspending the seal from the document, it still rests in its original zinc skippet or seal box.

Upon the death of the next monarch, King William IV, a warrant dated 23 June 1837 was sent to Newfoundland authorizing the continued use of the then Great Seal.[13] If this was different from the George IV seal just discussed, examples do not appear to have survived. It is probable, however, that in common with those for the other British North American colonies, the William IV Great Seal Deputed of Newfoundland was single-sided and intended for impression directly onto the surface of the document.

With the accession of Queen Victoria we enter upon a completely different situation, as from then on a good number of impressions of the great seals deputed of Newfoundland have been preserved. The date-letter on the silver seal die for her reign [5.3] is 1838-39, and so we may conclude that it came into use for Newfoundland during that year or very shortly thereafter.[14] The seal matrix was made by the Chief Engraver to Her Majesty's Seals, Benjamin Wyon. It will be recalled that he belonged to that celebrated family who among seal engravers rank as do the family of Bach among composers.

The basic design of the Victorian seal for Newfoundland [5.4] became in due course the standard pattern, with local variations, not only for the remainder of the colonies of British North America, but also for almost all others of the Empire, certainly down to the middle of the century. One might, therefore, be permitted to call it the Newfoundland pattern for ease of reference. Based on a design first evolved during the reign of William IV for colonial deputed great seals, it comprised four basic elements.

The first element consisted of arms occupying the upper third of the seal. These were made up of a shield of the royal arms of general purpose as borne since 1837, surrounded by the Garter and ensigned by the royal crown, interpreted in the manner favoured by Queen Victoria. The lion and unicorn supporters stood on scroll work entwined by a motto riband inscribed with the royal motto DIEU ET MON DROIT.

The second element comprised a somewhat elaborate frame designed in the manner of Chippendale. Within this is contained the allegorical scene and motto based on the obverse of the George IV seal, just discussed. There are, however, a few variations of detail and interpretation worthy of note. Some rigging and a bowsprit are added to the vessel, and the roses, thistles, and shamrocks are removed from the border of the shield supported by Britannia. Further, she is portrayed in that diaphanous manner common to most allegorical female figures on late eighteenth- and early nineteenth-century

5.3 Sterling silver female die of the Great Seal
Deputed of Newfoundland of Victoria, engraved by
Benjamin Wyon (officially defaced)
Tonnochy: no. 263

5.4 Wax proof impression of the Great Seal
Deputed of Newfoundland of Victoria
BL: Detached Seals XCVIII.9

5.5 Female die of the Great Seal
Deputed of Newfoundland of Edward VII
Tonnochy: no. 264

5.6 Paper impression of the Great Seal
Deputed of Newfoundland of Edward VII
Royal Mint, London. Crown copyright

official seals. In fact, while chronologically the seal is Victorian, from the point of view of aesthetics it is the product of the artistic taste of the late Georgian and Regency period which lasted on into the new reign until that ethos had developed which we regard as typically Victorian. Outside the frame at more or less the centre points are included roses to the left and a thistle and shamrock to the right.

The third element of the seal is the legend which, starting at the middle left and going round the top of the seal, reads VICTORIA DEI GRATIA BRITANNIAR · REG · F · D.

The fourth and final element concerned the remainder of the legend which reads, starting at the middle left and going round the bottom of the seal, SIGILLUM TERRAE NOVAE INSULAE (The Seal of the Island of Newfoundland).[15]

The seal is single-sided and was intended for impression directly onto the surface of a document. The diameter was 2⅜ inches (60 millimetres).

In subsequent chapters it will be seen that the Newfoundland pattern was followed for the other colonial deputed great seals in British North America under Queen Victoria. The elements which varied from colony to colony concerned the panel within the Chippendale-like frame and that part of the legend which ran round the lower part of the circumference, both of which referred to the area concerned. The sole exception was the Seal of British Columbia, for which the design was completely different (see chapter 11).

The seal of Newfoundland for the reign of King Edward VII basically follows the Newfoundland pattern [5.5 and 5.6]. The crown in this case above the royal arms is in the imperial form favoured by that monarch. In the allegorical scene, waves of the sea are added to the background, while Britannia's shield is rendered without a border and the manner in which she is portrayed is a return to the essentially classical treatment of the George IV seal. Mercury has the traditional wings attached to his feet, and the fisherman is represented as of the period with a short-back-and-sides hair cut, while the collar of his shirt is modelled on that of a naval rating. The frame round the lower panel is now more à l'art nouveau. The rose, thistle, and shamrock are somewhat higher up than on the Victorian seal. A Tudor rose is placed at the base of the frame. The legend reads, starting at the lower left, EDWARDVS VII D · G · BRITT · ET TERRARVM TRANSMAR · QVAE IN DIT · SVNT BRIT · REX F · D · IND · IMP · and, at the foot of the seal, NEWFOVNDLAND.[16]

For King George V the seal was identical with that of his father save for the beginning of the legend, which is GEORGIVS V [5.7].[17]

The reign of King Edward VIII was too brief to have allowed for the engraving of a great seal deputed of Newfoundland particular to that sovereign.

With the accession of King George VI a new deputed great seal was made [5.8]. The interpretation and placing of the royal arms were much the same as before; Mercury, Britannia, and the fisherman are contained, once again, in the lower panel. This is surrounded by a modification of the Edward VII and George V art nouveau frame, but unlike theirs this is inscribed NEWFOVNDLAND. However, the rose, thistle, and shamrock rising from either end of the royal motto scroll have been transmuted into sprigs of unspecified vegetation. The arms, the panel, and the frame, while similar to those on the two preceding seals, are somewhat smaller. This was necessitated by the much larger legend, which is placed on a ribbon for the first time. Starting at the upper left, it reads GEORGIVS VI · DEI · GRATIA · MAG · BR · HIB · ET TERR · TRANSMAR · QUAE IN DIT · SVNT

5.7 *Copper counterpart of the Great Seal Deputed of Newfoundland of George V Royal Mint, London. Crown copyright*

5.8 *Copper counterpart of the Great Seal Deputed of Newfoundland of George VI, in use up to 1963 Royal Mint, London. Crown copyright*

BRIT · and then, continuing at the centre left and down towards the base of the seal, on a separate piece of ribbon, · REX · FIDEI · DEFENSOR · IND · IMP. The diameter of this seal is 2³/₁₀ inches (59 millimetres).[18]

On 31 March 1949, Newfoundland became the tenth province of Canada. One of the early orders in council of the Lieutenant Governor of Newfoundland was to provide for the continued use of this seal until a new provincial deputed great seal could be engraved.[19] This followed the implications of section 136 of the British North America Act, 1867, and the precedents established, under similar circumstances, by New Brunswick, Nova Scotia, and British Columbia (see chapters 7, 9, and 11). However, nothing was done about getting a new seal at the time and, indeed, King George's deputed great seal continued to do service for the next fourteen years, notwithstanding the fact that within three years of the order in council the king was dead and he had been succeeded by Her present Majesty.

The matter was not, apparently, raised again until 1955, when on the sixth anniversary of the union the Minister of Provincial Affairs asked if, in view of the changed constitutional status of Newfoundland, it were not appropriate to adopt a new seal. He suggested that the design might follow the tradition of many of the other provinces and comprise the armorial bearings of Newfoundland along with the inscription 'Province of Newfoundland' or, on the other hand, retain basically the existing pattern but with a similar inscription, as 'there seems to be a general desire to preserve as many of our old customs as possible.'[20]

Two years passed, during which the matter 'was referred to the Department of the Attorney General where it was evidently lost sight of.'[21] By 1958, however, the Executive

Council had 'definitely decided' to retain, if possible, the basic design as used in New-foundland up to then with a change of inscription appropriate to the reigning sovereign. There was, however, the question of the propriety of the retention of the royal arms of general purpose upon the seal, and so the Newfoundland government consulted the Secretary of State of Canada[22] and the College of Arms on this matter.[23] Both came independently to the same conclusion and advised that the more approp-riate armorial element in the great seal would be the Arms of Newfoundland.[24] The advice from the College of Arms settled the matter,[25] and on 30 June 1961 the Executive Council authorized the Minister of Provincial Affairs to arrange for the making of a new Great Seal Deputed of Newfoundland which was to include the provincial arms and an appropriate reference to Her Majesty inscribed round the border.[26] The Crown Agents in London were duly asked to have the seal engraved, and in time and at a cost of £100.10.0d[27] the new and present Great Seal Deputed of Newfoundland arrived and was taken officially into use by an order in council on 3 July 1963.[28] The seal has the provincial shield of arms, crest, motto, and supporters, the latter standing on a com-partment or grassy mound [5.9]. Beneath on a scroll is the word NEWFOUNDLAND. The legend band has upon it a scroll which runs from the middle left round the top of the seal and down to the middle right, and which is inscribed · ELIZABETH II D · G · CANADAE REGINA · .[29] The diameter of the seal is 2½ inches (64 millimetres).

The influence of the Great Seal Deputed of Nova Scotia (see figure 7.8) upon the design is obvious, although the Newfoundland seal cannot be compared to the Nova Scotia seal for strength of sigillographic design. The Newfoundland seal is unique among the seals of the Canadian provinces in that it contains a specific reference to the reigning monarch.

Privy seal of the Lieutenant Governor

The Lieutenant Governor of Newfoundland has a privy seal [5.10] which he uses when sealing proclamations, commissions to notaries public, and the like. It is impressed over a paper wafer (generally gold) in the usual manner for privy seals, that is to say, in the upper left-hand corner of the document.

Circular in shape, the seal bears in the centre the Newfoundland shield of arms, with the crest only. Round the edge, within an exterior rope design, runs the legend, which reads, starting at the centre left and continuing round the top of the seal to centre right, LIEUTENANT GOVERNOR; with NEWFOUNDLAND round the base of the seal, with a small mullet, or five-pointed star before and after the word. The seal is 1½ inches (38 mil-limetres) in diameter.

Privy seal of the Administrator

In the absence of the Lieutenant Governor from the province, and during the interim between Lieutenant Governors, an Administrator – usually the Chief Justice – assumes his duties. The Privy Seal of the Administrator [5.11] is oval in shape and is impressed onto wax (shellac). It is used officially for the same purposes as that of the Lieutenant Governor, and in the same position on documents. It is almost certainly Victorian in origin and consists of the royal arms of general purpose, hatched for tincture, on a

5.9 Impression of the Great Seal Deputed of Newfoundland of Elizabeth II, in use since 1963
Author's collection

5.10 Privy seal of the
Lieutenant Governor of Newfoundland
Author's collection

5.11 Wax impression of the privy seal
of the Administrator of Newfoundland
Author's collection

circular shield which is surrounded by the Garter, and ensigned by the royal crown in the form favoured by Queen Victoria. Round the edge the legend runs, starting at the upper-centre left and continuing over the top of the seal, ADMINISTRATOR, and round the base of the seal, starting at the lower-centre left, NEWFOUNDLAND. The diameter at the widest point, from top to bottom, is $1^{1}/_{20}$ inches (27 millimetres), and at the narrowest, $9/_{10}$ inches (23 millimetres).

It is an elegant and well-carved seal.

FLAGS

Flag of the Lieutenant Governor

The official flag of the Lieutenant Governor is the Union Badge (Jack), in oblong form, debruised or charged at the centre by a circular device as approved by King Edward VII in 1904.[30] This consists of the Mercury, Britannia, and fisherman scene as on the deputed great seal – about which see above – with the addition of a scroll above the heads of the three figures inscribed TERRA NOVA. This scene is usually carried out in various tones of carnation with the hull of the boat coloured brown; Britannia's shield is decorated with the Union Badge (Jack) in its proper colours. The exergue contains the phrase: HAEC TIBI DONA FERO, as on the deputed great seal. This whole device is surrounded by a wreath of green laurel complete with red berries. The official flag of the Lieutenant Governor is regulated by the Statutes of Newfoundland.[31]

Provincial flag

The flag of the province of Newfoundland is the Union Jack (see plate 22.5), which was adopted by legislation in 1931.[32]

The Honble G.A. Frecker, LLD, Minister of Provincial Affairs, Captain Ambrose J. Shea, Private Secretary to the Lieutenant Governor, and A.E. Hemmens, Sergeant-at-Arms of the House of Assembly, have all helped generously in connection with this chapter. F. Burnham Gill, Provincial Archivist, has been untiring in his efforts to assist with its preparation, and I am further indebted to him for having read the chapter in manuscript.

NOTES

1 i.e. proper

2 CA: Heralds 1.437. The text of the original letters patent appears in schedule A of the Newfoundland Coat of Arms Act, 1957.

3 CA: Miscellaneous Grants 4.7

4 For further details on this subject see Conrad M.J.F. Swan (York Herald of Arms), 'American Indians in Heraldry,' *The Coat of Arms* 12 (July 1971) pp. 96-106 and 12 (October 1971) pp. 148-59.

5 CA: Heralds 1.437b

6 6:33; also St Luke 12:31

7 CA: 14 Garter, p. 449: Governor of Newfoundland to Jas. H. Thomas, PC, MP, Secretary of State for the Colonies, 4 November 1924

8 Ibid. p. 452: Garter to Under Secretary of State for the Colonies, 18 February 1925

9 PRO: CO 195, no. 17, p. 117

10 Ibid. p. 146

11 Ibid. pp. 287-90

12 PANL: Detached Great Seal Deputed of Newfoundland, George IV

13 PRO: CO 854/3 (1837-40, Circulars – Colonial Department) ff. 36-9v

14 Tonnochy: no. 263

15 BL: Detached Seals XCVIII.9. This is in excellent condition and is a wax impression made from the original seal prior to its defacement (see Tonnochy: no. 263).

16 Tonnochy: no. 264, undefaced

17 Royal Mint, London: male copper counterpart

18 Royal Mint, London: male copper counterpart

19 Provincial order in council 15 (1949) dated 9 April 1949

20 PANL: A-61, Department of Provincial Affairs: memorandum of the Honble Myles Murray, Minister of Provincial Affairs, 31 March 1955

21 Ibid. J.S. Channing, Deputy Minister of Provincial Affairs, to the Private Secretary, Government House, 7 September 1957

22 Ibid. the Honble Myles Murray, Minister of Provincial Affairs, Newfoundland, to the Honble Henri Courtemanche, Secretary of State of Canada, 29 August 1958

23 Ibid. J.G. Channing, Deputy Minister of Provincial Affairs, to Rouge Dragon Pursuivant of Arms, 18 January 1960

24 Ibid. the Honble Henri Courtemanche, Secretary of State of Canada, to the Honble Myles Murray, Minister of Provincial Affairs, Newfoundland, 19 September 1958, and J.P. Brooke-Little, Bluemantle Pursuivant of Arms, to J.S. Channing, Deputy Minister of Provincial Affairs, 11 March 1960

25 Ibid. memorandum to the Executive Council by the Minister of Provincial Affairs, 7 October 1960

26 Provincial order in council 34 (1960)

27 PANL: A-61, Department of Provincial Affairs: Director of Supply to Deputy Minister of Provincial Affairs, 1 March 1963

28 Provincial order in council 285 (1963)

29 ELIZABETH II DEI GRATIA CANADAE REGINA (Elizabeth II by the Grace of God, Queen of Canada)

30 *Revised Statutes of Newfoundland,* 1952, An Act Respecting a National Flag for Newfoundland and Colours to be worn by Vessels, c. 272 (see schedule)

31 Ibid. as amended by An Act to Amend the National Flag Act, 22 June 1954

32 An Act Respecting a National Flag for Newfoundland, 1952

CHAPTER 6

Quebec

ENSIGNS ARMORIAL

During the French regime, New France had no arms particular to itself. The arms of dominion and sovereignty – those ensigns of general purpose – which applied have been discussed in chapter 3.

Nevertheless, during the existence of New France, both before and after it became a royal colony in 1663, various mercantile corporations were introduced to the area, and in some instances even administered the colony on behalf of the Crown – for instance, La Compagnie des cent associés (1627-63), later known as La Compagnie de la Nouvelle France, which, as a typical seventeenth-century proprietary company, performed for New France many of those functions soon to be carried out by the Hudson's Bay Company for Rupertsland and other northern areas. La Compagnie des cent associés, while it had an official seal (see figure 6.2), does not appear to have had arms.[1]

Even after New France was declared a royal colony, other companies were empowered to function there, and while they were not exclusively viceregal in the sense that La Compagnie des cent associés was, nevertheless their powers and duties were extensive. As often as not in certain spheres they had administrative authority delegated to them under the Crown in respect of its North American territories.

The classic example of such a company was La Compagnie des Indes occidentales, which functioned in Canada between 1664 and 1674. The extent of its wide-ranging authority is reflected in the fact that it was empowered to place its arms not only on coins and cannons, but also on seals, signets, public buildings, and vessels. The blazon of the company's ensigns armorial, as granted by article 32 of its royal charter of foundation in May 1664, is as follows:

Arms: *azure, semy of fleurs-de-lis or;* the shield of arms is ensigned by *une couronne tréflée* [2]
Supporters: *on either side a savage habited and holding in the exterior hand a bow all proper* [plate 2.1]

A further company which functioned in Canada, from about 1719, was La Compagnie d'occident (the successor to La Compagnie des Indes orientales), for which the armorial bearings were:

Arms: *azure, a fleur-de-lis or*
Crest: *a fleur-de-lis or*
Supporters: *on the dexter, Peace symbolized by a woman in classical clothes holding a palm branch in her exterior hand, all proper; and on the sinister, a like figure symbolizing Plenty holding a cornucopia in her exterior arm, all proper*
Motto: FLOREBO QUOCUMQUE FERAR (I shall flourish wherever I am brought) [3] [plate 2.2]

The motto is a pun on that symbol *par excellence* of France and the French, the fleur-de-lis in the arms and crest, and echoes the refreshing and magnificent self-confidence of this nation at about this time. The inscription, GLORIAM REGNI TVI DICENT (They shall speak of the glory of thy kingdom), [4] surrounding the royal arms on the reverse of the 1670 silver 15 sols piece of New France (see figure 3.8) is a further example. [5]

The third and last of these companies to be considered here is the Compagnie perpétuelle des Indes, the inheritor of a twenty-five year monopoly in Canadian beaver pelts. The armorial bearings of this company were:

Arms: *vert, on a pile undy argent, a seated male figure symbolic of a river resting the sinister arm on a cornucopia and holding a (?) trident with the dexter hand all proper, a chief azure, semy of fleurs-de-lis or, in base a barrulet also gold.* The shield of arms is ensigned by the coronet of a French Duke proper
Supporters: *on either side a savage habited holding a bow in his exterior hand proper*
Mottoes: SPEM AUGET OPESQUE PARAT [6] (She augments hope and provides riches) and FLOREBO QUOCUMQUE FERAR (I shall flourish wherever I am brought)

Passing to the British Colonial period, there was no official assignment of arms particular to Quebec, to its successor, Lower Canada, or to this area when joined with Upper Canada to form the united Province of Canada. It was not, in fact, until the year following Confederation that, along with the other foundation provinces, Quebec received arms by royal warrant dated 26 May 1868. The blazon is: *or, on a fess gules, between in chief two fleurs-de-lis azure, and in base a sprig of three leaves of maple slipped vert, a lion passant guardant or* [7] [plate 16.2].

The allusions are obvious. The blue fleurs-de-lis on gold attest the origin of Quebec and its first name, New France. The reversal of tinctures of *France Modern* is simply to obtain a good, balanced heraldic design, the fess and maple leaves being coloured. The gold lion against a red background comes from the arms of the grantor. In fact Quebec, along with New Brunswick and Prince Edward Island, is among the very few provinces

6.1 Arms used for Quebec since 1939

in the British Empire ever to have been assigned a part of the royal arms of general purpose in this form.[8] The sprig of green maple was included 'it being commonly used as a distinctive Provincial badge ... [and] ... as the most characteristic natural product of' Quebec. Fortunately we know what was in the mind of the original designers from this quotation from the *Memorandum Explanatory of the proposed Armorial Bearings for the Provinces and Dominion* prepared for the Canadian Delegates' Conference in London in 1868.[9]

In 1939 one notes the appearance of new tinctures for this basic design: *per fess azure and or, on a fess gules, a lion passant guardant also gold, between in chief three fleurs-de-lis of the same, and in base a sugar maple sprig with three leaves vert, veined also gold* [6.1].[10]

It will be noted that in outline the arms remain about the same, but there are three substantial differences: first, the fleurs-de-lis are increased to three in number; second, they are changed to gold and placed on a blue background; and third, gold veins are added to the maple leaves. It is this design which has been used consistently by the Province of Quebec since 1939.

From the point of view of technical armory this design cannot be faulted; whether one prefers the 1868 or 1939 tinctures is really a matter of personal preference. However, when one passes from theoretical aspects of design to consider the question of authority upon which this change was based, one cannot but be less happy. The process by which the change was attempted was by a provincial order in council.[11] Search as one will in the British North America Act in those sections which specify provincial powers, and indeed in any other acts, whether imperial or federal, or in any royal warrants, one fails to find the investing of any province with the power to create or

6.2 *Seal of La Compagnie des cent associés (Les Archives des Ursulines de Québec)*

alter arms. Indeed, this is as one would expect, as authority in arms emanates solely from the sovereign authority. The logic of these principles was not lost upon the federal government, as witness the 1967 Centennial Fountain on Parliament Hill in Ottawa, where Quebec is identified by the arms for that province as established by the royal warrant of 1868.

It must also be remembered, however, that a similar attempt by British Columbia in 1895 and by Manitoba in 1870 – both of which cases will be discussed in the chapters on those provinces – did not assist Quebec to a full appreciation of the exact situation in these matters. Presumably, however, when the Quebec order in council was considered in 1939, the fact that both British Columbia and Manitoba had in the meantime placed their armorial position *en règle* by means of royal warrants had escaped attention. It may well prove difficult to explain the 1939 Quebec provincial order in council save on this premise.

It was not until 1883 that the motto JE ME SOUVIENS (I remember) began to be used. Its author was Eugène Taché, who included it upon his architectural designs for the Legislative Buildings at Quebec. These plans were approved on behalf of the provincial government following an order in council of 22 January 1883. [12]

SEALS

Seals of public authority in New France

The first seal used in New France in token of public authority was that of La Compagnie des cent associés.

An example of this very rare seal is preserved in the Monastère des Ursulines in Quebec [6.2]. It has deteriorated much since the nineteenth century and only a portion now remains. Judging by the extant fragment, the diameter of the obverse was probably 2⁹/₁₆ inches (65 millimetres). This side still shows, against a background semy of fleurs-de-lis, a classical figure symbolic of religion, holding in the right hand a plain Latin cross. From sketches made of the seal in the last century, we know that this was a female figure standing on waves, and that in her left hand she held a lily stalk. Within two plain concentric circles the legend read ME · DONAVIT · LVDOVICVS · DECIMVS · TERTIVUS 1627 (Louis XIII granted me [the Company] 1627). A scalloped outer edge completes the design of the obverse.

The reverse of the impression bears a smaller counter-seal, of which the diameter is 1³/₁₆ inches (30 millimetres). This side shows a sailing ship upon waves. It has two masts, with a sail billowing from the foremast towards the left, while symbolic wind blows from the inner legend band on the right. On top of the rear and smaller mast is a cock, and the hull is decorated with clover arabesques. The legend round the upper part of the seal reads IN · MARI · VIÆ · TVÆ[13] (Thy paths [are] upon the sea). A scalloped pattern completes the outer edge of the sea.[14]

In 1663 New France became a royal province, and the Sovereign Council (Conseil souverain) was established. The official seal of this body consisted of a shield of arms of *France Modern,* that is to say three fleurs-de-lis, placed two and one, ensigned by a representation of the Royal Crown of France [6.3]. The latter is shown as a jewelled circlet upon which are set five visible fleurs-de-lis; arches rise from these and meet at the centre; naturally, the rear portion of the crown is only suggested in the design. The seal is oval in shape and measures 1¹/₄ inches (32 millimetres) at its widest point. The total design is contained within a frame of pellets.[15] This seal was one-sided and was impressed onto wax (shellac) placed directly on the face of the document concerned.

It will be seen that the general design was basically as found in the counter seal of the Great Seal of France for Louis XIV, with the exception that the supporting angels are not included on the Seal of the Sovereign Council of Quebec.

Apparently the custody of the seal passed to each member of the council for a fixed period, as we gather from the following minute of 18 June 1664: 'Le Sceau des armes du Roy nostre Sire a esté ce jourd'huy déposé ez mains du sieur de la ferté Conseiller en ce Conseil pour le remettre au desir de l'ordonnance du 18e octobre dernier.'[16]

In time this supreme agency of government for New France became known as the Superior Council (Conseil supérieur), and accordingly a somewhat different seal came into use [6.4]. A shield of arms of *France Modern* ensigned by a royal crown formed the central motif, along the lines of the seal just discussed, but there were additions in the form of two orders and a legend. The collar of the Order of St Michael surrounds the shield, and outside this is placed that for the Order of the Holy Ghost, details of which have been discussed in chapter 3. Both collars pass behind the crown, which ensigns the shield directly. Round the outer edge of the upper part of the seal runs the legend NOVVELLE FRANCE. Oval in shape, the seal measures 1¹/₄ inches (32 millimetres) at its widest point. As in the previous instance, this seal was one-sided and was impressed onto wax (shellac) directly on the face of the document.[17]

Save for the legend, the general design of this seal is akin to several royal seals of the period, such as the round Small Seal (Petit Sceau) and the oval Secret Seal (Sceau secret) of Louis XIV.[18]

6.3 Seal of the Conseil souverain, New France
ANQ: NF.25, no. 147

6.4 Seal of the Conseil supérieur, New France
ANQ: NF.25, no. 1630

6.5 Seal of the Jurisdiction
de Montréal, New France
ANQ: NF.21.15 (1700-23)

6.6 Seal of the Jurisdiction
des Trois-Rivières, New France
ANQ: NF.23.18

During the French regime, Canada was divided into three governments or administrative territories, centred around the towns of Quebec, Trois-Rivières, and Montreal, grouped under the Governor General, the Intendent, and the Conseil souverain (later the Conseil supérieur). None appears to have had a local seal comparable with those of the latter conseils, but seals of a somewhat judicial nature were used. That for Montreal [6.5] was circular in shape with a shield of *France Modern* ensigned by a royal crown and surrounded with the legend, starting at the upper right, IVRISDICTION DE MONTREAL, all within two concentric circles. The seal was 1 inch (25 millimetres) in diameter and was impressed onto wax directly adhering to the face of the document.[19] The seal for Trois-Rivières [6.6] was oval in shape, and ⁷/₈ inch (22 millimetres) in height. A shield of arms of *France Modern* was ensigned by a royal crown; two plain concentric ridges containing a reel design form the outer edge of this seal, which has no legend.[20] Acadia also had its own government, but so far no seals have come to light similar to those just described for Montreal and Trois-Rivières.

Great seals deputed of Quebec, Lower Canada, and Quebec

Consequent upon the transfer of New France to the British Crown, in accordance with the Treaty of Paris of 1763, a deputed great seal was required for the government of this colony. Accordingly, as such matters concerned them, the Board of Trade in London worked towards a suitable design. By October, eight months after the signing of the treaty, they were ready to recommend the general lines to be followed in the engraving, with the result that on the 5th of that month the Privy Council ordered His Majesty's Chief Engraver of Seals to prepare a draft of a seal for 'the Province of Quebec.' It was to have

on the One Side His Majesty's Effigies, pointing to a Chart of that part of America through which the River of St. Lawrence flows, including the Gulph and with this Legend or Motto underneath, Extensae gaudent agnoscere Metae; and this Inscription around the Circumference, Sigillum Provinciae nostrae Quebecensis in America; and on the Reverse His Majesty's Arms, Crown, Garter, Supporters and Motto with this Inscription round the Circumference, Geo. III Dei Gratia Magnae Britanniae, Franciae et Hiberniae Rex, Fidei Defensor Brunsvici et Luneburgi Dux, Sacri Romani Imperii Archi Thesaurarius et Elector.[21]

In due time this seal was produced and taken into use [6.7]. In the Collection de pièces judiciaires et notariales at the Provincial Archives, Quebec, an excellent example is preserved.[22] The treatment of the reverse is in accordance with the customary design for the British American colonies of the period. On a shield are placed the royal arms of the period 1714-1801, that is to say: *quarterly, 1, England impaling Scotland; 2, France Modern; 3, Ireland; 4, Hanover.* The Garter, inscribed HONI SOIT QUI MAL Y PENSE, surrounds the arms which are ensigned by a representation of the royal crown. The lion and unicorn supporters stand upon a scroll bracket through which is threaded the motto scroll inscribed DIEU ET MON DROIT. Two thin concentric circles divide this design from the legend band, which reads, starting at the upper right, GEORGIUS · III · D · G · MAG · BRI · FR · ET · HIB · REX · F · D · BRUN · ET · LUN · DUX · S · R · I · AR · THES · ET · PR · EL. It will be noted that the Latin contractions of the royal style and titles follow the usual form at this time with the exception that PR (Princeps) is inserted before EL (Elector) at

6.7 *Obverse and reverse of the Great Seal Deputed of Quebec, 1763*
BL: *Detached Seals XLV.4 and Royal Mint, London. Crown copyright*

the end of the inscription (see appendix A). A narrow wreath of stylized foliage forms the outer edge of this side of the seal.

The obverse follows the widely observed tradition for British American and West Indian colonies of the period, with the sovereign, in this instance George III, as the subject of a symbolic composition. While this was common practice further south, the 1763 seal for Quebec is unique in this regard as far as Canadian colonial seals are concerned, as subsequent chapters will show. George III, crowned, in coronation robes and wearing the Collar of the Order of the Garter, stands on the right-hand side. With a sceptre in his right hand he indicates on a map the location of the province for which he had recently assumed responsibility. The map, which hangs over a stand, shows eastern North America from Newfoundland southwards to New York. The treatment is one of great elegance and is in the best eighteenth-century tradition. The exergue contains the motto from Statius: EXTENSAE GAUDENT AGNOSCERE METAE,[23] for which a possible translation is 'The extended boundaries rejoice to acknowledge [him, i.e. George III].' The legend, which starts at mid left, reads SIGILLUM · PROVINCIAE · NOSTRAE · QUEBECENSIS · IN · AMERICA · (The Seal of Our Province of Quebec in America) contained within the general composition by a plain circle which extends from one end of the floor upon which the king stands round the upper part of the seal and so down to the other end of the floor. A narrow wreath of foliage completes the outer edge of the seal. A proof impression in red wax of this side of the seal is preserved in the British Library. Save for a certain chipping of the edge it is in excellent order.[24] The diameter of the seal is 4½ inches (115 millimetres). Impressions were made on wax covered with paper in accordance with the usual practice in British America.

6.8 *Obverse and reverse of the Great Seal Deputed of Lower Canada of George III, 1793 Royal Mint, London. Crown copyright*

This 1763 seal did duty for Quebec until the Constitutional Act of 1790 brought into being Upper and Lower Canada, which began their separate existences on Boxing Day of the following year.

Accordingly, Thomas Major, 'Engraver of Seals to His Majesty,' was instructed to engrave a new seal. By 30 April 1793 he had completed his work and, according to his bill, on the obverse had included as a 'Device an Oak Tree with some branches cut off a Pruning knife on the ground a river and ships at Anchor, at a distance a Town and Church on a rising hill' [6.8]. For the engraving he charged £70.0.0d which, together with 43 ounces of silver at 5/6 per ounce, duty at 6d per ounce, and a Shagreen case with silver clasps for the seal, came to a grand total of £84.8.0d.[25]

It would seem likely that the view was intended to be Quebec City as seen from a point across and somewhat down river from Lévis — possibly based on the engraving of c.1700 inscribed 'A Paris chez Chereau,' which was shown in the Pageant of Canada exhibition at the National Gallery of Canada in 1967.[26]

In the exergue of the seal is placed the motto from Horace: AB · IPSO · DUCIT · OPES · ANIMUMQUE · FERRO,[27] which one might translate as 'It derives power and courage from the steel itself.' In the original, Hannibal is praising the dauntless virtue of the Roman race, and so transposed it could signify that Lower Canada derives power (wealth) and courage from the division of the country (symbolized by the pruning knife lying on the ground near the tree on the seal) into Lower and Upper Canada. The whole design is contained within a plain circle which forms the inner edge of a legend band inscribed SIGILL · PROV · NOS · CAN · INF · .[28] A narrow wreath of foliage forms the outer edge of the seal.

6.9 *Obverse and reverse of the Great Seal Deputed of Lower Canada, 1817*
ANQ: Petites Collections, M-8

6.10 *Obverse and reverse of the Great Seal Deputed of Lower Canada of George IV, 1828*
Fuller Collection 4/1 and PAC: PDP

The reverse contains a shield of the royal arms as for the first seal of George III for Quebec (1763), in other words as borne from 1714 to 1801. Surrounded by the Garter the shield is ensigned by a royal crown. However, in contrast to the first seal, one notes that the crown rests upon an architectural feature above the shield, and the bracket upon which the lion and unicorn stand is a much more solid construction featuring a shell motif. The royal motto, inscribed DIEU ET MON DROIT, entwines round this bracket. A further change is that the Rose and Thistle 'grow' from behind the shield and appear between the lion and the crown, and the crown and the unicorn, respectively.

A plain circle contains this armorial design and is broken by the cross on top of the crown, which, in turn, forms the final stop, as it were, for the legend band. This reads GEORGIUS · III · D · G · MAG · BRI · FR · ET · HIB · REX · F · D · BRUN · ET · LUN · DUX · S · R · I · AR · THES · ET · EL. As will be recalled, this is exactly the same as for the first seal of George III for Quebec, except that the abbreviation PR (Princeps) has been omitted before EL (Elector) at the end of the legend. A narrow wreath of stylized foliage forms the outer edge of this seal, the diameter of which is 4¼ inches (108 millimetres). This seal was impressed through paper onto wax.[29]

This first Great Seal Deputed of Lower Canada was despatched on 6 May 1793 together with a royal warrant authorizing its use.[30]

As has already been discussed, because of the Union of Great Britain and Ireland in 1801, the royal arms were altered. Briefly, it will be recalled, *France Modern* was removed; thereupon *England* filled the first and fourth quarters, *Scotland* moved into the second quarter, *Ireland* remained in the third, and *Hanover* was accommodated upon an inescutcheon ensigned by an electoral bonnet. It does not appear, however, that deputed great seals for any of the Canadian provinces were prepared bearing these arms.

However, owing to the further change in the royal arms in 1816 consequent upon Hanover being declared a kingdom, a fresh seal had to be prepared for Lower Canada. It will be recalled that the change involved the replacement of the electoral bonnet by a royal crown over the inescutcheon of Hanover.

An order was apparently given for the preparation of such a seal in anticipation of this change, as by December 1815 Nathaniel Marchant had presented his bill for £60.0.0d to the Lords Commissioners of the Treasury for his engraving of a new silver seal for Lower Canada.[31]

Fifteen months later Earl Bathurst, Secretary of State for War and Colonies, sent this seal [6.9] to Sir John Sherbrooke, Captain General and Governor in Chief of Canada, for use in Lower Canada.[32]

Basically the obverse is the same as for the first seal for Lower Canada except that the legend begins with SIGIL rather than SIGILL and the stops between the abbreviations consist of cinquefoil stylized flowers.

On the other hand the reverse has undergone considerable change. The shield shows the royal arms as borne from 1816 to 1837 with the inescutcheon of *Hanover* ensigned by the royal crown of that kingdom. The Garter and the lion and unicorn supporters occupy their accustomed places. The royal crown ensigning the shield is lower and somewhat more squat and angular than previously. Gone are the rose and thistle between the supporters and the crown, and the bracket for the supporters to stand upon.

In its place is the royal motto scroll, inscribed DIEU ET MON DROIT, entwined about a wreath of roses, thistles, and shamrocks.

The whole design is contained within a plain circle which forms the inner edge of the legend band. This is inscribed, starting at the bottom left of the seal, GEORGIUS TERTIUS · DEI GRATIA · BRITANNIARUM REX · FIDEI DEFENSOR · (the final stop being a quatrefoil stylized flower).[33] A narrow wreath of conventionalized foliage forms the outer edge of the seal. The diameter is 4¼ inches (108 millimetres).

Within three years of the arrival of this seal in Lower Canada, George III was dead and he was succeeded by his son, George IV. Following the usual procedure, Earl Bathurst, the Secretary of State for War and Colonies, forwarded a warrant for Lower Canada authorizing the use of the seal of the late king until another was transmitted.[34]

In fact, the George III seal continued to fulfil its function in the purposes of day-to-day government for another eight years, at least, as will be seen from its attachment to the twenty-one year lease to John Murray of a lot in the seigneury of Notre-Dame-des-Anges, dated 8 August 1828.[35] Indeed, it was not until that year that the George IV Great Seal Deputed of Lower Canada [6.10] was despatched.[36]

The obverse was basically as for the preceding seal, with its view of a city on a hill across a river upon which are five square-rigged ships of the period at anchor, and, to the left, a sloop. The church in the distance on the George IV seal has a tall tower topped by an architectural lantern. The oak tree in the foreground is much as before except that the branch stump projecting over the river is considerably smaller. The legend is exactly the same as for George III's second Great Seal Deputed of Lower Canada, save that whereas that one has stylized cinquefoils for all the stops, George IV's has a quatrefoil as the final one at the top of the seal. The motto in the exergue is as before. The outer edge of the George IV seal consists of a bead and reel design instead of stylized foliage.

The reverse is almost identical with its predecessor. However, the interpretation of the royal crown is quite different to all others appearing on Canadian seals during this reign. Indeed, it is much more like that favoured by Her present Majesty in having the pearls on the arches clearly visible and the arches rounded rather than angular. The royal titles begin at the upper left and read GEORGIUS · QUARTUS · DEI · GRATIA · BRITANNIARUM · REX · FIDEI · DEFENSOR (with a quatrefoil as the final stop). The outer edge is the same as for the obverse. The diameter is 4½ inches (114 millimetres). This seal was impressed onto wax through paper.[37]

Within two and a half years of the issue of the George IV seal, the king was dead; he was succeeded by his brother, King William IV, on 26 June 1830. In the usual manner, the existing seal of the deceased sovereign was authorized for continued use until a new one could be prepared.[38]

Some two years later this was forthcoming and was accompanied by a royal warrant dated 1 November 1832 by which it was to be taken into use. In the following week, as this was to be a single-sided seal, unlike its predecessors, the Under Secretary for the Colonies told the Governor General of Canada that a press was being despatched so that it could be used appropriately for impression directly onto the surface of documents.[39]

In general, what had been distributed over two surfaces on previous seals was now brought onto one side [6.11]. The upper half was occupied by the royal arms as borne from 1816 to 1837, hatched in part. Surrounded by the Garter, ensigned by a royal

6.11 *Proof impression of the Great Seal*
Deputed of Lower Canada of William IV, 1832
BL: *Detached Seals* CXLVIII.43

6.12 *Great Seal Deputed of*
Lower Canada of Victoria, 1839
BL: *Detached Seals* CXLVIII.84

crown, the shield is supported by the lion and unicorn, which stand upon the motto scroll, inscribed DIEU ET MON DROIT. A wreath of oak to the left and laurel to the right is placed outside the Garter.

The lower part of the seal is filled with the customary view across the river found on all seals for Lower Canada; in this one, however, the large ships are reduced to four in number. The motto in the exergue is as before. All is contained within a narrow circular frame, to the left and right of which, respectively, are placed a rose and shamrocks, and a thistle and shamrocks.

A simple circle contains the total armorial and pictorial elements of the design and also forms the inner edge of the legend band. This is inscribed, starting at the left middle and going round the top of the seal, GULIELMUS IV D · G · BRITANNIAR · REX F · D ·; and starting once again on the left-hand side and continuing down round the bottom of the seal: SIGILL · PROV · CANADAE INFERIORIS.[40] The upper and lower portions of the legend are separated by cinquefoil stops. A plain circle completes the outer edge. A proof impression of this seal, the diameter of which is 2½ inches (64 millimetres), is preserved at the British Library.[41]

Upon the death of William IV and the accession of Queen Victoria, a royal warrant was despatched, in the customary manner, authorizing the continued use of this great seal until one was made available for the new queen.[42] In due time this was despatched in February 1839 with the request that William IV's seal be returned for defacing in the usual way.[43]

The design of the seal of Queen Victoria for Lower Canada [6.12] was in accordance with what has been referred to before as the Newfoundland pattern (discussed in detail in chapter 5). The total area occupied by the royal arms of general purpose was reduced from about one half to one third of the whole design, and the local element contained in the lower panel was increased proportionately. This comprised a panoramic scene similar to all those which occur on the seals of Lower Canada, and is closest to that on the second seal of George III (1817). The motto in the exergue is as before. Roses and shamrocks appear from behind and outside the shield to the left and a thistle and more shamrocks to the right.

The royal titles are engraved round the upper circumference of the seal, starting at the centre left: VICTORIA DEI GRATIA BRITANNIAR · REG · F · D; and starting once again at the lower left and reading down round the bottom of the seal: SIGIL · PROV · CANADAE INFERIORIS.[44] A plain outer circle round the circumference completes this seal, of which the diameter is 2½ inches (64 millimetres).[45]

Within two years of the taking into use of this seal, it was made obsolete by the creation of the Province of Canada on 10 February 1841. The details of the seal issued for that arrangement of government will be discussed in the chapter dealing with Upper Canada and Ontario.

Upon Confederation the Province of Quebec came into being, and section 136 of the British North America Act provided that

until altered by the Lieutenant Governor in Council, the Great Seals of Ontario and Quebec respectively shall be the same, or of the same design, as those used in the Province of Upper Canada and Lower Canada respectively before their Union as the Province of Canada.[46]

As far as Quebec was concerned this referred to the 1839 seal appointed for use in Lower Canada upon the accession of Queen Victoria, just discussed. However, as the Secretary of State for the Colonies admitted to the Governor General in 1869, 'the provisions of the 136th section appear to have escaped observation till quite recently,'[47] with the result that a completely different seal was, in fact, provided for use in Quebec immediately following Confederation [6.13].

This seal consists of the royal arms of general purpose, as borne since 1837, on an oval shield surrounded by the Garter. The royal helm, crest, and mantling are included. The lion and unicorn supporters stand on a ribbon inscribed with the motto DIEU ET MON DROIT.

A decorative circle of pellets contains the armorial achievement. Outside this, between two concentric plain circles, is the legend which, starting at the centre base, reads THE SEAL OF THE PROVINCE OF QUEBEC. Outside this band a milled edge with a final plain circle completes this seal, of which the diameter is 2 inches (51 millimetres). The brass female die is preserved at the British Museum.[48]

The intention was that this seal should be for immediate use while a more elaborate one was prepared.[49] One was, in fact, approved by a United Kingdom Order in Council some six weeks before Confederation was to take place,[50] but it was subsequently decided that this design was not consistent with the arms proposed for Quebec, and so the Chief Engraver of Her Majesty's Seals was asked to prepare a fresh design in that following year.[51]

Ultimately, the new deputed provincial great seal was ready, and the queen at Osborne House issued her warrant on 7 May 1869 for its use in Quebec and the return of the interim seal so that it could be defaced in the usual way.[52]

6.13 *Brass female die, officially defaced, of the temporary Great Seal Deputed of Quebec, 1867-9 Tonnochy: no. 266*

6.14 *Proof impression of the Great Seal Deputed of Quebec, 1869 BL: Detached Seals CXLVIII.87*

This seal [6.14], like those of the other three foundation provinces, consists of a broadly based shield of the royal arms of general purpose, hatched in part, ensigned by a royal crown with, on a scroll encircling three sides of the shield, the motto DIEU ET MON DROIT. Beneath this is placed, on a heater-shaped shield, the Arms of Quebec, also hatched in part, and the whole is contained within a quadrilobial frame in the manner of fourteenth-century reticulated tracery, with the upper and lower arches pointed and the side ones rounded. The deep moulding of this frame contains four-petalled stylized flowers and pellets placed alternately. The background is heavily diapered with a fretty and quatrefoil design. A circular band embellished with pellets passes beneath the extremities of the frame, and there is a similar band on the outer edge of the seal. Between these two concentric bands is enscribed the legend which reads, starting at the upper right hand, THE · SEAL · OF · THE · PROVINCE · OF · QUEBEC. The diameter of this seal is 2½ inches (64 millimetres).[53]

The composition of this seal for the foundation provinces is one of great dignity, certainly an example of Pugin gothic at its best. While one should never read history backwards, nevertheless one is tempted to feel that an opportunity for imaginative and sensitive understanding was missed in not having the inscription on the legend band in the French language – a change that was authorized by article 4 of chapter 18 of the Revised Statutes of Quebec in 1925.

The design of the present seal [6.15] has remained basically as for that of 1869, save that since the change in provincial arms in 1939 a broadly-based shield in the lower lobe of the seal has displayed that design. The legend now reads LE · SCEAU · DE · LA · PROVINCE · DE · QUEBEC. As before the diameter is 2½ inches (64 millimetres).[54]

6.15 *Present Great Seal*
Deputed of Quebec (post 1939)
Author's collection

6.16 *Personal seal of Pierre de Voyer,*
Vicomte d'Argenson, Governor of New France
ANQ: NF.25.1, no. 38

Cachets des gouverneurs and privy seals

A well-established tradition, dating from the days of New France, underscores the use *ex-officio* by French and then British governors and now by the lieutenant governors of seals bearing their own personal arms.

To select but a few examples, the French governors appended their personal seals alongside their signatures, as on the concession granted by Pierre de Voyer, Vicomte d'Argenson, Governor of New France, to Gabriel Lemieux in 1658[6.16]. His seal shows a quarterly shield: *1 and 4, [azure] two lions passant guardant crowned [or]* (Voyer); *2 and 3, argent, a fess [sable]* (d'Argenson) *over all in chief a label; ensigned by a coronet consisting of a jewelled rim surmounted by seven large pearls; on either side of the shield and crossed beneath it two palm branches.* Oval in shape, this seal measures half an inch (12.5 millimetres) at its highest.[55]

Towards the end of the French regime we note the seal of Charles, Marquis de Beauharnois, Governor of New France, upon an ordonnance of 1743 in connection with fishing and the Mingan Islands [6.17]. His oval seal, 1 inch (25 millimetres) in diameter at its highest, shows an oval shield bearing the arms: *argent a fess and in chief three martlets [sable]*. The shield is surrounded by a riband bearing the motto of the Order of St Louis, BELLICAE VIRTVTIS PRAEMIUM, and from this depends the badge of that order. The shield and motto riband are ensigned by the coronet of a marquis (a jewelled circlet surmounted by three strawberry leaves; on either side of the central leaf are clusters of three pearls, with a small pearl between each leaf and cluster). Eagles on either side act as supporters.[56]

6.17 *Personal seal of Charles,*
Marquis de Beauharnois, Governor of New France
ANQ: NF.25.52, 36 liasse, no. 1320

6.18 *Privy seal of James Murray,*
Governor of Quebec
ANQ: AP Petite Collection James Murray, 1760-6

Following the transfer of New France to the British Crown, the governors followed the British tradition of using their own personal arms upon privy seals. Accordingly, we find the first governor, James Murray, employing his seal [6.18] in this manner upon the appointment of André Bauchard as *sous-procureur* in 1763. The seal is three quarters of an inch (19 millimetres) at its highest and oval in shape. A rococo shield displays the arms *a crescent within a fetterlock and on a chief three estoiles.* The crest rises from an open helm in profile and comprises a *cubit arm charged with a spur rowel holding scroll in bend sinister.* The motto, placed in the Scottish manner on a scroll above the crest, reads DEUM · TIME (Fear God).[57]

In the chapter on Ontario we shall see that the use of privy seals was continued by the governors general during the United Province of Canada. Upon the creation of the Province of Quebec in 1867, the lieutenant governors followed this tradition and have continued to do so down to the present day.

FLAGS

Flag of the Lieutenant Governor

In 1870 the Lieutenant Governor of Quebec was authorized to fly 'when embarked' on boats and other vessels the Union Badge or Jack with the arms of the province placed on a white roundel or disc and surrounded by a garland of maple leaves.[58] This gradually came to be used both afloat and on land and remained the practice until the tenure of office of Sir Eugène Fiset (1940-50), who flew the Union Badge or Jack *without* the

6.19 Flag of the Lieutenant Governor, Quebec
(from c. mid-1950)

provincial arms, roundel, and maple leaf wreath in the centre.

His successor, the Honble Gaspard Fauteux (1950-8), introduced the practice of flying the Canadian Red Ensign at the Bois de Coulogne in order to identify it as a gubernatorial residence. Further, probably as early as mid-1950, he introduced the present flag for the Lieutenant Governor of Quebec [6.19]. This is oblong in shape and royal blue in colour. The centre is charged with a white disc or roundel which bears the provincial arms and motto as used since 1939, ensigned by a royal crown.

The present practice is to fly the Lieutenant Governor's flag on his car as well as from his residence and at the Parliament Buildings whenever he is present there.[59]

Provincial flag

On 21 January 1948 the provincial flag, frequently called the *fleurdelisé flag* [plate 23.4], came into being following a provincial order in council.[60] Two years later, it was the subject of an Act of the Legislature of Quebec.[61]

The blazon of this flag would be *bleu celeste, a cross between four fleurs-de-lis argent*. The proportions are six to four.

From the technical point of view this design is one of great beauty by virtue of its simplicity.[62]

I wish to express my special appreciation of the help received in the preparation of this chapter from SE le Cardinal Maurice Roy, CC, OBE, Archevêque de Québec, and HE Cardinal George Flahiff, CC, CSB, Archbishop of Winnipeg, without whose unremitting assistance parts of this chapter would never have been accomplished, as well as from RP René Baudry, Archives Publiques du Canada, Ambassade du Canada, Paris; S. Marcelle Boucher, Archiviste, Monastère des Ursulines, Québec; Mlle Doris Drolet, Ancienne-Lorette; Mme Micheline Gaulin-Larocque, Ste-Foy; RP Honorius Provost, Archiviste, Grand Séminaire, Québec; Group Captain Gabriel Taschereau, DFC, CD, RCAF, Executive Assistant and Aide-de-Camp to the Lieutenant Governor of Quebec.

NOTES

1 The following discussion on the three mercantile companies is based on the scholarly article on the subject by Robert Pichette, KM, 'Early French-Canadian Heraldry' in *Heraldry in Canada* 2 (September 1968) pp. 20-4.

2 Crest-coronet

3 The motto scans quite happily as the first part of a hexameter, stopping at a fourth-foot caesura. If classical, it is very well chosen, but I shall not be surprised if it obstinately refuses to reveal such an origin.

4 Psalm 145:11

5 Others will be found in that monumental work, *Histoire Dv Roy Lovis Le Grand Par les Medailles, Emblêmes, Devises, Jettons, Inscriptions, Armoiries, et autres Monumens Publics. Recuëillis, et Expliquéz par le Pere Clavde François Menestrier De La Compagnie De Iesvs* (Paris, I.B. Nolin 1689).

6 Presumably synthetic, yet classical in inspiration; obviously not verse and almost certainly not a prose quotation

7 CA: 163. 124

8 Saskatchewan bears a similar charge but the tinctures are reversed.

9 PAC: PDP, no. 622-6-1

10 Prior to 1939, upon occasion, the arms established by royal warrant in 1868 were depicted with the fleurs-de-lis increased from two to three. This, however, seems to have been a case of artistic licence rather than anything else.

11 9 December 1939, no. 2895

12 P.-G. Roy, *Bulletin des recherches historiques* (Lévis 1896) 2, p. 20

13 An adaptation of Psalm 76 (Vulgate 77):20 (*in mari via tua*)

14 Bureau des archives, Monastère des Ursulines, Quebec

15 ANQ: NF.25, Collection de pièces judiciaires et notariales, no. 147: 'Ordonnance du lieutenant général civile et militaire contre Rainville, l'obligement à payer une provision alimentaire à Charles Turgeon, 10 septembre 1681'

16 *Jugements et délibérations du Conseil Souverain de la Nouvelle-France* 1, p. 207

17 ANQ: NF.25, Collection de pièces judiciaires et notariales, no. 1630: 'Arrêt qui declare le congé défaut bien et dûment obtenu par Augustin Maguet, père, habitant de la Rivière des Prairies, contre Augustin Maguet, fils, 13 decembre 1751'

18 Louis Rouvier, *La Chancellerie et les sceaux de France,* second edition (Marseille, Impr. Marseillaise 1950)

19 ANQ: NF.21.15 (1700-23): 'Ordonnance de Jacques-Alexis de Fleury Deschambault, lieutenant général commis en la Prévôté de Montreal, 8 juin 1700'

20 Ibid. NF.23.18: 'Requête de Raymond Dizy de Champlain pour fair assigner Joseph Pizard de la Pouche, 6 mars 1752'; and see Gilles Heon, 'Un Sceau de conséquence,' *Heraldry in Canada* 7 (December 1973) pp. 12-13.

21 *Acts of the Privy Council of England, Colonial Series* 4, p. 573

22 ANQ: NF.25, Collection de pièces judiciaires et notariales, no. 4284: 'Commission erigeant le Gouverneur en Conseil en Cour d'Appel, 1 août 1776'

23 Slightly adapted from Statius, *Silvae* 5.2.26. Statius is comparing a young nobleman with a spirited race-horse of distinguished pedigree: 'illum omnes acuunt plausus, illum ipse volantem pulvis et *incurvae gaudent agnoscere metae*' (Each burst of applause stimulates him, and the very dust and the rounded turning-posts delight to acknowledge him as he flies past).

24 BL: Detached Seals XLV.4

25 Royal Mint, London: Royal Mint Record Book 1/15, p. 190

26 Reproduced in *A Pageant of Canada* (Queen's Printer, Ottawa 1967) p. 309

27 Horace, *Odes* 4.4.59-60

28 SIGILLUM PROVINCIAE NOSTRAE CANADAE INFERIORIS (The Seal of Our Province of Lower Canada); the stops between the Latin abbreviations consist of quatrefoil stylized flowers.

29 ANQ: Papiers de Léry, AP-C-23-10, no. 4: 'Commission nommant Charles de Léry Maître de Chancellerie du Bas-Canada, 10 mars 1817'

30 PAC: RG 4, A1, vol. 55, pp. 18171-2 through Dundas to Lord Dorchester, Governor of Lower Canada

31 Royal Mint, London: Royal Mint Record Book 1/18, p. 309

32 PRO: CO 43, vol. 24, p. 175 and PAC: G9, pp. 93-4: Earl Bathurst, Secretary of State for War and Colonies, to Sir John Sherbrooke, Captain General and Governor in Chief of Canada, 12 March 1817

33 ANQ: Petites Collections, M-8: 'Bail pour 21 ans à John Murray, d'un lot dans la seigneurie Notre-Dame-des-Anges, 8 août 1828'

34 PAC: RG 7, G1, vol. 11, p. 14: Earl Bathurst, Secretary of State for War and Colonies to the Officer Administrating (concerning Lower Canada), 9 February 1820

35 ANQ: Petites Collections, M-8

36 PAC: RG 4, A1, vol. S192, part 2: royal warrant for use of great seal in Lower

Canada, 30 January 1828

37 PAC: PDP: Detached Seal

38 PAC: RG 68, A, vol. 96, p. 46: royal warrant to Lord Dalhousie, 22 July 1830

39 PAC: RG 7, G1, vol. 25, p. 122: Lord Howick, Under Secretary of State for the Colonies, to Lord Aylmer, Governor General of Canada, 8 November 1832

40 SIGILLUM PROVINCIAE CANADAE INFERIORIS (The Seal of the Province of Lower Canada)

41 BL: Detached Seal CXLVIII.43. For an example of an impression of this great seal upon an actual document see ANQ: Petites Collections, P-3: 'Commission nommant Joseph Fran-Perrault greffier à la cour du Banc du Roi, 20 decembre 1838.'

42 PRO: CO 854/2 (1837-40, Circulars – Colonial Department) ff. 36-9v: Lord Glenelg, Secretary of State for the Colonies to Governor/Lieutenant Governor of Lower Canada, 23 June 1837

43 PRO: CO 854/2, f. 274: Marquess of Normanby, Secretary of State for the Colonies, to Sir John Colborne, 13 February 1839; for the draft warrant see CO 380/136, item 46.

44 SIGILLUM PROVINCIAE CANADAE INFERIORIS (The Seal of the Province of Lower Canada)

45 BL: Detached Seal CXLVIII.84

46 The British North America Act, 1867, 30 and 31 Vic., c. 3

47 PRO: CO 43/676, ffs. 318-21r: Earl Granville, Secretary of State for the Colonies to Sir John Young, Bt., Governor General of Canada, 23 August 1869

48 Tonnochy: no. 266, heavily defaced. For a good impression see ANQ: Petites Collections, D-7: 'Nomination au Service Civil de J. William Dunscomb, de Francois Vézina et de Caspard Drolet, 22 janvier 1869.'

49 PRO: CO 42/678, ff. 101-2v: minute paper for Sir F[rederic] Rogers, 31 December [1869]

50 22 May 1867

51 PRO: CO 324, vol. 170, pp. 279-80: Duke of Buckingham and Chandos, Secretary of State for the Colonies, to Lord President of the Council, 27 July 1868

52 PAC: RG 7, G21, vol. 157, file 282A: royal warrant dated 7 May 1869

53 ANQ: Petites Collections, F-2: 'Nomination de J.B. Romauld Fiset et d'Alfred Bouillon comme coroners conjoints pour le district de Rimouski, 10 août 1897'

54 ANQ: Grands Formats: 'Lettres patentes nommant Sir Thomas Chapais membre du Conseil Exécutif de la Province de Québec, 14 juillet 1938'

55 ANQ: NF.25.1, no. 38: 'Concession par le gouverneur à Gabriel Lemieux d'une place sur le quai de Champlain, 26 août 1658'

56 ANQ: NF.25.52, 36 liasse, no. 1320: 'Ordonnance en forme de règlement pour la pêche sur les Isles de Mingan, 4 octobre 1743'

57 ANQ: AP Petite Collection James Murray, 1760-6: 'Procuration validée par le gouverneur James Murray, en faveur de André Bouchard qui est appointé comme sous-procureur, 29 septembre 1763.' General James Murry, seventh son of the fourth Lord Elibank does not appear to be on record either at the Lyon Court (where one would expect to find his matriculation) or at the College of Arms, as entitled to the arms displayed on the seal he used.

58 PRO: CO 43/157 Despatch no. 191: Lord Kimberley, Secretary of State for the

Colonies, to Sir John Young, Bt., Governor General of Canada, 16 July 1870

59 The sizes are: large – 66″ (1.68 m) x 34″ (.86 m), diameter of roundel 26″ (.66 m); small – 11″ (279.4 mm) x 6″ (152 mm), diameter of roundel 4″ (102 mm). The design of this flag *may* be a conscious parallel to the governor general's flag, with all that such would imply. However, both such a thesis and the actual authority for this flag have yet to be demonstrated.

60 No. 72

61 14 Geo. VI, c. 3, 1950: 'Loi concernant le drapeau officiel de la Province de Québec'

62 This flag has not yet been recorded at the College of Arms.

CHAPTER 7

Nova Scotia and Cape Breton Island

ENSIGNS ARMORIAL

By a charter passed under the Great Seal of Scotland and dated 29 September 1621,[1] King James VI of Scotland and I of England granted the lands which lay between Newfoundland and New England to the poet and statesman, Sir William Alexander, soon to be Earl of Stirling and Viscount of Canada.[2] The grant was to further his proposed plantation or colony, and thus formed the legal, constitutional, and historical basis for the rise and development of New Scotland, or Nova Scotia, as it came to be called. The vicissitudes of its early history need not detain us here, save to note in passing that a beginning was made under Alexander himself in 1629 with two colonies and under Sir Thomas Temple from 1654 to 1667. The French, for their part, disputed with vigour the right of existence of this new British colony in North America, and it was not until the Treaty of Utrecht in 1713 that they finally conceded peninsular Nova Scotia to the British Crown.[3]

It is known that arms for Nova Scotia were already in existence in 1625; this is evident from the following passage in the patent dated 28 May of that year creating Sir Robert Gordon the first Baronet of Nova Scotia:

Et quod dictus dominus Robertus, et sui haeredes masculi praescript habebunt, et habere et gerere in perpetuum dehinc poterint, vel in paludamentis, vulgo lie cantoun in yr coit of armis, vel in scutis, vulgo scutcheons, pro eorum arbitrio, *arma regni Novae Scotiae* nimirum [italics mine].[4]

We cannot be more specific as to the date upon which the Arms of Nova Scotia were assigned because the registers of Scottish arms suffer from a *lacuna* between the manuscript of Sir David Lindsay, Lyon King of Arms 1591-1621, and the present Lyon register commenced in 1672 in obedience to the act of that year of the Scottish Parliament. What happened to these precious documents from a period wracked by civil war and other disturbances has been the subject of much speculation and learned discussion, and fascinating though these investigations are they cannot detain us here.[5] Suffice it to say that between the years 1805 and 1810 (the actual entry is undated) the armorial bearings of Nova Scotia [plate 17] were re-entered in the new register of the Lyon Court at Edinburgh; their blazon is as follows:

Arms: *argent, a cross of St Andrew azure, charged with an inescutcheon of the royal arms of Scotland*
Crest: *on a wreath of the colours, a branch of laurel and a thistle issuing from two hands conjoined, the one armed and the other naked proper*
Supporters: *on the dexter, an unicorn argent, armed crined and unguled or, and crowned with the imperial crown proper, and gorged with a coronet composed of crosses paty and fleurs-de-lis, a chain affixed thereto passing through the forelegs and reflexed over the back gold; on the sinister, a savage holding in the exterior hand an arrow proper*
Motto: MUNIT HAEC ET ALTERA VINCIT (One defends, the other conquers).[6]

It will be noticed that the tinctures of the national Arms of Scotland have been transposed for New Scotland so that a blue saltire of St Andrew's Cross rests on a silver background. An inescutcheon or small shield of the Royal Arms of Scotland is placed in the centre. The crest is formed by sprigs of laurel and thistle supported by two hands, one in armour and the other bare, joined in friendship. These, taken with the motto, possibly signify that the King of the Scots – represented by the hand in armour and the thistle – would defend his liegemen engaged in conquering the difficulties to be met in Nova Scotia – represented by the bare hand and laurel sprig (symbol of peace, triumph, conquest); in other words, that the result of strong government is peaceful development.

The supporter to the dexter, the crowned unicorn, is from the royal achievement of Scotland. That to the sinister, 'a savage,' is capable of considerable latitude of interpretation. It can be emblazoned as anything from a hair-covered creature not unlike the popular conception of Darwin's missing link to a bearded Hercules girded about the loins with leaves or animal skins, such as the sinister supporter in the armorial achievement of HRH the Duke of Edinburgh. It is probable, however, that what the Stuart monarch had in mind was a North American Indian, as usually conventionalized by heraldic artists in the seventeenth century. Certainly, this is the legitimate interpretation used in representations of this armorial supporter of Nova Scotia today. If this type of rendering accords with the original intention, then this supporter probably affords the first example of the specific influence of British colonial endeavours in armory, and so the beginning in British heraldry of that large and varied range of devices including different races, flora, fauna, and objects from the four corners of the Empire and Commonwealth. On the other hand, if this conjecture is not correct, then primacy of place passes, without a doubt, to the armorial supporters of Newfoundland, as already indicated in the chapter on that province.[7]

It will be noted that the helm for the armorial bearings of Nova Scotia is a royal helm,

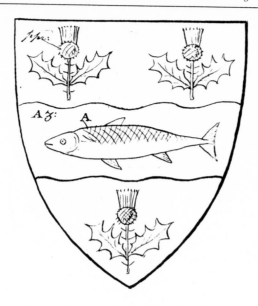

7.1 Pen and ink sketch of the arms assigned for Nova Scotia by royal warrant, 26 May 1868
PAC: PDP

that is to say, it faces the viewer, the opening is covered with bars, and the metal is gold. In fact, this is the only province entitled to such a privilege. The usual present-day practice is for a tilting helm – vizor closed and facing the viewer's left – to be used in connection with provincial arms. In the seventeenth century, however, when these arms were originally assigned, the use of a royal helm in connection with arms of particular purpose used in token of royal public authority overseas appears to have been the custom, if we are to judge by the complete achievement as assigned to Jamaica, for example.[8]

The ancient Arms of Nova Scotia have not, however, always enjoyed the undisputed place of honour which they do today, for in 1868 a most curious situation arose. By a royal warrant dated 26 May of that year, arms were assigned for the four provinces which had just come together to form the Dominion of Canada. For Ontario, Quebec, and New Brunswick, which had never had arms, this was most appropriate. For Nova Scotia, however, it meant the displacing of ensigns of public authority of some 243 years' standing by a completely new coat of arms: *or, on a fess wavy azure, between three thistles proper, a salmon naiant argent*[9] [7.1]. As these arms are technically sound, had they been assigned for a province which had never had ensigns of public authority, then none could have objected. But bearing in mind the historic and splendid complete achievement which they supplanted, one can only say that one's breath is taken away. Complete inadvertence seems to be the only explanation of how this could have come about, particularly in view of the very considerable knowledge of, and real sympathy for, things Scottish on the part of the queen. Most curious of all is the fact that when the provincial delegates were in London in April 1868 to discuss, among other matters, the arms about to be assigned, no objection appears to have been raised by the Nova Scotia representative. In fact, the delegates apparently took a real interest in these armorial matters and even went so far as to make an explicit request that the design of the arms proposed by Garter Young for Ontario be altered, which it was.[10]

The result was that the next month the arms for the four foundation provinces, approved by the delegates, were assigned by royal warrant, with such dire results for Nova Scotia. For some years, however, this situation does not appear to have occasioned general complaint. After World War I, however, interest developed in the restoration of the ancient Arms of Nova Scotia, and the cause found able advocates in such men as John A. Stewart, who campaigned with all that vigour characteristic of the Gael when taking up a cause.[11] Throughout the 1920s momentum in this direction increased, with the result that finally the government of Nova Scotia put forward a formal request for the restoration of the ancient arms. The federal government supported this and on 31 March 1928 requested the Secretary of State for Dominion Affairs to arrange for the annulment of the 1868 arms and the restoration of the Stuart armorial bearings of the province.[12] As their origin was Scottish, Lyon and Garter Kings of Arms settled between them the terms by which this was to be accomplished.[13] The result was the royal warrant dated 19 January 1929, whereby the seventeenth-century armorial bearings became once again the ensigns of public authority 'to be borne for the said Province of Nova Scotia upon Seals, Shields, Banners or otherwise, according to the Laws of Arms.'[14] It is of interest to note that because of the illness of King George V, it was the three Councillors of State who signed the warrant: Queen Mary, and her sons the Prince of Wales (subsequently King Edward VIII) and the Duke of York (subsequently King George VI).

SEALS

Great seals deputed of Nova Scotia

On 18 July 1622 the Lords of the Privy Council of Scotland directed that a seal should be made for Sir William Alexander as Lieutenant of Justice and Admiralty in New Scotland 'for the gritair solempnitie in useing of the saidis officeis.' The seal was to

have and on the ane syde his Majesteis armes within a shield, the Scottis armes being in the first place, with a close crowne above the armes, with this circomescriptioun – SIGILLUM REGIS SCOTIAE, ANGLIAE, FRANCIAE, ET HIBERNIAE, and on the other syde of the seale his Majesteis protrat in armour, with a Crowne on his heade, ane sceptour in the ane hand, and ane glob in the other hand, with this circomescriptioun – PRO NOVAE SCOTIAE LOCUMTENENTE ... [15]

Some six years later, on 18 March 1628, the Privy Council of Scotland ordered that a seal be made

of the office of the Admiraltie of New Scotland ... having a shippe with all her ornaments and apparrelling, the mayne saile onelie displeyed with the armes of New Scotland, bearing a saltoire with ane scutchon of the ancient armes of Scotland, and upoun the head of the said shippe careing ane unicorne sittand and ane savage man standing upoun the sterne both bearing the St Androes croce, and ... this circumscriptioun, SIGILLUM GULIELMI ALEXANDRI, MILITIS, MAGNI ADMIRALLI NOVI SCOTIAE ... [16]

7.2 *Obverse and reverse of the Great Seal Deputed of Nova Scotia of George II, in use 1730-67*
PANS: box 3, Land Grants (see note 25)

Neither dies nor impressions of these seals appear to have survived. Indeed, it is possible that the former were never engraved. However, be that as it may, these orders give a vivid impression of how the Scottish authorities conceived the sigillographic expression of public authority in that extended area of their responsibility, Nova Scotia. However, although, as mentioned before, settlements were attempted there on a number of occasions in the seventeenth century, the French contested each attempt with such force that it was not until the reign of Queen Anne that they finally conceded Nova Scotia to the British Crown by the Treaty of Utrecht.[17]

Within sixteen months of its ratification, the queen was dead, and so one would not expect a Nova Scotia seal for this last of the Stuarts to have been made. Indeed, her successor, George I, was to follow her to the grave before one was proposed by the Lords Commissioners of Trade and Plantations on 8 October 1728, 'there being as yet no Publick Seal for Nova Scotia.'[18] Accordingly, matters were set *en train* and within the surprisingly short period of fifteen months the seal was engraved, approved by the Privy Council, and ordered to be despatched.[19] The steps by which this was accomplished – including the direction that Virginia pay for it – have been discussed in chapter 2.

Happily, an example of an impression in wax of this Great Seal Deputed of Nova Scotia of George II is preserved in the Provincial Archives at Halifax [7.2]. The obverse consists of one of those panoramic and allegorical scenes which are a characteristic of the colonial seals of British North America in the eighteenth century. Dressed in tricorn hat, frock coat, breeches, stockings, and sword of the period, a British merchant trades for furs with an Indian, who appears to be represented in the stylized manner of that period. They stand, somewhat to the left, against a part of a coastline map of Nova Scotia, while at sea nearby sails a small fishing sloop.[20] It is an interesting combination of the one- and the three-dimensional. Something less than the bottom quarter of the seal is occupied by the exergue, in which is placed the motto TERRAE MARISQUE OPES (The resources of land and sea).

The legend round the edge of the seal, starting at the lower left, reads SIGILLUM · PROVINCIAE · NOST... NOV... SCOTIAE... AM... According to the instructions issued to John Rollos, the engraver of this seal, it was to read SIGILLUM PROVINCIAE NOSTRAE NOVAE SCOTIAE IN AMERICA.[21] An outer edge of stylized foliage completes the obverse of this seal.

The reverse consists of the royal arms in the usual form for the remainder of the American colonies of the period. The arms are as borne from 1714-1801, that is to say, *quarterly, 1, England impaling Scotland; 2, France; 3, Ireland; 4, Hanover,* and as discussed in chapter 3. The shield is surrounded by the Garter and ensigned by a royal crown. The lion and unicorn supporters stand on scroll work attached to which is a riband inscribed with the royal motto DIEU ET MON DROIT. A plain circle contains this design and is free of it save where it passes behind the base of the cross on top of the orb on the Crown. The legend, starting at the top of the seal just to the right of the orb and cross, reads GEORGIUS · II · D · ... MAG · BRI · FR · ET · HIB · ...EX · ... · D · BR ... N · ... S.R.I. AR ... ... T · PR · EL. Rollos was instructed to include the following inscription: GEORGIUS SECUNDUS, DEI GRATIA, MAGNAE BRITANNIAE, FRANCIAE ET HIBERNIAE REX, FIDEI DEFENSOR, BRUNSVICI ET LUNEBURGI DUX, SACRI ROMANI IMPERII ARCHTHESAURUS ET ELECTOR.[22] As the new king had longer titles than his predecessor, the engraver was specifically permitted to use his discretion in contracting the words when preparing seals.[23] It will be noted, however, that not only did he do so but in addition inserted PR (Princeps) before EL (Elector) at the end of the legend. As he also did this on the George II seals for the other American colonies at this time, we can only infer that the variation was made with due authority.[24] An outer circle of stylized foliage completes the edge of this great seal of Nova Scotia, of which the diameter is 4½ inches (115 millimetres).[25]

George II died on 25 October 1760 and, following the usual custom, his seal continued in use until a new one could be provided.[26] In fact this interim lasted a considerable time, for as late as 30 September 1767 we find the late king's seal still in use in connection with a land grant in Sackville Township,[27] although earlier that year, in April, a new seal for Nova Scotia had been approved by the Privy Council and ordered to be sent to the governor and the old one was ordered to be returned for defacing.[28]

This first seal of George III [7.3] has as its obverse a scene similar to that for the previous reign. From the bill presented for its making we learn that it represents 'the Country of Nova Scotia and a British Merchant trading with an Indian for Furs and also a Fishing Vessel Boat and Nett.'[29] The figures are somewhat more to the centre than in the previous seal. With all the heroic elegance of a Gainsborough, the merchant dominates the whole composition; dressed in tricorn hat, frock coat, knee breeches, stockings, shoes, and sword of the period, he stands with right hand on hip, the left hand pointing to furs carried by the Indian. The latter is rendered with feathered head-dress and kilt in that stylized fashion so often employed in portrayals of American Indians from the sixteenth to the eighteenth centuries. In this instance he is neither the 'noble savage' of Rousseau nor a native capable of surviving the rigours of hunting and

*7.3 Obverse (proof impression in wax) and reverse of the
Great Seal Deputed of Nova Scotia of George III, in use 1767-1818
Royal Mint, London (Crown copyright) and PANS: MS Docs. (see note 31)*

trapping in the local forests of the day. Rather he is a somewhat physically underde-veloped young man who would have been much more at home in the clothes of the merchant in front of him than standing semi-naked on this windy foreshore – or was it in reality a draughty London studio? Could he have been the same model as for the Indian on the reverse of the Great Seal of Virginia for this reign,[30] for on both occasions they wear (?) cloth kilts overlaid with feathers and their head-dresses are formed of ostrich feathers? We shall never know, save that the artist was probably as ignorant of North American ornithology and anthropology as, conversely, he was patently highly skilled as an engraver, for he produced a most excellent piece of workmanship in this seal.

The scene is completed with a beaver skin on the ground near the Indian; from the fishing sloop a man casts his net, while nearer land another rows in a dinghy. The exergue and motto are as for the seal of George II. The legend, starting at the lower left, reads SIGILLUM · PROVINCIAE · NOSTRIAE · NOVAE SCOTIAE · SIVE · ACADIAE · IN · AMERICA · (The Seal of Our Province of Nova Scotia or Acadia in America). Stylized foliage completes the outer edge of the obverse of this seal.

The reverse has the 1714-1801 royal arms as on the George II seal, but the treatment is slightly different in that the upper corners of the shield are placed behind the Garter, and the scroll work upon which the lion and unicorn supporters stand is somewhat more Chippendale. The legend for the first George III seal is the same as for the previous one except that II becomes III, and PR (Princeps) is omitted at the end. The diameter is 4⅜ inches (111 millimetres).[31]

As mentioned in chapter 3, the royal arms were altered upon the Union of Great

7.4 *Obverse (proof impression in wax) and reverse of the*
Great Seal Deputed of Nova Scotia of George III, in use from 1818
Fuller Collection 4/1 and PANS: box no. 4 (see note 34)

Britain and Ireland in 1801 when *France Modern* was removed from the second quarter and *Scotland* placed there instead, and the arms of *Hanover* were placed on an inescutcheon over all ensigned by an electoral bonnet. Accordingly, royal warrants were issued for the colonies authorizing the temporary continued use of existing seals,[32] although the warrant for Nova Scotia does not seem to have survived. Certainly the first great seal of George III for this province was still being used in 1812, and if the apparent experience of the other colonies is a guide, then a deputed great seal engraved with the royal arms and electoral bonnet was never issued for Nova Scotia.

In 1816, Hanover having become a kingdom, the royal arms were changed once again, with the substitution of a royal crown for the electoral bonnet above the inescutcheon. Accordingly, a sterling silver seal die was duly engraved by Thomas Wyon, Chief Engraver of His Majesty's Seals, and completed by 23 November 1818 [7.4]. In his bill to the Lords of the Treasury he described the obverse as having an 'English Merchant, Trading with an Indian – for skins, a ship and a view of the Country, at a distance, on the other side the Royal Arms.' Complete with a red case and impressions for the office, it cost £85.13.11d.[33]

The design on the obverse was a new interpretation of the merchant and Indian scene. On this seal, the European wears a cut-away coat and a stumpy, narrow-brimmed hat of the period – almost a top hat. Far from being something of a magnificent pro-consul, as on the first George III seal, he has now been reduced to a rather undistinguished travelling salesman. In this instance it is the Indian who dominates the composition. Wearing a feather head-dress of the stylized form, he stands holding a pelt. Between the two men lies a trunk, while further to the left a fishing net dries over a

7.5 *Impression of the Great Seal Deputed of Nova Scotia of William IV, in use 1832-9 PANS: Land Papers, 1838 (see note 39)*

7.6 *Proof impression in wax of the Great Seal Deputed of Nova Scotia of Victoria, in use 1839-79 BL: Detached Seals XCVIII.6*

frame. To the right, behind the Indian, a rowing boat is beached. The background consists of a vessel – probably a trading brigantine – with sails furled lying at anchor in a bay or river on the far side of which tall firs rise from a rocky shore. Unlike the obverse on the previous seals of Nova Scotia, the treatment on this one is three-dimensional throughout. As on the other seals the motto TERRÆ MARISQUE OPES occurs in the exergue. This whole design is contained within a plain circle which forms the inner limit of the legend band. Starting at the upper right, the legend reads SIGILLUM PROVINCIÆ NOSTRÆ NOVÆ SCOTIÆ SIVE ACADIÆ IN AMERICA. The outer edge comprises a fillet of stylized acanthus leaves.

The reverse shows the royal arms in their 1816-37 form. The legend is simplified and reads, starting at the upper right, GEORGIUS TERTIUS DEI GRATIA BRITANNIARUM REX FIDEI DEFENSOR. [34] The diameter is 4 inches (102 millimetres).

Upon the death of George III on 29 January 1820, the 'Seal used during the Reign of His late Majesty within the Province,' that is to say the one just described, was sanctioned for continued use until a new one could be provided for his successor, George IV. [35] In due time one was presumably forthcoming, as upon the death of George IV the continued service of the 'Seal made use of in the Province of Nova Scotia in America during the lifetime of Our dear Brother the late deceased King' was provided for. [36] However, neither the matrices nor impressions of a George IV seal have come to light so far.

The next sovereign was William IV, and his seal for the province was despatched with a royal warrant for its use on 1 November 1832. [37] In common with those of the other British North American colonies the Great Seal Deputed of Nova Scotia of William IV [7.5] was single-sided for impression directly onto the surface of the document. It consisted of the royal arms of the 1816-37 design surrounded by the Garter, which in turn was flanked by a branch of oak to the dexter and a branch of laurel to the sinister. The shield of arms was ensigned by a royal crown. The lion and unicorn supporters are in their accustomed places and stand upon a motto scroll inscribed DIEU ET MON DROIT.

The lower part of the seal contains, in a circular frame, basically the same merchant and Indian scene and exergue with motto as found on the obverse of the 1818 Great Seal Deputed of Nova Scotia. In the space on either side of this frame are arranged a rose, a thistle, and shamrocks to the left, and more shamrocks and thistles to the right. A plain circle contains the armorial and symbolic scene.

Around the circumference are placed the royal style and titles, starting at the centre left and going round the top of the seal: GULIELMUS IV D · G · BRITANNIAR · REX F · D ·. Starting again at the centre left and running down the lower part of the legend band is the inscription SIGIL · NOVAE SCOTIAE ET PROM · BRIT · (probably, SIGILLUM NOVAE SCOTIAE ET [INSULAE] PROMONTORII BRITANNIAE − The Seal of Nova Scotia and Cape Breton Island). A plain circle forms the outer edge of the seal, of which the diameter is 2 1/4 inches (58 millimetres).

Upon the death of the king, the Secretary of State for the Colonies sent, in the usual manner, a further royal warrant dated 22 June 1837 authorizing the continued use of the William IV seal for Nova Scotia until another was provided,[38] it continued to be used during the next twenty months.[39]

By February 1839, the new seal was ready.[40] Like the other seals of the British North American provinces then in existence, the Great Seal Deputed of Nova Scotia for Queen Victoria [7.6] was single-sided and of the Newfoundland pattern, the permanent elements of which have been discussed in detail in chapter 5. The local elements, both the scene contained within the Chippendale-like frame and the legend, are as on the William IV seal. A plain circle completes the outer edge of the seal, of which the diameter is 2 3/8 inches (60 millimetres).[41]

This seal did duty for the greater part of the reign of Queen Victoria. With the advent of Confederation, however, an imperial order in council of 22 May 1867 approved certain devices for a new seal of Nova Scotia upon her joining with the other three foundation provinces to form the new dominion.[42] During the succeeding months it was decided to change the design in order to incorporate the new arms proposed for the province,[43] and it was this seal [7.7] which was finally decided upon and sanctioned by royal warrant dated 1 May 1869. Basically, it was the same as for Ontario, Quebec, and New Brunswick. That is to say, a shield of the royal arms of general purpose was placed in the centre of a quadrilobial frame, in the lower, and pointed, lobe of which were placed the new Arms of Nova Scotia as authorized by the royal warrant of 26 May 1868, discussed earlier in this chapter; around the circumference ran the legend THE · SEAL · OF · THE · PROVINCE · OF · NOVA · SCOTIA · (the lower arch of the quadrilobial frame protrudes into the legend band after PRO). The diameter is 2 1/2 inches (64 millimetres).[44]

It was not for another decade, however, that this seal was actually brought into use in Nova Scotia. The reason for this extraordinary situation stemmed from a rather complicated series of events of which the main points were as follows.

By section 136 of the British North America Act it was specifically provided that certain seals were to be used in Ontario and Quebec until altered by their respective lieutenant governors in council. The necessity for this arose from the fact that from the legal point of view those two provinces were new creations out of the former Province of Canada. At the time of Confederation they had, therefore, no separate seals and so were authorized by the British North America Act to use the same seals, or seals of the same design, as had been used by Upper and Lower Canada. This was obviously an interim measure until it was possible to provide permanent Great Seals Deputed of Ontario and of Quebec. That the historical sequence of events for the two provinces was not quite as envisaged by this act is discussed in the appropriate chapters.

As far as Nova Scotia was concerned, the Act was silent. Further, the royal warrant of 26 May 1868 assigned arms to Nova Scotia but said nothing about a seal. Nevertheless, a seal was engraved for this province, along with others for the dominion and the other three provinces, and sent to Ottawa by the Colonial Secretary accompanied by a despatch dated 8 May 1869.[45]

At this point Sir John A. Macdonald, as Minister of Justice, had second thoughts and accordingly submitted a memorandum on the subject in the following June. He felt that 'there can be no doubt that Her Majesty has the sole power to order and to change at will the Great Seal of the Dominion. A question, however, arises, whether, under the British North America Act, 1867, and under the altered position of the Provinces caused by that Act, the power to fix the Great Seals for those Provinces does not rest elsewhere [i.e. at Ottawa in the Governor General in Council].'[46]

Earl Granville, Colonial Secretary, having studied this memorandum was of the opinion that the British North America Act in no way removed from Her Majesty the power of altering the Great Seal Deputed of Nova Scotia. He felt, however, that all provinces should be on the same footing and that their respective lieutenant governors should be vested with the power to alter the great seals deputed of their provinces from time to time. The only problem he foresaw was the method by which this should be done, whether by an Act of the local legislature concerned assented to by the Crown, or by an Imperial Act.[47]

While this correspondence was proceeding between Ottawa and London, nothing could be done as far as Nova Scotia was concerned, and it was not until 24 November 1869 that the Secretary of State for the Provinces sent a copy of these letters to the Lieutenant Governor of Nova Scotia, and, in accordance with the decision of the Canadian Privy Council, ordered that the new seal be adopted for the province.[48] By the end of the first week in December it had been delivered to Halifax, and the Lieutenant Governor promised to return the old seal to Ottawa by 'the first available opportunity.'[49] However, the Executive Council obviously had other ideas on the subject, for at a meeting held in February[50] a minute was passed noting the contents of the letters and continuing:

While freely recognising the right of Her Majesty the Queen to change and alter the Great Seal of the Province at pleasure, [they] respectfully submit that, as the people of Nova Scotia are warmly attached to the Seal, which, for a long period of time was used in sealing all Provincial documents under their old and highly-valued constitution, the Government be permitted to retain the old Seal instead of adopting the new one, a course which will obviate the necessity of either Imperial or Local legislation on the subject.[51]

A copy of this minute was duly sent to the Secretary of State for the Provinces, who said

7.7 *Proof impression in wax of the Great Seal*
Deputed of Nova Scotia, in use 1879-1930
BL: *Detached Seals CXLVIII.88*

7.8 *Copper counterpart of the Great Seal*
Deputed of Nova Scotia, in use from 1930
Royal Mint, London. Crown copyright

that he would submit it to the Governor General for onward transmission to the Colonial Secretary, if thought appropriate.[52]

Nothing further was, in fact, done about this by Ottawa,[53] and Nova Scotia continued to use its old seal. Indeed, the matter seems to have been forgotten about during the next seven years until a decision of the Supreme Court of the province in 1877 called into question the validity of this seal.[54] Naturally considerable alarm ensued for, by implication, all land grants since 1869, as well as the Assembly itself, the Acts of two Parliaments and of the Law Courts and other institutions created thereby, were all called into question. There was no dalliance on this occasion. The files of Government House were combed, not only by the Private Secretary but by the Lieutenant Governor himself, in an effort to turn up every relevant paper for laying before the Legislature.[55] Telegrams flashed between Halifax, Ottawa, and London.[56] The Colonial Secretary immediately brought in the Law Officers of the Crown so as to have their opinion, and in the meantime promised that 'of course anything necessary to be done, which can be done here, will be done.'[57]

At Ottawa the House of Commons passed an Address on 12 March calling for copies of all correspondence between, on the one hand, the imperial and dominion governments, and, on the other, the dominion government and that of Nova Scotia concerning the great seal deputed of that province since Confederation.[58]

Back at Halifax, the Legislature then in session – not quite knowing if indeed they were – passed an Address to the Queen in which they recapitulated the facts of the matter. They ended with a request that steps be taken to remove all doubt concerning the validity of 'all Acts, Instruments, and things done and passed under the old Seal', and further stated that if the Lieutenant Governor in Council could be vested with the power of altering and changing the seal then his 'first act under such authority would be to adopt such Seal as your Majesty shall direct.'[59]

Mercifully, the agony was finally relieved by the Law Officers in London. They pointed out that as the warrant of 7 May 1869 for the use of the new seal was merely directive, documents sealed with the old seal of Nova Scotia were not invalidated. Further, they held that the federal Parliament was competent to empower lieutenant governors to alter the great seals deputed of their respective provinces, from time to time. The Law Officers further recommended that, although this was not strictly necessary, such legislation should declare all documents sealed with the former seal of the relevant province to be valid.[60]

As a consequence, Ottawa moved with a speed which might well be described as meteoric in Parliamentary annals. A bill was drafted, introduced, debated, passed through both Houses, and had received the royal assent by 28 April 1877 – less than a month after the Law Officers' opinion had been received. This Act respecting the Great Seals of the Provinces of Canada, other than Ontario and Quebec[61] embodied precisely the points advised.

So empowered by this Act, the Lieutenant Governor of Nova Scotia by an order in council dated 21 November 1878, decreed that the seal 'now in the possession of the Lieutenant Governor'[62] engraved with the new Arms of Nova Scotia would be taken into use, in accordance with the royal warrant of 1 May 1869.[63] Accordingly, some four weeks later the Honble Adams George Archibald, Lieutenant Governor, issued a proclamation to the effect that on and after 1 January 1879, this was to be the Great Seal Deputed of Nova Scotia.[64]

For the rest of that century and into the next, this seal did duty. However, as explained earlier in this chapter, a movement gradually developed in the province for the restoration of the ancient Stuart Arms of Nova Scotia. When this was finally accomplished in 1929, a provincial order in council directed that by proclamation forthwith the present seal of Nova Scotia [7.8] be brought into use on, from and after 15 September 1930.[65]

The seal is circular in shape. The design consists of the complete armorial achievement of Nova Scotia save for the motto. The supporters stand on a compartment or grassy mound upon which are shown a thistle of Scotland and may-flowers of Nova Scotia. Around the lower half of the circumference runs a scroll which bears the legend PROVINCE OF NOVA SCOTIA. The diameter is 3 inches (76 millimetres).

The Lieutenant Governor is the Keeper of the Great Seal Deputed of the Province;[66] the Provincial Secretary is the custodian of the matrices. The provincial statute dealing with the great seal is The Lieutenant Governor and Great Seal Act, chapter 166 of the Revised Statutes of 1967.

Privy seal of the Lieutenant Governor

The Lieutenant Governor of Nova Scotia uses a privy seal on certain categories of official and semi-official documents. This either takes the form of the personal arms of the governor[67] or some other device such as a cypher.[68]

FLAGS

Flag of the Lieutenant Governor

The official flag of the Lieutenant Governor of the province consists of the Union Flag or Jack charged at the centre with a plate or white heraldic disc. This in turn is charged with the shield of arms of the province. Round the edge of the plate is arranged a wreath of green maple leaves. (See plate 22.4 for the basic design; the shield of arms varies for the province concerned.)

Provincial flag

The flag of the province of Nova Scotia [plate 23.1] consists of the arms as displayed on the shield, but bled out so as to occupy rectangular flag the breadth of which is three-quarters of the length. The authority for this flag rests in the royal warrant of 19 January 1929 by which the ancient arms were restored 'to be borne for the said Province of Nova Scotia upon Seals, Shields, Banners or otherwise according to the Laws of Arms.'[69]

SEALS OF CAPE BRETON ISLAND

Deputed great seals

Between 1784 and 1820 Cape Breton Island was a separate colony. Accordingly a great seal was required for the administration of government, and by 7 February 1785, Thomas Major, HM's Engraver of Seals, had completed his commission to engrave the first seal of Cape Breton Island [7.9]. It was made of 11 ounces, 3 pennyweights of silver, and together with the duty on the metal, the shagreen case to be used for keeping it when not in use, and Major's charges for engraving, the total bill came to £29.3.9d.[70]

The design, according to Major, shows 'Fishing Vessels in a Rocky Bay defended by a Fortress.'[71] Above this scene in the sky, as it were, is a circular scroll inscribed SIGIL · INS · PROM · BRIT · (of which the extended form was probably SIGILLUM INSULAE PROMONTORII BRITANNIAE − The Seal of the Island of Cape Breton). Beneath, in the exergue, is the motto FORTUNA · NON · MUTAT GENVS (Circumstance does not change our origin). Two plain concentric circles form the outer and inner edges of the legend band, which reads, starting at the top right, GEORGIUS · III · D · G · MAG · BRI · F · ET · HIB · REX · F · D · BRUN · ET · LUN · DUX · S · R · I · AR · THES · ET · PR · ELEC · .[72] The diameter is 2¾ inches (70 millimetres).

This is of particular interest as it is the first Canadian example of a single-sided deputed great seal and in this instance was usually impressed onto wax directly onto the document concerned.[73] It is the forerunner of all those single-sided deputed great seals which are now in general use in this country although their usual method of impression is *en placard* and without the use of wax. The North American precedent for the Cape Breton seal is to be found in the great seals deputed of New Jersey, which from as early as the reign of Queen Anne were of this type.[74]

On 25 February 1785 Lord Sydney, the Home Secretary, sent the seal to the Lieuten-

7.9 *Proof impression of the single-sided Great Seal Deputed of Cape Breton Island of George III, in use from 1785 Royal Mint, London. Crown copyright*

7.10 *Proof impression of the single-sided Great Seal Deputed of Cape Breton Island of George IV Royal Mint, London. Crown copyright*

ant Governor of Cape Breton Island along with the warrant which authorized its use.[75] As it contained none of the usual armorial details, one would not expect any new seals to be issued upon the various changes of the royal arms during the reign of George III. However, from the Royal Mint Record Books one notes the copy of a bill for £25.0.0d submitted by Marchant for the engraving of a silver seal 'with ivory handle, red case, box and impression for Office' for Cape Breton completed on 30 January 1816.[76] We know nothing of the details of the design except that, as it was provided with a handle, it must have been, like its predecessor, a single-sided seal. Had it been double-sided, in place of a handle it would have had some form of stem attached to the upper and lower matrices in order to secure it to the press.

The last seal of Cape Breton is that of George IV [7.10], which, like its predecessors, is single-sided. The design in the centre, while different from that on the George III seal, is nevertheless conceived along similar lines; the design shows sloops, as before, but in addition there is a small schooner at the lower left, and other craft, difficult to identify, sail in the background. Sloops were local craft fitted with one mast and a fore and aft rig. These extremely fine sea boats were used extensively for fishing as well as for other purposes up and down this part of the North American coast from the mid-seventeenth century onwards for something like the next two centuries.

The vessels on the George IV seal are placed before a fortress which rises to the left, built upon a rocky coast. The Union Jack flies from a flag pole above the battlements.

Above this scene is a circular scroll inscribed SIGIL · INS · PROM · BRIT · . The same motto occurs in the exergue as on the first seal of George III, while all of this is contained within a plain circle. The legend reads, starting at the upper right, GEORGIUS QUARTUS ·

DEI · GRATIA · BRITANNIARUM · REX · FIDEI · DEFENSOR · (a laurel wreath forms the final stop). Stylized foliage forms the outer edge of the legend band and seal. The diameter is 2³/₄ inches (70 millimetres).[77]

Whether in fact this seal was ever used is a moot point as Cape Breton ceased to be a separate colony in 1820. So far, at least, no documents bearing it have been identified.

Privy seals

As in other colonies of the period, privy seals appear to have been used in Cape Breton Island. A specific example is that of Brigadier General N. Nepean, President of His Majesty's Council for Cape Breton Island which, impressed in the usual manner in the upper left-hand corner, occurs on an ordinance for the raising of revenue by an 'import on rum and other Spirituous Liquors,' dated 20 February 1809.[78]

In connection with this chapter I owe a special debt of gratitude to the following: Brigadier General the Honble V. de B. Oland, KStJ, ED, KM, Lieutenant Governor of Nova Scotia for most generous hospitality at Government House, Halifax; C. Bruce Fergusson, DPhil, MA, Provincial Archivist, whose untiring efforts have made the preparation of this chapter possible; C.L. Beazley, Special Consultant, Province House, Halifax; C.E. Thomas of Halifax; the Rev D.F. Arnold, St Paul's Church, Halifax; and my colleagues in Edinburgh, Sir James Monteith Grant, KCVO, Lord Lyon King of Arms, Malcolm Innes of Edingight, MA, Marchmont Herald of Arms, Lyon Clerk and Keeper of the Records, Court of the Lord Lyon, and Major David Maitland-Titterton, TD, Ormond Pursuivant.

NOTES

1 Printed in *Royal Letters, Charters, and Tracts, relating to the Colonization of New Scotland, and the Institution of the Order of Knights Baronets of Nova Scotia, 1621-1638* (Edinburgh, The Bannatyne Club 1867) pp. 1-15

2 14 June 1663: see G.E. Cockayne (Clarenceaux King of Arms), *The Complete Peerage* 12 (London, St Catherine Press 1953) p. 279

3 For a detailed discussion on these early settlements see G.P. Insh, *Scottish Colonial Schemes 1620-1686* (Glasgow, Maclehose, Jackson 1922) pp. 3, 78-90; and for further views see T.H. McGrail, *Sir William Alexander First Earl of Stirling* (Edinburgh and London, Oliver & Boyd 1940) pp. 105-23, and appendix C.

4 *The Register of the Great Seal of Scotland*, vol. 8, f. 287, charter no. 790 (Reg. Mag. Sig. vol. 51, fo. 34)

5 Those interested in this sad episode in Scottish heraldic history might refer to Sir Thomas Innes of Learney, *Scots Heraldry* (Edinburgh, Oliver & Boyd 1956) chapters 5 and 6, and J.H. Stevenson, *Heraldry in Scotland* (Glasgow, James Maclehose and Sons 1914) 1, p. 115 ff.

6 CLL: Public Register of All Arms and Bearings in Scotland (vol. 1, f. 485) 1805-10. An ancient source for the motto seems unlikely. The fact that hands occur in the crest explains why one has the forms *haec* and *altera* in the motto, as *manus* is feminine.

7 For a further discussion on this subject see Conrad M.J.F. Swan (York Herald of Arms), 'American Indians in Heraldry,' *The Coat of Arms* 12 (July 1971) pp. 96-106, and 12 (October 1971) pp. 148-59.

8 CA: Walker's Grants II.5 on or before 3 February 1661/62

9 CA: I 63.124

10 PRO: CO 324, vol. 170, pp. 229-231: F[rederic] Rogers at Downing Street to Sir Charles Young, Garter King of Arms, 29 April 1868

11 J.A. Stewart, *The Arms of Nova Scotia* (Glasgow, St Andrew Society 1921)

12 CA: 14 Garter, ff. 354-6

13 CA: 14 Garter, ff. 360-3

14 CA: I 79. 258-9

15 David Masson, ed., *The Register of the Privy Council of Scotland* (Edinburgh 1877-98) 13, pp. 14-15

16 Ibid. second series (1899-1908) 2, p. 271

17 Signed 11 and ratified 18 April 1713; see the original treaty, PRO: SP 108/73.

18 PRO: CO 218/2 Nova Scotia 1720-49 B, pp. 122-3: Lords Commissioners of Trade and Plantations to King George II, 8 October 1728

19 *Acts of the Privy Council of England, Colonial Series* 3, p. 249: 22 January 1730

20 For the detailed instructions given to John Rollos, the engraver of this seal, see *Calendar of State Papers: Colonial America and West Indies*, 1728-9, p. 356, item 673: HM Warrant to John Rollos, 22 April 1729.

21 Ibid.

22 Ibid.

23 PRO: 324/11 Plantations General, May 1722-February 1733, p. 53: order to John

Rollos, HM's Seal Cutter, to prepare new seals for American plantations, 17 November 1727

24 For example, the Great Seal Deputed of George II for Virginia; see Royal Mint, London, for wax impression.

25 PANS: box 3, Land Grants: Grant to Edward Barron, Jr., of four shares in the Township of Sackville, 30 September 1767

26 The royal warrant authorizing this was promised on 29 October 1760; see PANS: MS Docs., vol. 30, doc. 36: Lords Commissioners for Trade and Plantations to Governor of Nova Scotia.

27 See note 25 above.

28 *Acts of the Privy Council of England,* Colonial Series 5, p. 86: 13 April 1767

29 Royal Mint, London: Royal Mint Record Book 1/12, p. 85, dated 17 March 1766

30 Royal Mint, London: wax impression

31 PANS: MS Docs.: pardon to Jane Tolmy for the crime of petit larceny, 21 October 1774. There is an excellent wax impression of the reverse of the first George III Seal at the Royal Mint, London.

32 For example, PAC: RG 7, G1, vol. 53, p. 452: Portland at Whitehall to Hunter, Governor of Upper Canada, 10 January 1801

33 Royal Mint, London: Royal Mint Record Book 1/20, p. 169

34 PANS: box no. 4: commission to Edward James as Justice of the Inferior Court of Common Pleas for the County of Lunenburg, 29 April 1823

35 PANS: MS Docs., vol. 63, f. 100: covering letter of royal warrant to Earl of Dalhousie, Lieutenant Governor of Nova Scotia, 9 February 1820

36 Ibid. vol. 67, doc. 34, dated – July 1830, signed by William IV

37 PANS: MS Docs., vol. 69, doc. 28: covering letter for royal warrant, Viscount Goderick, Secretary of State for War and Colonies, to Sir Peregrine Maitland, KCB, 1 November 1832

38 PRO: CO 854/2 (1837-40, Circulars – Colonial Department) ff. 36-9v: Lord Glenelg, Secretary of State for the Colonies, to Sir Colin Campbell, Governor of Nova Scotia, 23 June 1837; and PANS: MS Docs., vol. 75, f. 151 and f. 153: royal warrant dated 22 June 1837

39 For example, see PANS: Land Papers, 1838: land grants to George Hartling, dated 23 January 1838, and Edward James, dated 27 April 1838

40 PANS: MS Docs., vol. 77, f. 67: Marquis of Normanby, Secretary of State for War and Colonies, to Sir Colin Campbell, KCB, Governor of Nova Scotia, 23 February 1839, and ibid. ff. 69-70: royal warrant dated 4 February 1839

41 BL: Detached Seals XCVIII.6: a proof impression in wax in excellent condition

42 PRO: CO 324, vol. 170, pp. 279-80: Duke of Buckingham and Chandos to Lord President of the Council, 27 July 1868

43 Ibid.

44 PANS: Harris Papers: seal on the commission to Reginald V. Harris as King's Counsel, 30 October 1922, and see BL Detached Seals CXLVIII.8.

45 *Sessional Papers,* vol. 9 (vol. X). Fourth Session of the Third Parliament of the Dominion of Canada. Session 1877. No. 86, p. 4: Earl of Granville, Secretary of State for the Colonies, to Sir John Young, Bt., Governor General of Canada, 8 May 1869

46 PRO: CO 42/676, ff. 322-7r: memorandum by Sir John A. Macdonald, 25 June 1869

47 PRO: CO 42/676, ff. 318-321r: Earl Granville, Secretary of State for the Colonies, to Sir John Young, Bt., Governor General of Canada, 23 August 1869

48 *Sessional Papers* (see note 45 above) pp. 8 and 9: 16 November 1869.

49 Ibid. p. 10: Major General Sir Hastings Doyle to Secretary of State for the Provinces, 7 December 1869

50 2 February 1870

51 *Sessional Papers*, (see note 45 above) p. 11

52 Ibid. p. 12: Secretary of State for the Provinces to Lieut. Gen. Sir Hastings Doyle, Lieutenant Governor of Nova Scotia, 14 February 1870

53 Ibid. p. 45: Report of a committee of the Privy Council of Canada, 5 April 1877

54 In the case of the precedence of J.N. Ritchie as Queen's Council 1877, in which three out of five of the judges of the Supreme Court of Nova Scotia declared that the Great Seal of Nova Scotia then in use was illegal. For the judgments, given on 26 March 1877, see *Sessional Papers* (see note 45 above) p. 25 ff.

55 *Sessional Papers* (see note 45 above) p. 24: Adams G. Archibald, Lieutenant Governor of Nova Scotia, to the Provincial Secretary, 5 March 1877

56 Ibid. p. 14: Earl of Dufferin, Governor General of Canada, to Earl of Carnarvon, Colonial Secretary, 9 March 1877; Secretary of State for the provinces to Lieutenant Governor of Nova Scotia, March 14; the Honble P.C. Hill to the Honble W.B. Vail, Clerk of the Council of Nova Scotia, March 17

57 Ibid. Earl of Carnarvon, Colonial Secretary, to Earl of Dufferin, Governor General of Canada, 13 March 1877 (wire)

58 Ibid. pp. 1-50: 'Return and Supplementary Return to Address. Correspondence relating to the Great Seal of the Province of Nova Scotia being affixed to Documents requiring the same. Printed by Order of Parliament, Ottawa, 1877'

59 'Address to the Queen's Most Excellent Majesty. Passed by the Legislature of Nova Scotia at the Session in 1877.' Printed in ibid. pp. 43-5

60 Ibid. pp. 47-8: Earl of Carnarvon, Colonial Secretary, to Earl of Dufferin, Governor General of Canada, 29 March 1877

61 40 Vic., c. 3

62 This had apparently been in the possession of the Lieutenant Governor from its delivery in 1869; see PANS Vertical MS, file 'Nova Scotia Seal,' no. 62: Private Secretary to the Lieutenant Governor of Nova Scotia to the Provincial Secretary, 22 September 1877

63 Order in Council, 21 November 1878, in Stewart, *The Arms of Nova Scotia*, pp. 32-3

64 PANS: Vertical MS, file 'Nova Scotia Seal': proclamation by the Honble Adams George Archibald, PC, CMG, Lieutenant Governor of Nova Scotia, 17 December 1878

65 Order in council, 29 August 1930

66 See oath of office of a lieutenant governor

67 For example, PANS: MS Docs.: appointment by Sir Andrew Snape Hamond, Lieutenant Governor of Nova Scotia, of the managers of a lottery to build a public school in Halifax, 21 September 1781

68 As with the privy seal of Brigadier General V. de B. Oland, KSTJ, ED, BA

69 CA: I 79.258-9

70 Royal Mint, London: Royal Mint Record Book 1/15 (1797-1804), p. 189: bill of
    Thomas Major, HM's Engraver of Seals, to the Lords of the Treasury, 1799

71 Ibid.

72 Royal Mint, London: wax impression; the motto is from Horace, *Epode* 4-6.

73 PANS: MS Docs.: document dislayed on wall of ground floor: sealed land grant of
    four lots in the town of Sydney to Archibald Charles Dodd, 16 February 1789. For
    an example impressed over paper as well as a wafer of wax, see *ibid. Cape Breton
    Island of* (2) Militia Commissions, Commissions of the Peace etc., 1787-1820, no.
    16: commission appointing Richard Stout to be a Commissioner of Escheats and
    Forfeitures in Cape Breton Island, 25 June 1807 (good impression).

74 P. Walne, 'The Great Seal Deputed of New Jersey,' *Proceedings of the New Jersey
    Historical Society* 79 (October 1961) pp. 223-31

75 PRO: CO 218, vol. 12, p. 6: Lord Sydney, Home Secretary, to the Lieutenant Gover-
    nor of Cape Breton Island, 25 February 1785

76 Royal Mint, London: Royal Mint Record Book 1/18, p. 309

77 Royal Mint, London: wax impression

78 PANS: MS Docs., Cape Breton Ordinances, 1786-1820. The impression is not very
    clear but the shield of arms includes a mullet in the dexter canton, and the crest is a
    goat trippant.

CHAPTER 8

Prince Edward Island

ENSIGNS ARMORIAL

Until 1769, the Island of Saint John or Saint John's Island was part of Nova Scotia, but in that year separate government was provided for it as a colony in itself. Thirty years later, in 1799, its name was changed to Prince Edward Island in honour of the Commander-in-Chief of British North America at that time, Prince Edward, Duke of Kent and Strathearn, the father of Queen Victoria.[1] In 1864 its capital, Charlottetown, became the scene of the beginning of those series of discussions and conferences which started with a view to a Maritime Union and finally resulted in Canadian Confederation in 1867. For various local reasons, however, Prince Edward Island did not join this new state for another six years. As a result, the then colony was not a recipient of arms in 1868 as were the other foundation provinces, Ontario, Quebec, New Brunswick, and Nova Scotia. In fact, Prince Edward Island was without arms until they were assigned by a royal warrant dated 30 May 1905.[2]

On that occasion the following were assigned,

Arms: *argent, on an island vert, to the sinister an oak tree fructed, to the dexter thereof three oak saplings sprouting all proper, on a chief gules, a lion passant guardant or* [plate 15.1]
Motto: PARVA SUB INGENTI (The small under the protection of the great)[3]

As will be seen from the later discussion on the seals of this province, the arms were largely inspired by the tree and sapling design to be found on the great seals deputed of Prince Edward Island, from its first one in 1769. Indeed, this design came to be regarded, it would appear, in the popular mind at least, as the device if not the 'arms' of the province notwithstanding the fact that no arms had been assigned during the Colonial or early dominion period.[4] The government of Prince Edward Island gave expression to this fact when it issued the well-known 'Tree Cent' in 1871 which embodied this basic design.[5] An Assistant Provincial Secretary asserted, also, that the three young trees or saplings were always regarded as the three counties of the province: Kings, Queens, and Prince.[6] The larger tree to the right, when considered in the context of 1769 when it first appeared on the great seal, was obviously intended to represent Great Britain. The inscription PARVA SUB INGENTI in the exergue of the seal would seem to bear out this contention. Following Confederation with Canada on 1 July 1873, Prince Edward Island could reinterpret from whence the immediate protection came, and so keep this phrase as its motto.

The result of these various historical circumstances was that the arms assigned in 1905 included, on a silver background, three oak saplings to the dexter and a large oak tree to the sinister, all rising from a green island – a device that was particularly appropriate in view of the geographical circumstance of the province. Across the top of the shield was placed a gold lion passant guardant on a red background from the arms of both Prince Edward, after whom the province was named, and King Edward VII, by whom these arms were assigned.

SEALS

Great seals deputed of the Island of St John, subsequently Prince Edward Island

Within six weeks of the provision of a separate government for the Island of St John, an order in council was made on 14 July 1769, for the design of a seal to include

on the one side, a representation of a large spreading oak, with a shrub under it and the legend or motto underneath PARVA SUB INGENTI and this inscription round the circumference SIGILLUM INSULAE SANCTI JOHANNIS IN AMERICA and on the reverse His Majesty's arms, crown, garter and supporters.[7]

Following these instructions Thomas Major, the king's Engraver of Seals, submitted his design, which was approved on 4 August following.[8] For reasons which will be mentioned later, the seal dies do not appear to have survived, but from the bill Major submitted for his work to the Lords Commissioners of the Treasury on 21 October 1769 we know that it followed the specific directions laid down by the council and that, in addition, as was customary, the legend of the reverse contained the style and titles of George III in Latin.[9]

A proof impression in wax of the obverse of this seal is preserved at the Royal Mint, London, albeit somewhat damaged [8.1]. The oak and saplings rise from a piece of landscape. Beneath in the exergue is placed the motto, taken from Vergil, PARVA SUB INGENTI.[10] A plain circle contains this design and forms the inner edge of the legend band, which is inscribed, starting at the upper right, SIGILLUM · INSULAE · SANCTI · IOHANNIS · IN · AMERICA ·. An outer edging of stylized foliage, probably acanthus, completes this seal, of which the diameter is 4¹/₅ inches (107 millimetres).

Judging from the examples which are extant, all subsequent great seals deputed of

*8.1 Obverse and proof impression of the reverse of the
Great Seal Deputed of the Island of St John of George III, 1769
Royal Mint, London. Crown copyright*

this colony and then province have contained this oak and sapling motif. The 1769 design is handsome, with a great and sturdy oak, complete with a plenitude of acorns, filling the greater part of the surface, while the young saplings shelter under its branches. The whole conception is very much in the manner of John Constable, the celebrated landscape painter.

A proof impression of the reverse of the 1769 seal is also preserved at the Royal Mint. The treatment of the arms and the positioning and contraction of the royal style and titles are in the usual form found at this period in British North America.

The matrices of this seal were made of 50 ounces, 1 pennyweight of sterling silver and they were supplied with a 'Shagreen case lined with velvet and Silver Clasps,' the total cost for the engraving and for providing the silver and the box being £85.8.6d. [11]

Within six years of the arrival of this seal in the colony, the American Revolution broke out and the seal was carried away from the island, never to be returned, by New England privateers from Marblehead, Massachusetts, when they raided Charlottetown on 17 November 1775. [12] How government was conducted without the deputed great seal is not apparent, but presumably some provision had to be made even of an *ad interim* nature.

By 1801, following the union of Great Britain and Ireland to form one kingdom, the royal arms, style, and titles were altered, making a new seal necessary. However, until it could be prepared for the colony, now called Prince Edward Island, [13] it is probable that a royal warrant was issued authorizing the continued use of the existing deputed great seal, as for the other colonies of British North America, although such a warrant for Prince Edward Island does not appear to have survived. Further, as with the other

8.2 Obverse and reverse of the Great Seal Deputed of Prince Edward Island of George III, 1815
Executive Council Secretariat, PEI

British North American colonies of the period no seal embodying the royal arms as laid down in 1801 appears to have been made for Prince Edward Island.

However, such a seal was made for the colony in anticipation of the further armorial changes about to be enjoined following Hanover's becoming a kingdom, for on 12 December 1815 Nathaniel Marchant, engraver, submitted a bill to the Lords Commissioners of the Treasury for 'engraving pair of Seals for Prince Edward's [sic] Island, red case and 2 boxes with impressions for Office – £52.0.od.'[14]

An impression of this seal through paper onto wax in the usual manner of the time is extant [8.2].[15] The obverse contains the large spreading oak tree and saplings as on the 1769 seal, together with the same motto in the exergue. The legend, however, starting at the upper right, reads SIGILLUM · INSULÆ · PRINCIPIS · EDWARDI · IN · AMERICA ·, all contained within a fillet of stylized acanthus leaves. The diameter is 4 inches (102 millimetres) [8.3].[16]

The reverse shows the royal arms in their 1816-37 form along with the recitation of the royal style and titles on the legend band, starting at the lower left: GEORGIUS TERTIUS DEI GRATIA BRITANNIARUM REX FIDEI DEFENSOR.

On 29 January 1820, George III died, and eleven days later, following the usual procedure, a circular was almost certainly sent from London, as for the other colonies, enclosing a royal warrant authorizing the use of the deputed great seal of the late king until another could be provided.

Judging from an obverse proof impression preserved in the Fuller Collection at the University of London Library, a seal for the new king, George IV, does appear to have

8.3 *Proof impression of the obverse of*
the Great Seal Deputed of Prince Edward Island
of George III, 1815
Fuller Collection 4/1

8.4 *Proof impression of the obverse of the Great*
Seal Deputed of Prince Edward Island of George IV
Fuller Collection 4/1

been engraved [8.4].[17] This shows basically the same oak and sapling design as originated on the 1769 seal, but the interpretation is quite different and shows a much more mature, even knarled, oak with luxuriant undergrowth. The motto in the exergue remains the same. The legend, starting at the upper right, reads SIGILLUM · INSULÆ · PRINCIPIS · EDWARDUS · IN · AMERICA ·, all contained within a border of stylized foliage. The diameter is 4⅕ inches (107 millimetres).

Following the death of George IV in 1830,[18] presumably the customary circular was sent permitting the continued use of the existing great seal deputed of the colony until a new one could be prepared. However, so far neither a warrant for this nor a seal of William IV for Prince Edward Island seems to have survived. Nevertheless, one appears to have been in use during his reign – of whatever design – for immediately after his death a warrant was sent to the colony (on 23 June 1837) permitting the use of the existing seal of Prince Edward Island pending the engraving of one for Queen Victoria.[19]

By an order in council of the young queen dated 4 February 1839, a seal for Prince Edward Island was sanctioned [8.5] and took the general form of the Newfoundland pattern, the permanent elements of which have been discussed in detail in chapter 5. For Prince Edward Island, the panel contains a large oak tree to the right with three saplings (not necessarily oak) to the left, all rising from a grassy mount. As before, the exergue contains the motto PARVA SUB INGENTI. The inscription round the circumference embodying the local reference reads, starting at slightly less than mid-point on the left and reading downwards round to a corresponding point on the right edge of the

8.5 Proof impression of the Great Seal Deputed
of Prince Edward Island of Victoria, 1839-1949
BL: *Detached Seals XCVIII.8*

8.6 Great Seal Deputed of
Prince Edward Island since 1949
Author's collection

seal, SIGILLUM INSULAE PRINCIPIS EDVARDI. The seal is single-sided, 2²/₅ inches (61 millimetres) in diameter, and impressed directly onto the surface of the document concerned.

This seal continued to be used until 26 April 1949, when the present great seal deputed of the province was authorized [8.6].[20] The design of the latter consists of a broad based shield of the provincial arms as granted in 1905 with the motto PARVA SUB INGENTI placed on a scroll beneath. Round the circumference of the seal, between a rope-like design on the outer edge and a series of dots on the inner edge, is inscribed the legend, starting a little to the left of the base of the seal, GREAT SEAL OF THE PROVINCE OF PRINCE EDWARD ISLAND. The seal is single-sided and 2²/₅ inches (61 millimetres) in diameter; impressions are made directly onto the surface of the document.

Privy seal of the Lieutenant Governor

Privy seals have been used by the lieutenant governors of Prince Edward Island in the past, but it does not appear to have been the custom to do so since about 1900.[21]

FLAGS

Flag of the Lieutenant Governor

The official banner or flag of the Lieutenant Governor of Prince Edward Island is similar in design to that of most of the other provinces (see plate 22.4 for the basic design). The Union device or Jack is rectangular and is debruised in the centre with a plate, that is to say a white disc, charged with a representation of the shield of arms of Prince Edward Island within a wreath of green maple leaves.[22]

Provincial flag

The provincial flag is a banner of the arms [plate 23.2]. That is to say, it comprises the design usually borne on a shield 'bled out' so as to fill up a rectangular shape. This is surrounded by a symbolic fringe, gules and argent, so that the overall measurements are six feet in the fly and four in the hoist.[23] The legal basis for this flag stems from the royal warrant of 30 May 1905 assigning the arms.

I am most grateful to Earle K. Kennedy, Clerk of the Executive Council, Prince Edward Island, who despite his official duties gave generously of his time and knowledge in connection with the preparation of this chapter. J.W. Macnutt, Private Secretary to the Lieutenant Governor, and Douglas B. Boylan, Provincial Archivist, have also assisted.

NOTES

1 By an Act for altering and changing the name of this Island, from Saint John to that of Prince Edward Island, 1798; General Assembly of the Island of Saint John, approved by George III in Council, 1 February 1799, and proclaimed by Major General Edmund Fanning, Lieutenant Governor and Commander-in-Chief of Prince Edward Island, 13 June 1799

2 CA: I 74.228

3 Neither crest nor supporters have been assigned, so far, for this province.

4 Minute of meeting of the Lieutenant Governor in Council, 24 March 1905

5 The authority for this 'Tree Cent' is An Act to Establish a Decimal system of Currency on this Island (passed 17 April 1871) sec. 5, cap. 5

6 CA: 14 Garter, f. 227: Arthur Newbury, Assistant Provincial Secretary, PEI, to Joseph Pope, Under Secretary of State, Ottawa, 23 November 1904

7 PRO: CO 226, vol. 1, pp. 135-8

8 Ibid. pp. 143-6

9 Royal Mint, London: Royal Mint Record Book 1/12, pp. 111-13

10 Vergil, *Georgics* 2.19: 'pullulat ab radice aliis densissima silva / ut cerasis ulmisque: etiam parnasia laurus / *parva sub ingenti* matris se subiicit umbra.' (Others, like elm and cherry, have a thick undergrowth / Cropping up from their roots: the Parnassian bay-tree also, / When tiny, shelters beneath the immense shade of its mother.)

11 Royal Mint, London: Royal Mint Record Book 1/12, pp. 111-13

12 Lorne C. Callbeck, *The Cradle of Confederation* (Fredericton, NB, Brunswick Press 1964) p. 74 ff.

13 PRO: CO 189, vol. 10, part 2, p. 204: J. King to Edmund Fanning, Lieutenant Governor, sends order confirming act to change name of island to Prince Edward Island, 5 February 1799.

14 Royal Mint, London: Royal Mint Record Book 1/18, p. 309

15 Preserved in the offices of the Executive Council Secretariat/Provincial Archives, Prince Edward Island

16 Fuller Collection: 4/1

17 Fuller Collection: 4/1

18 26 June 1830

19 PRO: CO 854/2 (1837-1840, Circulars – Colonial Department) ff. 36-39v

20 Order in council, Prince Edward Island, 26 April 1949

21 I am indebted to Earle K. Kennedy, Clerk of the Executive Council of the Province of Prince Edward Island, for this information.

22 Specific authority for this has not been located so far, but without doubt it is implied in the Order of the Queen in Council, 7 August 1869, and the Canadian order in council, 28 February 1870, concerning *inter alia,* a flag for each of the lieutenant governors of Ontario, Quebec, Nova Scotia, and New Brunswick. Lord Kimberley, Secretary of State for Colonies, to Sir John Young, Bt., Governor General of Canada, 16 July 1870 (Canada no. 191), indicates approval of the final design, see PRO: CO 43/157.

23 An Act Respecting a Provincial Flag, Chapter 11, Laws of Prince Edward Island, assented to 24 March 1964

CHAPTER 9

New Brunswick

ENSIGNS ARMORIAL

It was not until Confederation that arms were assigned for New Brunswick, along with Ontario, Quebec, and Nova Scotia. This was effected by royal warrant dated 26 May 1868.[1] The blazon is *or, on waves a lymphad or ancient galley with oars in action proper on a chief gules, a lion passant guardant or* [plate 16.1]. The inspiration for the major part of this design flows naturally from that of the great seals deputed of New Brunswick from its foundation in 1784. On these, about which more later, the local element, as it were, comprised a ship on water and in the arms this has been interpreted by means of a conventional heraldic ship, or lymphad. It has been suggested that the eighteenth-century ship used in the seals referred to 'the vessels which brought the Loyalists to the Province,'[2] and that the conventionalized version assigned in the arms alluded to 'New Brunswick's prominence at that time in ship-building.'[3] Both are reasonable conjectures.

Across the upper part of the shield is a broad red band, or chief, upon which is a gold lion passant guardant. This is a charge and combination to be found in the Arms of the Duchy of Brunswick, *gules two lions passant guardant in pale or,* which, at the time of the foundation of the province, was one of the hereditaments of the British Crown.

No motto was assigned along with the arms in 1868, but for some time now it has been the custom to place on a scroll beneath the shield the motto SPEM REDUXIT, which might be translated as 'It restored hope.' As will be seen below, this dates from 1784-5, when it was engraved on the obverse of the first seal of New Brunswick.

9.1 *Obverse and reverse of the 1785 Great Seal Deputed of New Brunswick of George III*
PANB: MYO/CB4/3 (see note 9)

9.2 *Obverse (proof impression) and reverse of the 1817 Great Seal Deputed of New Brunswick of George III*
Fuller Collection 4/2 and Legislative Library, Fredericton (see note 12)

SEALS

Great seals deputed of New Brunswick

By August 1784 matters were *en train* towards providing a seal for the newly created province of New Brunswick.[4] Five months later this sterling silver instrument of government in its shagreen case with silver clasps[5] was on its way,[6] and in time was duly received.

The design of the obverse of this 1785 seal of the province [9.1] comprised 'a settlement on the Banks of a River on whose sides are growing lofty Fir Trees and a Ship sailing up the River,' according to Thomas Major who made the seal die and charged £70.0.0d for his work.[7] The ship is three masted and square rigged, with all sails furled except the fore and main topsails. There is a row of small cabins and a wharf in front of the trees, and between this and the ship three rowing boats apparently ply.

Beneath this scene, in the exergue, is the motto, almost certainly an adaptation from Horace, SPEM REDUXIT.[8] A plain circle contains all this and forms the inner edge of a band. This, in turn, bears the legend which, starting at the upper right of the seal, reads SIGILL · PROVINCIAE · NOV · BRUNS · (SIGILLUM PROVINCIAE NOVI BRUNSVICENSIS – The Seal of the Province of New Brunswick). A circle of stylized foliage completes the outer edge of the legend band. The seal's diameter is 4½ inches (115 millimetres).[9]

Contemporary evidence as to the precise symbolism of this design appears to be lacking. However, bearing in mind the circumstances which brought about the foundation of the province, it seems not unlikely that the troubled journeyings of the Loyalists to a new haven which restored hope may well have been in the mind of the authorities when they ordered the engraving of this seal. At least this seems to be borne out by the description given by a former Colonial Secretary in which he said that the seal was 'engraven on one side with a Representation of a Ship sailing up a river on the Borders of which is a new settlement with lofty Pines on each Side destined to Naval purposes.'[10] Certainly, the trees as rendered on the obverse of this seal would make excellent masts.

The reverse of the 1785 seal bears the royal arms in almost precisely the same form as for the Quebec seal of 1793 described in chapter 6.

It will be recalled that with the union of Great Britain and Ireland in 1801 the royal arms, style, and titles were modified accordingly. As was to be expected, royal warrants were issued authorizing the continued use temporarily of existing seals in British North America, and presumably this was done for New Brunswick although, to date, it has not been possible to locate the actual royal warrant issued to this end. Further, as with all other North American colonies, it does not appear that a seal was provided for New Brunswick showing the royal arms as borne immediately following the union of Great Britain and Ireland, that is to say with the inescutcheon of Hanover ensigned by the electoral bonnet.

Within a few years the royal arms were altered once again, in 1816, upon Hanover being declared a kingdom, with a royal crown being substituted for the electoral bonnet above the inescutcheon. Accordingly, on 12 March 1817 Earl Bathurst, Secretary of State for War and Colonies, sent a circular royal warrant to the Governor of New Brunswick authorizing the new seal consequent upon these changes in the royal arms.[11]

The obverse of this 1817 seal of George III [9.2] is almost identical with the first seal for

9.3 Obverse and reverse of Great Seal Deputed of New Brunswick of George IV
PANB: MYO/CB4/8 (see note 14)

this province except that the stops on the legend band are not simple pellets but small cinquefoils with a somewhat larger quatrefoil with extended lateral petals as the principal stop at the top of the seal between the words BRUNS and SIGILL.

The reverse, with the royal arms, style, and titles, is the same as for the other deputed great seals of this area at this time − for example, that of Nova Scotia discussed in chapter 7 − with the inescutcheon of Hanover ensigned by the royal crown of that kingdom with its characteristic ten arches.[12] The diameter of this seal is 4¼ inches (108 millimetres).

Following the usual custom, this seal of George III continued to be used after his death, until 1822 at the least.[13]

Ultimately, a new seal for his successor, King George IV, was forthcoming [9.3].[14] The only difference here is in the obverse; the ship is shown with a spanker on the mizzenmast, and with her fore, main, and mizzen topsails all set and drawing ahead. Further, the legend band has quatrefoil stops with a larger final sextafoil stop at the head of the seal. The legend remains as for all the previous seals. The interpretation, however, is somewhat heavier than formerly and, therefore, less effective.

The reverse with the royal arms is almost identical with the 1817 seal of George III for the province. The legend on this seal commences, naturally, GEORGIUS QUARTUS but the remainder is as for the 1817 seal, except that it commences at the upper right and has a sextafoil as the final stop. The diameter of this seal is 4½ inches (115 millimetres).

Following the accession of the late king's brother as William IV, one notes the change from double-sided dependent seals to single-sided seals for impression directly onto the surface of the document.

9.4 *Great Seal Deputed of*
New Brunswick of William IV
PANB: REX/PA/ Ordinances (see note 15)

9.5 *Matrix of female die of the Great Seal Deputed*
of New Brunswick of Victoria, officially defaced
Tonnochy: no. 262

Accordingly, we find that the upper part of the William IV Great Seal Deputed of New Brunswick [9.4] comprises the royal arms as borne between 1816 and 1837. The shield is ensigned by a royal crown and surrounded by the Garter. Outside the latter, to the dexter, is a branch of oak and to the sinister a branch of laurel. The shield is supported by the lion and unicorn and these stand on a motto scroll insribed DIEU ET MON DROIT. Beneath these ensigns of sovereignty is placed the local element – the design of the 1785 obverse placed in a plain circular frame. The only difference is that in the exergue of this design a small quatrefoil is placed beneath the motto SPEM REDUXIT. Outside this panel, on either side, are, to the left, a rose, a thistle, and shamrocks, and, to the right, thistles and shamrocks.

The legend band is contained within two concentric plain circles and inscribed, starting at the centre left and running round the top of the seal, (quatrefoil) GULIELMUS IV D · G · BRITANNIAR · REX · F · D ·, and starting once again from the same point and going round the bottom of the seal, SIGILLUM PROVINCIAE · NOV · BRUNS (quatrefoil).[15] The diameter of this seal is 2³/₁₀ inches (59 millimetres).

The king died on 20 June 1837, with the result that his seal had to be authorized for use in connection with the government and service on behalf of the new sovereign, Queen Victoria, until a new seal could be provided. Accordingly, three days later, the Secretary of State for the Colonies, Lord Glenelg, forwarded a circular royal warrant to Harvey, Governor of New Brunswick, to this end.[16]

When the seal for the new queen was forthcoming [9.5] it was engraved along the lines of the Newfoundland pattern, the permanent elements of which have been discussed in detail in chapter 5.

In this seal, the frame below the arms is filled with the ship scene and exergue, complete with the motto SPEM REDUXIT, as found so far with minor variations on all seals for New Brunswick since their inception in 1785. The interpretation of the ship follows that on the seal of George IV in that all three top sails are set. Further, in this instance the flag flying from the stern has a Union Jack which occupies about one half of the total area of the bunting and not just the canton, or upper left-hand corner. [17] The legend reads, starting at the upper left and going across the top of the seal, VICTORIA DEI GRATIA BRITANNIAR · REG · F · D · and then, starting once again at the left and going round the bottom of the seal, SIGILLUM PROVINCIAE NOV · BRUNS ·. The diameter is 2⁷/16 inches (62 millimetres).

This remained the great seal deputed of the province until Confederation and, apparently, for some two and a half years after New Brunswick had joined the dominion while she awaited the delivery of a new seal. A design for this had been approved by an imperial order in council as early as 22 May 1867. What the details were, do not, unfortunately, appear to have survived. We do know, however, that during the following year it was decided to create a new design – the one which was eventually used – and this was settled by 27 July of that year. [18]

The basic conception of what may be termed this Confederation Great Seal Deputed of New Brunswick [9.6] was the same as for the other three foundation provinces. Within a quadrilobate frame, upon which are placed four leaved stylized flowers alternately with pellets, the upper and lower lobes of the frame pointed and the lateral ones rounded, is placed a shield of the royal arms of general purpose ensigned by the royal crown. Beneath and on either side of the shield is a scroll inscribed with the motto DIEU ET MON DROIT. Beneath this, in the lower pointed lobe, are the Arms of New Brunswick on a heater-shaped shield. The background is a diaper design of lattice with fleurs-de-lis in the interstices. A circular band engraved with pellets passes outside and beneath the extremities of the lobes of the quadrilobate frame, and a similar band completes the outer edge of the seal. Between the two is placed the legend. Starting at the upper right it reads THE SEAL OF THE PROVINCE OF NEW BRUNSWICK. The point of the lower lobe of the quadrilobate frame intersects the legend band after PRO and the point of the upper lobe of the quadrilobate frame intersects the legend band after BRUNSWICK and forms the final 'stop,' as it were. The diameter of the seal is 2⁴/5 inches (71 millimetres).

This seal was authorized by Queen Victoria by a royal warrant dated 7 May 1869 and brought into use 'on, from and after the first day of January [1870] for the sealing of all things whatsoever which pass the Great Seal of this Province, and for Her Majesty's Service in this province' by a proclamation issued by the Lieutenant Governor of New Brunswick two days before it came into service. [19] The die was renewed in 1939 with the same design. [20]

The Lieutenant Governor of the Province is the Keeper of its deputed great seal, [21] which he entrusts to the Provincial Secretary as its traditonal day-to-day custodian. The die is physically housed in the latter's department and it is there that documents pass under this seal. [22]

Privy seal of the Lieutenant Governor

As has been seen already, it has long been the custom for governors and administrators

9.6 *Proof impression of the Confederation*
Great Seal Deputed of New Brunswick, 1868
BL: Detached Seals CXLVIII.86

9.7 *Privy seal of Thomas Carleton, Captain*
General and Governor in Chief of New Brunswick
PANB: REX/PA/Proclamations

to use a privy seal — as distinct from the deputed great seal committed to their care —
under certain circumstances when acting *ex officio.*

An early example in New Brunswick is the privy seal of Thomas Carleton, Captain
General and Governor in Chief of New Brunswick [9.7]. There is a good example of
this, preserved in the Public Archives of the province, on the proclamation by which he
announced his commission as governor on 22 November 1784.[23] It is impressed directly
onto the surface of the document, in the upper left-hand corner, with a wafer on the
reverse side of the document.

The seal consists of a heater-shaped shield of which the upper edge has double scallop
in the eighteenth-century manner. This bears the arms of Carleton, *ermine, on a bend
sable, three pheons argent,* and the crest, *on a wreath of the colours argent and sable, a dexter arm
embowed habited gules lined argent, holding in the hand an arrow point to the dexter proper.*[24]
Two palm branches, crossed beneath the lower point of the shield, rise up on either
side. The whole design is contained within a circular wreath of stylized foliage, which
also forms the outer edge of the seal. The diameter is 1 1/2 inches (38 millimetres).

A different type of privy seal is to be found in use by Major General Sir Howard
Douglas, Bt., Lieutenant Governor and Commander in Chief of the Province of New
Brunswick [9.8]. This might best be described as a non-personal as distinct from a
personal privy seal. By that is meant that whereas the personal privy seal contains the
personal arms of the governor concerned, a non-personal privy seal contains a device
other than personal arms or monogram. In the case of Sir Howard, the design comprised the ship on water between tree-lined shores to be found on the obverse of the
1785 great seal of the province, complete with motto SPEM REDUXIT in the exergue.

9.8 Privy seal of Major General Sir
Howard Douglas, Bt., Lieutenant Governor and
Commander in Chief of New Brunswick
PANB: REX/TR Treasury Warrant

9.9 Present-day privy seal of
the Lieutenant Governor of New Brunswick
Author's collection

There is no other inscription at all on the seal; the diameter is 1³/₅ inches (41 millimetres). A good example is to be found on a warrant of Sir Howard dated 6 March 1826 that abolished the payment of travelling expenses to attornies attending the Supreme Court; this is preserved in the Public Archives of New Brunswick.[25]

In a sense, therefore, it will be noted that this non-personal privy seal of Sir Howard Douglas is a forerunner of the present day privy seals of, for example, the lieutenant governors of this province as well as of Newfoundland, Ontario, and Manitoba.

The present-day privy seal of the Lieutenant Governor of New Brunswick [9.9] comprises the arms of the province ensigned by a royal crown. These are contained within a circle of pellets which forms the inner edge of the legend band. This is inscribed, starting at the upper left and going over the top of the seal, LIEUTENANT GOVERNOR, and commencing once again at the centre left and going down round the bottom of the seal, PROVINCE OF NEW BRUNSWICK. The outer edge of the legend band consists of a rope design. The diameter of this privy seal is 1⁷/₁₀ inches (43 millimetres).

FLAGS

Flag of the Lieutenant Governor

The official flag of the Lieutenant Governor of New Brunswick consists of the Union Flag in the centre of which is placed a plate, or white heraldic disc, charged with a shield of the provincial arms (see plate 22.4 for the basic design). A garland of green maple leaves follows the edge of the plate. A golden bow and scroll are sometimes placed at the base of the garland where two stems of the maple cross.[26]

This flag is flown at Government House, and from the Legislative Buildings whenever the Lieutenant Governor is in Fredericton. It is also flown from public buildings throughout the province whenever he happens to be in residence.

Provincial flag

When Queen Victoria assigned arms for New Brunswick by royal warrant on 26 May 1868, authority was thereby granted for them to be borne not only on seals but also on banner and flags. It was not, however, until 1965 that the official display of the arms in flag form was decided upon. This was accomplished by a proclamation of the Lieutenant Governor of New Brunswick dated 24 February 1965, with immediate effect.

The design of the provincial flag consists, therefore, of the Arms of New Brunswick bled out so as to fill a banner, the proportions of which are four by length and two and one-half by width [plate 23.3]. The chief – the broad red band charged with a gold lion across the top of the arms – occupies the upper third of the flag, and the remainder of the charges – the lymphad, waves, and gold background – the other two-thirds.[27]

When writing this chapter I received invaluable assistance from Robert A. Pichette, KM, sometime Executive Assistant to the Premier of New Brunswick; Hugh A. Taylor, Provincial Archivist; and B.W. Bathe, Assistant Keeper, Department of Water Transport, Science Museum, London; Mrs T.C. Barker, Official Secretary to the Lieutenant Governor of New Brunswick, and Frank Ayres, Sergeant-at-Arms of the Legislative Assembly, have also kindly helped.

NOTES

1 CA: 163.123-5, 26 May 1868

2 W.F. Ganong, 'Insignia of New Brunswick,' *Acadiensis* 3 (1903) p. 137

3 Ibid. p. 138

4 PAC: RG 7. G8B, vol. 1, pp. 5-12: Lord Sydney, Secretary of State, to Thomas Carleton, Governor of New Brunswick, 21 August 1784

5 Royal Mint, London: Royal Mint Record Book 1/15 (1797-1804): Bill of Thomas Major, HM's Engraver of Seals, to the Lords of the Treasury [prior to 23 November] 1799

6 PRO: CO 189, vol. 10, f. 25: Lord Sydney to the Governor of New Brunswick, 25 February 1785

7 Royal Mint, London: Royal Mint Record Book, 1/15 (1797-1804). This bill also indicates that the seal was made of 50 ounces, 7 pennyweights of silver (which cost £14.5.3³/₄d); the duty paid was 6d per ounce, £1.5.1d; and the cost of the shagreen case with silver clasps in which to keep the seal was £1.5.0d.

8 Horace, *Odes* 3.21.17: 'tu *spem reducis* mentibus anxiis / virisque et addis cornua pauperi / post te neque iratos trementi / regum apices neque militum arma.' The poet is addressing a cask of vintage wine: 'You restore hope to troubled minds, and give strength and courage to the poor man who after [drinking] you, fears neither angry potentates nor the weapons of war.'

9 PANB: MYO/CB4/3: letters patent granting Crown Land to John King, 27 October 1813. A proof impression of this obverse side of the 1785 seal is preserved at the Royal Mint.

10 Ganong, 'Insignia of New Brunswick,' p. 140

11 PAC: RG 7, G8B, vol. 5, pp. 225-9: Earl Bathurst, Secretary of State for War and Colonies, to Major General George Stachey Smyth, Lieutenant Governor of New Brunswick, 12 March 1817

12 Legislative Library, Fredericton, New Brunswick: File on Seals: commission to William Henry Minchin to be Clerk of the Crown in the Supreme Court of Judicature of New Brunswick, 21 September 1822

13 Ibid.

14 PANB: MYO/CB4/8, unattached seal

15 PANB: REX / PA / Ordinances: ordinance of Sir Archibald Campbell, Lieutenant Governor of New Brunswick, repealing certain ordinances *in re* Court of Assize and Nisi Prius, 30 January 1836

16 PRO: CO 854/2 (1837-40, Circulars – Colonial Department) ff. 36-9v: Lord Glenelg, Secretary of State, to Harvey, 23 June 1837

17 The female die of this seal, officially defaced, is preserved at the British Museum; see Tonnochy: no. 262; and also for a proof impression in wax see BL Detached Seals XCVIII.7.

18 PRO: CO 324, vol. 170, pp. 279-80: Duke of Buckingham and Chandos, Secretary of State for the Colonies, to Lord President of the Council, 27 July 1868

19 Dated 28 December 1869. Published in the *Royal Gazette of New Brunswick*, 29 December 1869

20 I am informed by a senior civil servant in Fredericton.

21 And in his absence, the Administrator; see the text of the oaths of office of the Lieutenant Governor and of the Administrator of the Province of New Brunswick. I am indebted to M.M. Hoyt, QC, of the Legislative Council, Fredericton, for the text of the two oaths.

22 Regulated by the Great Seal Act; see *The Revised Statutes of New Brunswick* 1952, chapter 100.

23 PANB: REX / PA / Proclamations

24 CA: Peers III.30. It will be recalled that he was the brother of Lt. Gen. Sir Guy Carleton, Baron Dorchester.

25 PANB: REX / TR Treasury Warrant, 6 March 1826

26 Order of the Queen-in-Council, 7 August 1869, and the Canadian order-in-council, 28 February 1870. Lord Kimberley, Secretary of State for Colonies, to Sir John Young, Bt., Governor General of Canada, 16 July 1870 (Canada no. 191), indicates approval of the final design; see PRO: CO 43/157.

27 Legislative Library, Fredericton: original proclamation of the Honble J. Leonard O'Brien, Lieutenant Governor of New Brunswick, 24 February 1965

CHAPTER 10

Ontario

ENSIGNS ARMORIAL

Deputed great seals were duly assigned for both Upper Canada and the Province of Canada, but neither had arms. Indeed, not until the year following Confederation were arms provided for Ontario, along with Quebec, Nova Scotia and New Brunswick, by a royal warrant dated 26 May 1868.[1] This instrument assigned the following ensigns for the Province of Ontario: *vert, a sprig of three leaves of maple slipped or, on a chief argent, a cross of St George.*

By this time, the maple leaf was firmly established as emblematic of Canada and, in fact, since 1854 had been an heraldic charge, having been so granted in the arms of Sir Louis Hypolite La Fontaine, Bt., Chief Justice of Lower Canada.[2] As a consequence, the Canadian authorities specifically requested its inclusion in the Arms of Ontario in place of the wheat sheaf suggested by the then Garter King of Arms[3]. [10.1]

To complete the effective simplicity of these arms, a chief of St George was added to the green field charged with three gold maple leaves on a single stem. For a province which came into being out of loyalty to the Crown, the inclusion of this reference to the namesake and patron of the monarch to whom this loyalty was directed, George III, was appropriate. It also served to recall the country from which had derived so much of the constitution, the laws, and the methods of government which the founders of Upper Canada were determined to maintain. It certainly could not have been intended to reflect national origins in the province when the arms were assigned for Ontario, as the Irish greatly outnumbered the English at that juncture.[4]

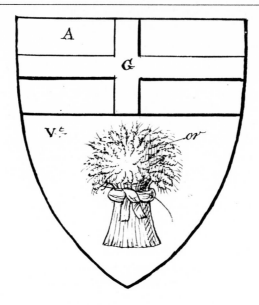

10.1 Pen and ink sketch of the arms proposed for Ontario, c. April 1868
PAC: PDP

It will be noted that on this occasion arms were assigned for Ontario, but not supporters. This gave rise to an enquiry some twenty years later by the Lieutenant Governor to the Secretary of State whether such might be borne.[5] The Privy Council of Canada thereupon appointed a committee to investigate the matter. Examining the papers on the subject they doubted if such authority had ever been given and so recommended that the College of Arms be approached with a view to the ultimate assignment of supporters.[6] This suggestion, however, does not appear to have been acted upon and it remained for Sir James Whitney, the Prime Minister of Ontario, some twenty years later to obtain a further royal warrant, dated 27 February 1909, by which King Edward VII added to the ensigns for the province and assigned crest, supporters, and motto.[7] [plate 19] For these the blazons are as follows:

Crest: *upon a wreath of the colours a bear passant sable.* That is to say, on a wreath of twisted silk coloured gold and green, a black bear in a walking position with its right foreleg raised from the ground
Supporters: *on the dexter side a moose, and on the sinister side a Canadian deer, both proper.* On the left-hand side to the viewer is placed a moose, and on the right-hand side a Canadian deer, both in their natural colours. Both these animals, like the black bear in the crest, are indigenous to the province
Motto: UT INCEPIT FIDELIS SIC PERMANET[8]

This recalls once again the United Empire Loyalist origins of the province and may be translated, 'As loyal it began, so loyal it remains.'
The originator of the design of the crest, supporters, and motto was Edward Marion

Chadwick, the well-known Toronto barrister of the period and author of *Ontarian Families*.[9]

SEALS

Great seals deputed of Upper Canada

Upon the creation of Upper Canada a seal for the province was authorized by a royal warrant dated 28 March 1792.[10] [10.2] The die was made of 45 ounces, 10 pennyweights of sterling silver by Thomas Major, His Majesty's Engraver of Seals, who charged £70.0.0d for his work, which he had finished by 7 March of that year.

When submitting his bill for this to the Lords of the Treasury he described the obverse as including 'the Calumet of Peace with the Anchor and Sword of State encircled by a Crown of Olives.'[11] The sword, point upwards, is placed in saltire with the anchor, flukes downwards; over these, the feathered pipe, with its bowl uppermost, rests vertically. A line from the anchor ring passes round the sword and back under the shaft of the anchor and tip of the pipe. Above all this is a representation of the royal crown, while beneath are two cornucopiae, the tips of the horns in saltire. In the upper right-hand part of the total design is a canton of the Union Flag, which, as it pre-dates 1801, contains no St Patrick's Cross.[12]

Around the edge of the obverse of the seal are two concentric circles. The inner band bears, starting at the upper right, the motto, which is from Horace, IMPERI · PORRECTA · MAJESTAS · CVSTODE · RERVM · CAESARE[13] (which might be translated as 'The greatness of the empire is extended under the guardianship of the Sovereign'). In the outer band is the legend, starting also at the upper right: SIGIL · PROV · NOS · CAN · SUP (SIGILLUM PROVINCIAE NOSTRAE CANADAE SUPERIORIS — 'The Seal of Our Province of Upper Canada'). The dividing lines between the central design and the motto and between the motto and the legend are plain; that on the outer edge of the legend and seal consists of stylized foliage, possibly Acanthus.

The whole conception of the obverse of this seal is refreshingly simple and in marked contrast to those elaborate allegorical scenes so popular on Colonial American seals of the eighteenth century. Can one take this as an earnest of a fresh start in the then wilderness of Upper Canada by those Americans who had sacrificed so much to maintain the ideal of organic social development? A few symbols of constitutional and patriotic loyalty, of alliance and determination, are gathered together in a pleasing design. The cornucopiae are doubtless intended to stand for the benefits and products which will follow the development of the province. Fruit is there in abundance, even the vine, and who would begrudge the engraver's introduction of what appears to be a pomegranate — at the base of the right-hand trophy — and the pineapples as splendid finials? Symbolism need not be trammelled by the requirements of geography and climate.

There occurs in the Simcoe Papers of the Ontario Archives a sketch of this side of the seal together with a description by, apparently, the ever loyal and gallant Lieutenant Governor of the day, Lieutenant Colonel John Graves Simcoe [10.3].[14] The description is in blazon form which doubtless stems from the fact that he seems to have considered these the arms of the province.[15] In fact no arms were ever assigned for Upper Canada.

10.2   *Obverse (proof impression) and reverse of the 1792 Great Seal Deputed of Upper Canada of George III*
Royal Mint, London (Crown copyright) and PAO: S3892(b)

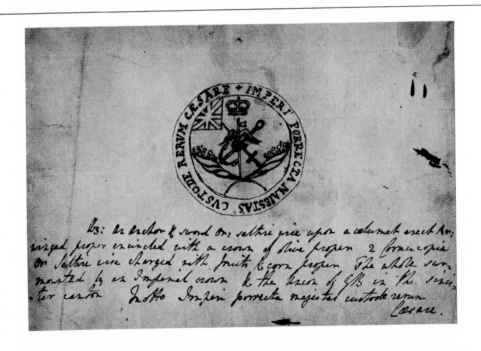

10.3   *'Arms' of Upper Canada, with description apparently in John Graves Simcoe's handwriting*
PAO: ACC 3304

The tinctures ascribed by Simcoe were, apparently, of his own creation. The sketch of this side of the seal follows the general lines of the design, but he transposes the canton of the Union from the upper right to the upper left. This and one or two other discrepancies probably arose from the difficulties in making a drawing from the actual metal seal die, when these are reversed so that when impressed onto wax they leave the impression the right way round.

The reverse of the 1792 great seal contains the royal arms in the usual form for all the deputed great seals of British North America at that time. The shield bears the royal arms as borne from 1714 to 1801, which we have already discussed in chapter 3, and is encircled by the Garter, which is ensigned by the royal crown. The lion and unicorn support the shield and stand upon a Chippendale-like cartouche through which is entwined a ribbon bearing the royal motto. The legend band round the edge reads GEORGIUS · III · D · G · MAG · BRI · FR · ET · HIB · REX · F · D · BRUN · ET · LUN · DUX · S · R · I · AR · THES · ET · EL ·.[16] A plain circle divides the legend band from the armorial achievement, while stylized foliage — similar to that on the obverse — forms the edge of the legend band and seal. The diameter of the great seal is 4½ inches (115 millimetres).

The treatment of this reverse is something of a *tour de force* by the engraver. He has brought together an extremely complicated armorial design, an extensive legend, and various cartouches, all of which have been given a unity and a boldness which cannot fail to impress upon one the august nature of this instrument of government.

Following the union of Great Britain and Ireland in 1801, the royal arms were altered in the manner discussed in chapter 3, with the escutcheon of Hanover, ensigned by an electoral bonnet, being placed over all. Accordingly, on 10 January of that year a royal warrant was issued authorizing the continued use of the original great seal deputed of the province 'until another can be engraved and transmitted, with the new Ensigns Armorial on the Union with Ireland.'[17]

It does not appear, however, that such a seal was ever brought into use in Upper Canada, for the original 1792 seal went on being used well into the 1800s.[18]

Consequent upon Hanover's becoming a kingdom, the royal arms were modified once again in 1816 by the substitution of a royal crown for the electoral bonnet over the escutcheon of Hanover. Accordingly a royal warrant dated 10 February 1817 was issued authorizing a new seal for Upper Canada.[19] [10.4]

On this occasion the obverse was basically the same, with the calumet, crossed sword, and anchor design of 1792, but the Union canton was naturally modified to include the Cross of St Patrick.[20] However, the reverse displays the royal shield of arms consequent upon Hanover's becoming a kingdom. As before, this is surrounded by a Garter and ensigned by a royal crown of a somewhat more angular design. The lion and unicorn support the shield and stand upon a ribbon inscribed with the royal motto, DIEU ET MON DROIT. Arranged about this ribbon are roses, shamrocks, and thistles. The whole conception is somewhat simpler and less bold than the 1792 design. The new and shorter royal titles[21] are placed on the legend band round the edge of the seal, and read, starting at the bottom left, GEORGIUS TERTIUS DEI GRATIA BRITANNIARUM REX FIDEI DEFENSOR.[22] The treatment on either side of the legend band is the same as for the 1792 design. The diameter of this seal is 4½ inches (115 millimetres).

Upon the death of King George III on 29 January 1820, the usual custom was followed whereby a royal warrant was issued authorizing the continued use of the

10.4 *Obverse (proof impression) and reverse of the 1817 Great Seal Deputed of Upper Canada of George III*
Fuller Collection 4/1 and PAO: S3893(b)

10.5 *Obverse (proof impression) and reverse of the Great Seal Deputed of Upper Canada of George IV*
Fuller Collection 4/1 and PAO: S3895(b)

10.6 Great Seal Deputed
of Upper Canada of William IV
PAO: S3896

10.7 Proof impression of the Great Seal
Deputed of Upper Canada of Victoria
BL: Detached Seals CXLVIII.85

exisiting seal until it could be replaced by one for the new sovereign.[23] The new seal [10.5] was basically the same as the last seal of the late king, just described, but the legend on the reverse, which starts at the top right of the seal, reads GEORGIUS QUARTUS DEI GRATIA BRITANNIARUM REX FIDEI DEFENSOR.[24] The diameter of this seal was also 4½ inches (115 millimetres).

Once again, upon the death of King George IV, in accord with custom, his seal continued in use until a new one could be prepared following the accession of his brother, King William IV. This was finally achieved and authority for its use was sent from London on 1 November 1832.[25]

The delay in producing a new seal was longer than usual, doubtless because proposals were brought forward at this time to change colonial deputed great seals from double-sided seals in wax dependent from documents to single-sided impressions directly onto the surface of documents. The proposal was ultimately adopted and the resultant basic design of the William IV seals for British North America has already been discussed in detail in chapter 6. The local element for the new seal for Upper Canada [10.6] included, in the lower panel, the same design as on the obverse of the second seal of George III for Upper Canada, complete with the motto IMPERI · PORRECTA · MAJECTAS · CVSTODE · RERVM · CAESARE ·. In the spaces left on either side of the circular design, roses, thistles, and shamrocks are arranged.

The legend is contained within two plain concentric circles and reads, starting at the centre left-hand edge and going round the upper part of the seal, GULIELMUS IV D · G · BRITANNIAR · REX F · D ·, and, starting again at the centre left-hand edge and going round the lower part of the seal, SIGILL · PROV · CANADAE SUPERIORIS (SIGILLUM

PROVINCIAE CANADAE SUPERIORIS – 'The Seal of the Province of Upper Canada'). [26] The seal measures 2 inches (51 millimetres) in diameter.

One cannot help but feel that, by trying to include on a single-sided seal almost all the details which formerly were distributed over a two-sided seal, the innovators carried the day against the traditionalists by means of a compromise. This was not a happy solution, as it set the fashion for seals so complex that the details did not reproduce clearly unless great care was taken.

With the accession of Queen Victoria in 1837 a new seal [10.7] was produced and its use authorized when the Marquess of Normanby, Secretary of State for War and the Colonies, having procured the necessary royal warrant, sent it from Downing Street on 23 February 1839. [27] To a great extent the general design was like the seal of William IV, but the interpretation was along the lines of the Newfoundland pattern discussed in detail in chapter 5. The local element for the seal includes, in the lower panel, the design of the obverse of the second George III Great Seal Deputed of Upper Canada complete with motto. Round the edge of the seal is the legend, which is the same as for William IV except that the word VICTORIA is substituted for GULIELMUS IV and, naturally, REG[ina] for REX. [28] The diameter of this seal is 2 1/4 inches (58 millimetres).

Great Seal Deputed of the Province of Canada

The Rebellion of 1837 and Lord Durham's consequent and celebrated report brought about a radical constitutional change whereby Upper and Lower Canada ceased to exist as separate entities and were united to form the Province of Canada, which came into being on 10 February 1841. A particular seal was therefore required for the government and administration of this newly formed territory.

Following the passage of the Union Act, moves were initiated in September 1840 towards having one made. [29] The result was a seal [10.8] in which the central motif comprised two classical female allegorical figures within a quadrilobate architectural frame. Four-petalled stylized flowers are placed at intervals within the deep moulding of this frame. The left-hand figure holds a round shield-like structure upon which is the design of the obverse of the 1793 seal of Lower Canada with its view, which is probably of Quebec City. This fills the entire left-hand lobe of the frame. In the similar structure on the opposite side is figured the design from the obverse of the second seal of George III for Upper Canada, discussed above. Standing on the frame, in the upper part of the seal, the lion and unicorn support the shield of royal arms as borne since 1837 – but in this instance minus the Garter – ensigned by a royal crown. There is now no motto scroll. In the space between the frame and arms on the one hand and the inner edge of the legend band on the other are disposed roses, thistles, and shamrocks. Between two plain, concentric rings the legend reads, starting at the left middle of the seal and going upwards and around, VICTORIA D · G · BRITANNIARUM REGINA FID · DEF ·, and, commencing once again at the same point as before and going down round the lower edge of the seal, SIGILLUM PROVINCIAE CANADAE (The Seal of the Province of Canada). [30] The diameter is 3 inches (76 millimetres).

It is of interest to note that in his scholarly and, indeed, pioneer work on the great seals and arms of Ontario, George W. Spragge, Archivist of Ontario, suggested that this seal of the Province of Canada was the first one in this area to be single-sided. [3]

10.8 *Proof impression of the Great Seal*
Deputed of the Province of Canada
BL: Detached Seals XCVIII.5

10.9 *Brass female die of the temporary Great Seal*
Deputed of Ontario, 1867-9, officially defaced
Tonnochy: no. 265

Apparently, the seal of William IV for Upper Canada, just discussed, had not come to his attention.

Figure 10.8 shows a superb example of a mint impression in wax of Victoria's seal of the Province of Canada preserved in the British Library.[32] The details are finely rendered, and wax is undoubtedly the medium to show these to perfection. However, when the seal came to be impressed directly onto the surface of the document concerned, considerable distortion could result. An extreme example of this distortion is to be found on the grant in Orillia North of lot 13, concession 14, preserved in the Ontario Archives.[33]

Great Seal Deputed of Ontario

Until Confederation, the seal discussed above was used on all appropriate occasions for the Province of Canada. With the creation of the Dominion, however, the Province of Ontario came into being, and section 136 of the British North America Act provided that 'until altered by the Lieutenant Governor in Council, the Great Seals of Ontario and Quebec respectively shall be the same, or of the same design, as those used in the Province of Upper and Lower Canada respectively before their Union as the Province of Canada.'[34] As far as Ontario was concerned, this referred to the 1839 seal appointed for use in Upper Canada upon the accession of Queen Victoria and discussed earlier in this chapter.

However, as Earl Granville admitted to Sir John Young, Bt., in 1869, 'the provisions of the 136th section appear to have escaped observation till quite recently,'[35] with the result that a completely different seal was, in fact, provided for use in Ontario immediately following Confederation [10.9]. It will be recalled that Quebec had a similar experience.

The seal for Ontario consists of the royal arms of general purpose on an oval shield surrounded by the Garter, together with the royal helm and crest with mantling. The lion and unicorn supporters stand on a ribbon inscribed with the motto DIEU ET MON DROIT. A decorative circle of pellets contains the armorial achievement; outside this, between two concentric, plain circles, is the legend, which, starting at the centre base, reads THE SEAL OF THE PROVINCE OF ONTARIO. Outside this band a milled edge with a final plain circle completes this seal, which is 2 inches (51 millimetres) in diameter. The brass female die is preserved at the British Museum.[36]

This seal was taken into use by an order in council of the Province of Ontario on 7 August 1867[37] and was intended for immediate use while a more elaborate one was prepared.[38] A more elaborate one was, in fact, approved by a United Kingdom order in council some six weeks before Confederation was to take place,[39] but it was subsequently decided that its design was not consistent with the arms proposed for Ontario, and so the Chief Engraver of Her Majesty's Seals was asked to prepare a fresh design in the following year.[40]

Ultimately, the new seal [10.10] was ready and the queen at Osborne House issued her warrant for its use in Ontario and the return of the interim seal for defacing in the usual way.[41] This new seal was taken into use by a provincial order in council of 29 December 1869 to be effective from 1 January following 'for the Sealing of all things whatsoever which shall pass the Great Seal of the Province of Ontario and for Her Majesty's Service in this Province.'[42] So came into use the present Great Seal Deputed of Ontario.

The seal consists of a broadly based shield of the royal arms of general purpose ensigned by a royal crown, with the motto DIEU ET MON DROIT on a scroll encircling three sides of the shield. Beneath this are placed the arms of Ontario, and the whole is contained within a quadrilobate frame, the upper and lower arches of which are pointed and the side ones rounded. The deep moulding of this frame contains four-petalled stylized flowers and pellets placed alternately. The background is heavily diapered with a fretty and quatrefoil design. A circular band embellished with pellets passes beneath the extremities of the frame, and there is a similar band on the extreme outside edge of the seal. Between these two concentric bands is inscribed the legend which reads, starting at the upper right hand, THE · SEAL · OF · THE · PROVINCE · OF · ONTARIO. The diameter of this seal is 2½ inches (64 millimetres). The whole conception is Pugin gothic at its best − direct and bold in execution − the result is a seal of great dignity.

The Lieutenant Governor of the province is the official 'Keeper of the Great Seal of Her Majesty's Province of Ontario,'[43] while the Provincial Secretary is its day-to-day guardian. Tradition and convention have established its use and custody rather than Provincial Statute legislation, of which there is, apparently, none touching this subject. Generally, where an act provides that 'the Lieutenant Governor-in-Council may appoint,' the Great Seal Deputed of Ontario is applied in the name of the Queen. However, if the act reads 'the Lieutenant Governor may appoint,' then his privy seal is used. Nevertheless, by tradition there are appointments which have always conflicted with such definitions.

10.10 Facsimile of the Great Seal Deputed of Ontario from 1870

Privy seal of the Lieutenant Governor

The use of privy seals in Ontario dates from the earliest history of the area. One notes that, before the arrival of Simcoe, Lord Dorchester, Governor General in charge of what was to be Upper Canada, made use of such a seal [10.11]. This consisted of an oval shield of arms, *ermine on a bend sable, three pheons argent,* encircled by a ribbon upon which is the motto of the Order of the Bath, TRIA · JUNCTA · IN · UNO · (Three [probably kingdoms] joined in one). The shield is not only ensigned by the coronet of a baron complete with cap, but is supported by, to the dexter, *a beaver proper gorged with a mural crown [or],* and to the sinister *a like beaver gorged with a naval crown [also gold].* They stand partly on a motto scroll inscribed QUONDAM HIS VICIMUS ARMIS (We have conquered once with these arms)[44] and partly upon palm and olive branches placed in saltire behind the scroll. The whole design, a good example of eighteenth-century taste and elegance, is contained within a plain oval frame of 4³/₄ inches (121 millimetres) diameter at the widest.[45]

   With the founding of Upper Canada the use of privy seals continued, and we note by 1817 the appearance of what might be termed a non-personal privy seal. This consisted of the letters PS intertwined – presumably meaning privy seal – ensigned by a royal crown [10.12]. The design is contained within a plain circle which bore on its outer edge a legend the details of which cannot now be read save for the letter E at the upper left. This privy seal was used by the Administrator of the Province on a *Dedimus Potestatem* dated 19 July 1817. The diameter is 1¹/₄ inches (32 millimetres).[46] The importance of

10.11 Privy seal of Lord Dorchester, Governor General in charge of Upper Canada, 1788
PAO: S4751

10.12 Privy seal of Samuel Smith, Administrator of Upper Canada, 1817
PAO: S4494

10.13 Privy seal of Sir Charles Bagot, GCB, Governor General of the Province of Canada, 1841-3
PAO: S4752

10.14 Pre-1909 privy seal of the Lieutenant Governor of Ontario
PAO: S4816

this seal as an early precedent for the non-personal privy seals in current use in Ontario will be appreciated.

Passing to the Province of Canada, we find further examples of privy seals, including that of Sir Charles Bagot, GCB, Governor General [10.13], which is of particular interest in view of its singularity. It is oval in shape, greater in its width than in its height. The Arms of Bagot, *ermine two chevronels [azure]*, together with other quarterings, are marshalled on an oval shield which is surrounded by the Collar of the Order of the Bath. The crest of Bagot, *out of a ducal coronet a goat's head argent, attired [or]*, is placed above the shield. By virtue of the fact that he was a Knight Grand Cross of the Order of the Bath, Sir Charles's supporters stand on either side in their accustomed places, *a goat argent, attired [or], gorged with a ducal coronet [also gold]*. They stand upon a 'gas bracket,' around which is arranged the motto scroll inscribed ANTIQUUM OBTINENS (upholding tradition). [47] The diameter is 1 1/2 inches (38 millimetres) at its widest. [48]

Besides its shape, another unusual aspect of this seal is the fact that in addition to the armorial elements of the Governor General just described, the arms of his wife are included. She was Lady Mary Wellesley, eldest daughter of the third Earl of Mornington and so niece of the celebrated Iron Duke, the victor of Waterloo. The impressions of the seal are not as distinct in all details as one would wish, but the arms shown on Lady Mary's part of the achievement appear to be *quarterly, 1 and 4, Colley* (the original name of the Wellesleys), *[or], a lion rampant [gules], ducally gorged [also gold]* with other quarterings. [49] These are marshalled in the usual way for a matrimonial achievement; the shield is divided vertically down the centre, and the Arms of Bagot are placed to the dexter and those of Wellesley (Wesley) to the sinister. The shield is then surrounded by a wreath of laurel and placed *accollé*, that is to say leaning towards the shield of Sir Charles in such a way that the latter and the Collar of the Bath around it obscure the Bagot side of the matrimonial shield and display that of Wellesley.

Such an arrangement of the armorial bearings of husband and wife cannot be faulted – in fact it is excellent. However, as the seal was used *ex officio*, and as the purpose of arms is to identify, one might be tempted to conclude from the details of this official seal that Sir Charles and Lady Mary were joint Governors General, rather as King William III and Queen Mary II were both regnant. Such, of course, was not the case, as the office applied essentially to Sir Charles; indeed at that date the wife of a governor general was not even accorded the style of Her Excellency. We can only conclude that the use of a seal in this form was an oversight brought about, perhaps, by the connubial harmony of this distinguished couple.

Personal armorial privy seals continued to be used following the creation of the Province of Ontario; for example, that of the Lieutenant Governor, Donald Alexander Macdonald, was used on the warrant for the removal of Lucy Donald dated 25 June 1880. [50]

However, within a year one notes once again the appearance of what I have already termed a non-personal privy seal, although in this instance it was armorial [10.14]. The design consists of the Arms of Ontario, hatched in part, as assigned by royal warrant in 1868. The shield is pointed and heater-shaped, and it is ensigned by a royal crown which rises up into the legend band. The shield is contained within a plain circle which touches its three corners and passes behind the crown. In the spaces left on either side of the shield are inscribed the words PRIVY and SEAL, to the left and right respectively. The

10.15 Present-day privy seal of the
Lieutenant Governor of Ontario (post 1909)
Author's collection

legend band reads, starting at the lower left, LIEUTENANT GOVERNOR · ONTARIO ·. A plain circle completes the outer edge of this seal, of which the diameter is 1 1/16 inches (27 millimetres).[51]

Following the addition of supporters, crest, and motto to the armorial bearings of Ontario by royal warrant in 1909, the privy seal was redesigned to incorporate these elements, and this is the seal in use today [10.15]. In the centre is placed the provincial shield of arms, crest, supporters, and motto. Beneath the scroll of the latter, the phrase PRIVY SEAL is inscribed. This whole design is contained within a circle of pellets forming the inner edge of the legend band, which is inscribed, starting at the centre left of the seal, · LIEUTENANT GOVERNOR · and, on the lower part of the band, ONTARIO. The outer edge of the seal consists of a circle of rope design. The diameter is 2 1/10 inches (53 millimetres).

The categories of documents upon which the privy seal is applied have already been discussed.

FLAGS

Flag of the Lieutenant Governor

The official flag of the Lieutenant Governor of Ontario consists of a Union Flag or Jack in the centre of which is a round, white disc charged with the shield of arms of the province and surrounded by a garland of maple leaves coloured green (see plate 22.4 for the basic design).[52]

The authority for this stems from the order in council of Queen Victoria dated 7 August 1869 and a consequent order in council of the Governor General on 28 February following.[53]

Curiously enough, this flag ceased to be used from 1959 to 1965, during which period the Lieutenant Governor of the province used the Canadian Red Ensign, charged in the hoist beneath the canton of the Union with a plate, provincial arms, and garland as just described. However, following the adoption of Canada's national flag in 1965, the then Lieutenant Governor reverted to the original flag authorized in 1869/70, and this is flown today.

Provincial flag

With the advent of the National Flag of Canada, an official flag for the Province of Ontario was brought into being. The design, suggested by the provincial government, was prepared by Garter King of Arms in accordance with the practice and laws of arms. Her majesty the Queen having signified her approval of the design,[54] an Act of the Legislature of Ontario brought the provincial flag onto the Statute Books.[55] By proclamation, the act came into force on 21 May 1965.[56] The flag is the Red Ensign, in the proportions of two by length to one by width, with the shield of the provincial arms in the fly [plate 23.5].

I am indebted to the Honble Robert Welch, Provincial Secretary and Minister of Citizenship, Ontario, for assistance received when writing this chapter as well as to D.F. McOuat, Archivist of Ontario, who has also read it in manuscript and made helpful and valuable comments. John Cozens, sometime Chief, Protocol and Special Services; Janet Holmes, Canadiana Department, and Helen Ignatieff, Assistant Curator, Sigmund Samuel Collection, both of the Royal Ontario Museum, and Margaret Van Every, Picture Collector, Department of Public Records and Archives, have also helped greatly. Phillips MacKay Till, CA, Past President, Heraldry Society of Canada, despite a busy professional life, was never too occupied to answer by return of post any request I addressed to him in connection with this and other chapters.

NOTES

1 CA: 163.123-5

2 CA: Gts 51.184, 4 November 1854. For a discussion on the rise and development of this symbol see Conrad M.J.F. Swan (Rouge Dragon Pursuivant of Arms), 'The Beaver and the Maple Leaf in Heraldry,' *The Coat of Arms* 10 (July 1968) pp. 97-109.

3 PRO: CO 324, vol. 170, pp. 229-31: F[rederic] Rogers, to Sir Charles Young, Garter King of Arms, 29 April 1868; and see PAC: PDP: memoranda explanatory of the proposed armorial bearings for the Provinces and Dominion of Canada, c. April 1868.

4 *Census of Canada* 1870-1 (Ottawa 1873) 1, pp. 280-1

5 23 November 1887; see PAC: RG 2, 1, vol. 390: PC 1066 G A/B2, Report of Committee of Privy Council, 9 April 1888

6 Ibid.

7 CA: 175.261

8 This appears to be non-classical in origin; probably created for the occasion.

9 G.W. Spragge, 'The Great Seals and the Arms of Ontario,' *Ontario History* 51 (Winter 1959) p. 37, and Sir Bernard Burke, *History of the Colonial Gentry*, 1891 and 1895 (reprint London, Heraldry Society 1970) 2, p. 586

10 PAC: RG 68, vol. 150, p. 1: Dundas to Lieutenant Governor of Upper Canada (Simcoe was not appointed until July 1792).

11 Royal Mint, London: Royal Mint Record Book 1/15 (1796-1804) p. 190: bill of Thomas Major, HM's Engraver of Seals, to the Lords of the Treasury [before 23 November] 1799. Further costs enumerated in this bill include £12.10.3d for the silver; £1.2.9d as duty at 6d per ounce; and £1.10.0d for the shagreen case with silver clasps in which to keep the seal die.

12 Royal Mint, London: wax impression

13 Horace, *Odes* 4.15.14-15 and 17: 'per quas latinum nomen et italae / crevere vires, famaque et *imperi* / *porrecta maiestas* ad ortus / solis ab hesperio cubili/ *custode rerum caesare* non furor / civilis aut vis exiget otium, /non ira quae procudit ensis / et miseras inimicat urbis' ([He, Augustus, has restored the arts] by which the Latin name and the Italian power grew great: and the fame and majesty of the empire have been stretched out towards the sun's rising from his western couch. With Caesar as guardian of the world neither civil strife nor violence disturbs our tranquility, nor wrath which hammers out swords and menaces fearful cities).

14 Spragge, 'Great Seals ... Ontario,' p. 33

15 Ibid. In 1792 Simcoe requested medals 'with the Arms of Upper Canada' for distribution among the Indian chiefs.

16 PAO: s3892(b): seal on deed of grant dated 17 May 1805, from Record Group 1, Township Papers, Loughborough, lot 18, con. 9

17 PAC: RG 7, G 1, vol. 53, p.452: Portland to General Peter Hunter, Lieutenant Governor of Upper Canada, 10 January 1801

18 For example, see seal in note 16 above.

19 PAC: RF 1, E1, vol. 50, State Book F, p. 315: Earl Bathurst, Secretary of State for War and Colonies, to Francis Gore, Lieutenant Governor of Upper Canada, 10

February 1817

20 PAO: s3893(a), seal on commission of 21 July 1817, from Record Group 22, Court Records, series IIIB, box 17

21 Since 1 January 1801

22 PAO: s3893(b): seal on commission of 1817 from Record Group 22, Court Records, series IIIB, box 17

23 PAC: RG 7, G1, vol. 59, p. 218: Earl Bathurst, Secretary of State for War and Colonies, to Sir Peregrine Maitland, Lieutenant Governor of Upper Canada, 9 February 1820

24 PAO: s3895(b): seal on deed of grant of 4 September 1832, from Record Group 1, Township Papers, Brock, w6, con. 12

25 PAC: RG 7, G1, vol. 69, p. 304: Viscount Goderich, Secretary of State for War and Colonies, to Sir John Colborne, Lieutenant Governor of Upper Canada, 1 November 1832

26 PAO: s3896: seal on deed of grant of 25 April 1837, from Record Group 1, Township Papers, West Gwillimburg, lot 2, con. 7

27 PAC: RG 7, G1, vol. 91, p. 257: Marquess of Normanby, Secretary of State for War and Colonies, to Sir George Arthur, Lieutenant Governor of Upper Canada, 23 February 1839. The royal warrant was dated 4 February 1839; see p. 258.

28 PAO: s3897: seal on deed of grant of 23 January 1840, from Record Group 1, Township Papers, Williamsburg Township, w21, con. 8

29 PAC: RG 7, G1, vol. 49, pp. 228-30: Lord John Russell, Secretary of State for the Colonies, to Charles Edward (Poulett-Thompson) Lord Sydenham, Governor General of Canada, 11 September 1840

30 PAO: s3898: seal on Canada Company Papers, grant 65, dated 22 April 1848

31 Spragge, 'Great Seals ... Ontario,' p. 34

32 BL: Detached Seals XCVIII.5

33 PAO: s3899: seal on deed of grant from Record Group 1, Township Papers, Orillia N, lot 13, con. 14, dated 30 November 1863

34 The British North America Act 1867, 30 & 31 Vic., c. 3

35 PRO: CO 42/676, ff. 318-21r: Earl Granville, Secretary of State for the Colonies, to Sir John Young, Bt., Governor General of Canada, 23 August 1869

36 Tonnochy, no. 265. For a good impression see PAO: s3900: seal on Canada Company papers, grant 70, dated 8 September 1868.

37 PAO: RG 3, orders in council

38 PRO: CO 42/678, ff. 101-2v: minute paper for Sir F[rederic] Rogers, 31 December [1869]

39 22 May 1867

40 PRO: CO 324, vol. 170, pp. 279-80: Duke of Buckingham and Chandos, Secretary of State for the Colonies, to Lord President of the Council, 27 July 1868

41 PAC: RG 7, G21, vol. 157, file 282A: royal warrant dated 7 May 1869

42 PAO: RG 3, orders in council

43 From a copy of the oath of office of the lieutenant governor of Ontario kindly provided by the Honble Robert Welch, Provincial Secretary and Minister of Citizenship, with his letter of 9 July 1970 to the author

44 CA: Gts. 16.177

45 PAO: S4751, MSS, Macaulay Papers 1788: commission to Robert Macaulay as Captain of Militia in Kingstown and Ernest Town, 20 June 1788

46 PAO: S4494, misc. 1817

47 CA: Gts. 32.63

48 PAO: S4752, misc. 1842, env. 2: commission appointing John Haldane as ensign in the first regiment of Huron Militia, 10 September 1842

49 A.R. Wagner (Richmond Herald), *Historic Heraldry of Britain* (London, Oxford University Press 1948) p. 92

50 PAO: S4815, RG 8, Provincial Secretary's department, miscellaneous. The diameter of the seal is 1 3/16 inches (30 millimetres).

51 PAO: S4816, RG 8, Provincial Secretary's department, miscellaneous: transfer warrant for the removal of Cornelius Kelly, 10 January 1881

52 *Flags of All Nations* (London, HMSO 1958) 2, is in error in its depiction of the garland as ivy leaves.

53 For final approval of the design see PRO: CO 43/157: Lord Kimberley, Secretary of State for the Colonies, to Sir John Young, Bt., Governor General of Canada, 16 July 1870 (Canada, no. 191)

54 12 April 1965; see release by the Secretary of the Cabinet of Ontario, 21 May 1965. The actual design signed by Her Majesty may be seen in the permanent parliamentary exhibit rooms in the Parliament Buildings, Toronto.

55 The Flag Act, 1965: royal assent given 14 April 1965; description and shade of red indicated in the schedule of the act (British Admiralty Colour Code no. T 1144 for nylon worsted bunting and no. T 818A for other bunting)

56 Dated 13 May 1965; see *The Ontario Gazette* 98, 15 May 1965.

CHAPTER 11

British Columbia

ENSIGNS ARMORIAL

During the colonial period, deputed great seals were provided in the usual way for the administration and government of this area, and about these more will be said later in this chapter. It was not, however, until after Confederation that particular arms were assigned for British Columbia; this was accomplished by a royal warrant of King Edward VII dated 31 March 1906. The blazon reads as follows:

Arms: *argent, three bars wavy azure, issuant from the base a demi sun in splendour proper on a chief the union device charged in the centre with an antique crown or*[1] [plate 20.2]
Motto: SPLENDOR SINE OCCASU[2]

In association with these the following have long been used:

Crest: *upon an imperial crown proper a lion statant guardant imperially crowned or*
Supporters: *on the dexter, a wapiti stag proper; and on the sinister an Ovis Montana ram proper* (see 11.4 and 5)

In order to appreciate fully these singularly striking ensigns, a consideration of the historical background and circumstances of which they are the reflection is essential.

In the eighteenth and nineteenth centuries the destiny of the Pacific North West was anything but obvious. As a reaction to Russian exploration in Alaska from 1745 onwards, and the consequent foundation there of the colony of Russian America, Spain pushed up on the Pacific Coast from her bases in Mexico and California. In an effort to counteract this foreign danger and make good her claim to the entire seaboard of the

Pacific North West, Spanish officials got as far north as Nootka on Vancouver Island, and there they established a settlement on 24 June 1789 which they maintained until 23 March 1795.[3] Quite apart from the stimulus caused by the Russian presence in Alaska, this was but a logical northwards extension of their well-based dominions further down the coast in what are now California and Mexico.[4]

However, the British were also interested in the northerly reaches of this vast coast-line, and by the Nootka Convention of 28 October 1790 Spain agreed to abandon any claim to exclusive sovereignty northwards from California over that area which now includes British Columbia.[5]

In the meantime Russian exploration and the ever-widening search by the Russian American Company for sea-otter to satisfy the Chinese market continued. By 1806 they had got as far south as San Francisco Bay. By 1812 a permanent Russian settlement in California – complete with Redwood fort – had been established on the coast some eighteen miles north of Bodega Bay. In Spanish, it was called *Fuerto de los Rusos;* in English, Fort Ross.[6]

John Quincy Adams, later President of the United States, attests that when he was American Minister at St Petersburg in 1810, the Russians claimed that the coastline from Alaska down to the Columbia River was part of their possessions.[7] Eleven years later the tsar issued a ukase declaring all islands and coastal waters north of 51°, that is to say from a point just north of Vancouver Island, to be Russian territory, including the Queen Charlotte Islands and so on up the coast. Non-Russians were excluded from trading in this area and were to approach no nearer than one hundred Italian miles to the coastline.[8] Nine days later, on 13 September 1821, the charter of the Russian American Company was renewed and Russian sovereignty extended to the 'shores of north-west America which have from time immemorial belonged to Russia, commencing from the northern point of the Island of Vancouver, under 51 degrees north latitude to Behring Straits and beyond them.'[9]

Britain protested, and finally achieved the Convention of February 1825, whereby Russia agreed that the southern boundary of Alaska would start at latitude 54°40′ and then proceed northwards roughly along the boundary of what later became known as the Alaska Panhandle.[10]

The two contestants left to fill the vacuum so created were Great Britain and the United States. The conventions with Spain and Russia, far from investing any power with sovereignty over the contested area (the Oregon Territory as it came to be called), created a sort of waste or no-man's-land, the sovereignty of which could be held by any nation which effected settlement.[11]

During the second and third decades of the nineteenth century the open question was, therefore, whether the Americans or the British were to have the Oregon territory by virtue of discovery, exploration, and trading expectations. So well founded were the claims of each, and so hard did each side press its case, that between 1818 and 1846 the Oregon territory was open to British and American citizens alike. In the 1830s and 1840s large migrations of American settlers into the area encouraged considerable agitation for outright annexation of the whole territory by the United States.

Finally, however, by the Oregon Treaty of 1846 the United States and Great Britain agreed that the international boundary was to continue from the Rocky Mountains along the forty-ninth parallel of latitude to the Pacific and round the southern tip of

'Vancouver's Island.'[12] Accordingly, it was confirmed that *de jure* sovereignty over the immense area to the north of this parallel was to make it *British* rather than *American* Columbia.

At this juncture, consolidation was of primary importance. Accordingly, the Crown pressed the Hudson's Bay Company into an imperial role. By a royal grant dated 13 January 1849, Vancouver Island was handed over to the company, which was to develop it as a colony on behalf of the Crown.[13] Nine years later an Act of the Imperial Parliament erected the mainland into the Crown Colony of British Columbia.[14]

During this time, the 1850s and 1860s, the gold rush and the resultant flood of prospectors further complicated government. However, those who stood for the British connection maintained the *status quo* and led the colony – Vancouver Island had been united to British Columbia since 1866[15] – into a federal union with the new Dominion of Canada in 1871.[16]

Consequent upon this historical background, the desire to have tokens and emblems in the instruments of public authority which recalled the British roots of their constitutional position was but natural to the inhabitants of British Columbia. During the colonial period this had already been so, as witness the great seals from the beginning. In fact their consideration at this point will help to show how the present ensigns armorial borne and used by the province came into being.

SEALS

Great Seal Deputed of the Island of Vancouver and its dependencies

As mentioned earlier in this chapter, Vancouver Island first became a colony in 1849. Accordingly, a sterling silver great seal deputed of the colony was prepared by Benjamin Wyon, Chief Engraver of Her Majesty's Seals [11.1]. It has the hall-mark for the year 1849-50 and is now preserved in the British Museum.[17] It is basically of the Newfoundland pattern in that the royal arms occupy approximately the upper third. The shield, tricked in part, is surrounded by the Garter and ensigned by the royal crown. The lion and unicorn supporters are in their accustomed places and stand upon the upper part of a somewhat Chippendale-like frame. Beneath the arms, and twisted in and out of this part of the frame, is a motto scroll inscribed DIEU ET M[ON] DROIT (the word MON is partly obliterated by an official defacing mark). From the outer edges of the frame roses and shamrocks sprout on one side and a thistle and more shamrocks on the other.[18] Within the frame a trident and a caduceus are placed in saltire. Above these is a pine-cone, while beneath a beaver stands on a small grassy island; water occupies the remainder of the lower part of the frame. The allusions are obvious: the caduceus doubtless refers to commerce and industry, the trident to the maritime importance of the colony, and the cone to the vast stands of timber on the island, which is represented by the symbolic island on which the beaver stands. The beaver is possibly an allusion to the Hudson's Bay Company which was responsible for the administration of the Colony, as beavers occur in the company's arms. The legend round the upper circumference reads VICTORIA DEI GRATIA BRITANNIAR · REG · F · D · and then round the lower edge

11.1 Sterling silver female matrix (officially defaced) and proof impression of the Great Seal
Deputed of the Island of Vancouver and its Dependencies
Tonnochy: no. 268 and Fuller Collection 4/4

11.2 Impression in wax of the Great Seal
Deputed of the Colony of British Columbia
PABC: British Columbia Seal no. 55463

ISLAND OF VANCOUVER AND ITS DEPENDENCIES. [19] A plain outer circle completes this seal, of which the diameter is 2⁹/₁₆ inches (64 millimetres).

Great seals deputed of British Columbia

It will be recalled from an earlier part of this chapter that the Colony of British Columbia came into being in 1858 and that eight years later it was united with the Colony of Vancouver Island to form one colony under the name of the former. Accordingly, in 1866 the Great Seal Deputed of Vancouver Island ceased to be necessary. Following the usual custom it was defaced, returned to the United Kingdom, and finally deposited in the British Museum by the Lord President of the Council in 1876. [20]

The Great Seal Deputed of the Crown Colony of British Columbia [11.2] served for the united colony, and indeed continued in use even after Confederation as the first Great Seal Deputed of the Province of British Columbia without the word Colony being changed to Province. Following the usual custom in these matters, upon Confederation provision was made for the colonial seal to serve as the seal of the new province 'pending the provision of a Special Public Seal' in its stead. [21]

The colonial seal was single-sided for impression directly onto the surface of the document concerned at the upper left-hand corner, usually over a wax wafer covered by paper or vellum. [22] The seal shows Queen Victoria, wearing robes of estate and a tiara, seated on a throne with a sceptre in her right hand and an orb in her left. On either side of the arm-supports of the throne is placed the royal cypher, a crowned VR. In the exergue is a wreath with a rose in the centre, shamrocks to the right, and thistles to the left. A plain circle contains this whole design and with a similar outer circle forms the legend band which is inscribed, starting at the upper right, THE · SEAL · OF · THE · COLONY · OF · BRITISH · COLVMBIA ·. The diameter is 2 inches (51 millimetres). [23]

This seal is unique among single-sided colonial seals of British North America in having an effigy of the queen upon it. The whole conception is completely different from the Newfoundland pattern, which otherwise appears to have been of universal application as far as the colonies of this area are concerned. Indeed, in the context of British Imperial sigillography, there appear to have been only three dependent territories for which seals of this basic design, with minor variations, were established: the Colony of British Columbia, the Settlement of Honduras, [24] and the Island of Heligoland. [25]

In the latter part of the nineteenth century the royal crest, that is to say, the uppermost part of the complete armorial expression of supreme sovereign and parliamentary authority, came to be used in connection with British Columbia. This adjunct consists of a representation of the royal crown upon which stands a lion wearing a similar crown, as discussed in chapter 3. Two branches form a wreath about the crest; at times these are both laurel, and at others laurel to the left and oak to the right [11.3].

One notes this device again and again, as on the plaque in the Parliament Buildings, Victoria, commemorating the commencement of their construction on 7 June 1893. On this occasion the motto, SPLENDOR SINE OCCASU, forms part of the design. The device also occurs on shields on the end of a pair of stacks on the gallery of the Parliamentary Library, Ottawa (completed 1876), and here it is flanked by the initials B to the left and C to the right.

11.3 Device used for British Columbia in the latter part of the nineteenth century

When the arms and devices of more than the four foundation provinces were marshalled onto one shield in an attempt to form 'arms' for the Dominion, one frequently notes this same device (usually without the motto) placed in the dexter base quarter, as on the monument to Sir John A. Macdonald on the east side of Parliament Hill, Ottawa.

Bearing in mind that each quarter of these many-quartered shields for the Dominion was invariably (save in respect of the four foundation provinces) based on the major element which occurred in the great seal deputed of the province concerned, one might be tempted to conclude that British Columbia had a seal so constructed. In fact, we know that at that time the Colonial Great Seal Deputed of British Columbia, just discussed, was still in use, but a design containing a portrait of the queen could hardly have been included in a scheme of quarters.

Nevertheless, the occurrence of this wreathed royal crest design on the plaque in the Parliament Buildings at Victoria, just described, does cause one to ask whether in the 1890s before the 1896 seal, at least, a deputed great seal for British Columbia bearing such a device may not have been in use. Certainly, for that five or six year period I have seen no examples of documents impressed with the old colonial seal which did service for so many years after the Confederation of British Columbia with Canada. Subsequent research will, doubtless, fill in this lacuna.

Certain it is that by a provincial order in council of 16 September 1896[26] a new deputed great seal [11.4] was brought into being for British Columbia, in accordance with a federal statute of 1877[27] which empowered the provinces to change their seals from time to time. The design was armorial in form.[28] The royal crest, from the device frequently used at this time in connection with British Columbia, was retained but in the new seal it ensigned a shield. Upon this the field, or background, consisted of the Union Badge or Union Jack, as some would say, while across the upper part of the shield a broad band, or chief, included seven wavy parallel bars with a sun rising from the base of the chief over the bars. To the viewer's left a wapiti stag and to the right an *Ovis Montana* ram supported the shield. They stood upon a ribbon inscribed SPLENDOR SINE OCCASU. The legend of the seal read THE SEAL OF THE PROVINCE OF BRITISH COLUMBIA. The diameter of the seal was 3 inches (76 millimetres).[29] Good renderings of this design may be seen on the parapet about the principal entrance to the Parliament Buildings in Victoria, which was under construction at this time, and also over the Speaker's chair in the Legislative Chamber.

The author of this heraldic design was the Reverend Arthur John Beanlands, Rector and Canon Residentiary of Christchurch Cathedral, Victoria.[30] He was an armorial enthusiast and appears to have been the first resident of the province to receive a grant of arms.[31] Although he was naturally an amateur, the Canon conceived the design of the seal along most effective lines, which without a doubt reflected the singular position of the province in the Empire as then understood. The style, interpretation, and execution of the seal is a characteristically fine piece of work by Allan Wyon, FSA, Chief Engraver of Her Majesty's Seals, and a member of the celebrated family of seal engravers. A good proof impression of this seal is preserved in the Wyon Seal Collection at the College of Arms.[32]

Whether or not the provincial authorities at this time moved towards requesting that the sovereign exercise the royal prerogative and convert what was in reality purely an heraldic design on a deputed great seal into arms in fact, by due process of a royal warrant, is not obvious. Probably the answer is yes, such being the correct procedure in order to obtain the approval of one whose supreme authority in right of British Columbia was to be expressed in such armorial and sigillographic form. Whatever moves may have been made to this end came to nothing, and it was not until 1903 that the next steps were taken.

At this time the question of the arms of the Dominion was under discussion, and the Under Secretary of State of Canada, Joseph Pope, was interesting himself in this matter. He very much desired to be able to quarter the arms of all the provinces on one shield for the Dominion, and pressed those which had not done so up to that time to place themselves armorially *en règle*.[33] Pope had a clear grasp of the principles involved and fully appreciated that despite the confusion in the minds of many, arms and seals are quite distinct. Naturally, he was fully aware of the fact that the federal statute of 1877 invested the Lieutenant Governor in Council with the power to establish and to change the deputed great seal of his particular province at will. However, he further fully appreciated that that same statute said nothing about arms, and that for arms to be brought into being for a province of the Crown they must be assigned at the specific instance of the monarch personally, customarily by means of royal warrant, and be enrolled in the sovereign's College of Arms.

Apparently the provincial authorities took the point, for by an order in council of May 1904 they formally requested that the Secretary of State of Canada take the necessary steps to obtain such a warrant assigning as armorial bearings the heraldic design which had appeared on the great seal deputed of the province as authorized in 1896.[34]

11.4 Proof impression of the Great Seal
Deputed of British Columbia, 1896-1911
Author's collection

11.5 Proof impression of the Great Seal
Deputed of British Columbia since 1911
Author's collection

Formal negotiations with the College of Arms were, therefore, entered into, through the Secretary of State for the Colonies, by Joseph Pope, Under Secretary of State of Canada, on behalf of British Columbia; Ambrose Lee, Bluemantle Pursuivant of Arms, acted on the side of the College of Arms. Private and informal discussions, as formerly, continued between Pope and Lee and permitted a full exchange of ideas and advice to the common benefit of all over many years. [35]

Correspondence passed back and forth until December 1905 when Lee, now York Herald of Arms, wrote to Pope and enclosed a suggested design for the arms – the one finally assigned. He pointed out that the College of Arms would be

willing to retain the original main features of the design heretofore in use, if the B.C. Government will agree to their re-arrangement so as to place the Union device in the most important – instead of, as it now is, in the inferior – position on the shield, i.e. on the chief, the 'barry-wavy' and the sun being placed beneath ... over the charge in the chief would be placed an antique crown (such as is represented in early British and other coins). [36] All the symbolism to which B.C. is attached would by this means be retained and it would also be sufficiently in accordance with the Laws of Arms to put it within the duty of Garter to report in its favour. [37]

The British Columbia government concurred, with the result that when Pope wrote to York conveying this agreement to the rearranged design he could not refrain from adding, 'I think we may congratulate ourselves in having reached finality in these long negotiations with British Columbia,' [38] which he (Pope) had once felt constrained to describe as a 'recalcitrant Province'! [39] Need we doubt that Canon Beanlands, too, must have been extremely glad to have the design settled at long last and gratified that it was to be based on his own suggestions? By 31 March 1906 the royal warrant assigning arms for British Columbia had passed under the Sign Manual and Privy Seal of King Edward VII, as mentioned at the beginning of this chapter.

The warrant concerned only the arms which are borne for the province on shields or flags and also the motto. At an early date in the negotiations it had been decided by the provincial authorities not to seek the inclusion of the Wapiti and *Ovis Montana* ram as supporters nor the royal crest of general purpose of the sovereign as the crest for British Columbia.[40] No other Canadian province at that time had supporters and crest, although there was nothing against such additions in principle, and indeed within three years (1909) they would be authorized for Ontario, as has been seen in the chapter on that province.[41] However, as mentioned previously, Pope was primarily concerned with getting the arms of all provinces *en règle* so they could be marshalled together on a shield as the arms of the Dominion, and for such an exercise supporters and crest are irrelevant. Hence the exclusive concentration, in Pope's correspondence with York, upon arms for the provinces, and nothing else.[42]

From the assignment of the arms by royal warrant in 1906, discussion between the British Columbia authorities and the College of Arms has, from time to time, continued in order to seek a solution over the problem of a crest for the province – there is no problem over the supporters, in principle. In fact, according to Sir Richard McBride, when he was premier of British Columbia he agreed to one of the several possible solutions.[43] However, because of a change of provincial administration soon thereafter, this personal agreement was not translated into a formal request on the part of the British Columbia authorities that the agreed solution be implemented in the form of a royal warrant to assign crest and supporters as additions to the pre-existing arms and motto. Thus the matter still stands. As it is, therefore, still *sub judice,* I will refrain from further public discussion lest the outcome be prejudiced. It must suffice to say that as a Herald I am convinced that it is resolvable, and as a British Columbian it is a matter I have long wished to see resolved.[44]

Four years after the issue of the royal warrant a new great seal deputed of the province was ordered, and was finally entrusted to Allan Wyon, who had made the 1896 seal. Ultimately, it arrived from England and by an order in council of 15 May 1911[45] was approved, and the deputed great seal used up to that point ordered to be defaced, following the usual custom. It is this 1911 design which has been in use ever since on the Great Seal Deputed of the Province of British Columbia [11.5]. In the centre of the seal is a shield of the arms as assigned by the 1906 royal warrant, hatched in part to indicate the tinctures. This is ensigned by a representation of the royal crest – a royally crowned lion standing on a royal crown. The shield is supported to the dexter by a wapiti and to the sinister by an *Ovis Montana* ram, both of which stand upon a motto scroll inscribed: SPLENDOR SINE OCCASU. Behind the scroll is a wreath of roses, thistles, shamrocks, and maple leaves.

A circular border of cusping and another of cable pass round behind and are obscured in part by the crest, parts of the supporters, and the motto scroll. Outside this runs the legend scroll inscribed, starting at the upper right-hand side (with a decorative meander), THE · SEAL · OF · THE · PROVINCE · OF · BRITISH · COLUMBIA (the legend concludes with another decorative meander similar to the first). The horns of the ram are placed over this legend scroll and form the initial stop, as it were, while those of the wapiti perform a like function at the end of the inscription. A plain circle concludes the outer edge of the seal, the diameter of which is 3¹/₁₀ inches (79 millimetres).

Leaving all other considerations aside, from the point of view of design and execution, with the exception of the present seal of Nova Scotia, this Great Seal Deputed of British Columbia is, in my opinion, probably the finest example of its kind among Canadian seals of the twentieth century. It is bold, clear, and imaginative, with the various elements well placed so that the result is a seal of great dignity.

In accordance with his oath of office, the Lieutenant Governor is the 'Keeper of the Great Seal of Her Majesty's Province of British Columbia.'[46]

The Provincial Secretary is charged with the physical custody of the matrices in accordance with the Provincial Secretary Act (section 3), being 'the keeper of the Great Seal of the Province.'

Privy seal of the Lieutenant Governor

Up to the tenure of office by Sir Henri Joly de Lotbinière, from 1900 to 1906, a privy seal was used by Lieutenant Governors of the province in connection with such appointments as those of notaries public in accordance with the Act of 1888. Since Sir Henri's time, however, this does not appear to have been the custom in British Columbia.

FLAGS

Flag of the Lieutenant Governor

The official flag of the Lieutenant Governor consists of the Union Flag or Jack charged in the centre with an heraldic plate or white disc (see plate 22.4 for the basic design). This in turn bears a shield of the arms of the province with the motto SPLENDOR SINE OCCASU on a scroll beneath, the whole being enclosed within a wreath of green maple leaves with a golden bow in base.[47] The shape of the flag is oblong, being longer in the fly than in the hoist.

Provincial flag

The flag of the province consists of the provincial arms as they appear on the shield but 'bled out' so as to occupy the total area of the banner [plate 24.4].

The authority for this flag is specifically contained in the royal warrant of 1 March 1906,[48] while its proportions of five units in width by three in breadth were established by a provincial order in council of 20 June 1960.

Notwithstanding, many commercial flag makers seem determined to produce them in the proportions of two by one. The result, in my opinion, is a hideously distorted version of the arms of the province in banner or flag form so that the setting sun in base is reminiscent of a banana with rays. The moral of all this is that in making armorial flags good proportions are governed by the design of the arms concerned. The fact that many have their flags of certain proportions is no argument in specific instances where other proportions would set off the arms in question to perfection.

A beautiful realization of the Arms of British Columbia in banner or flag form was executed by the Royal School of Needlework and presented by the members of the armed forces and of the Royal Canadian Mounted Police stationed in the province to the people of British Columbia upon its centenary in 1958. The proportions are about one by one. It hangs in the Rotunda of the Legislature at Victoria.

I should like to recall the assistance generously and promptly given to me by the following in connection with this chapter, L.J. Wallace, Deputy Provincial Secretary; W.E. Ireland, when Provincial Librarian and Archivist; Comdr. C.S. Dixon, RCN (Rtd.), Secretary to the Lieutenant Governor; Rear Admiral M.G. Stirling, CD, RCN (Rtd.), Agent General for British Columbia, London; Professor W.J. Eccles, Department of History, University of Toronto; Christine R. Fox, Assistant Provincial Librarian; D.W.L. Tarasoff, Department of History, University of Victoria; Priscilla Knuth, Oregon Historical Society; and Joan Craig, Archivist, Hudson's Bay Company, London, who has read not only this but also the other chapters with which the history of the company is connected.

NOTES

1 CA: I 75.5

2 This motto is capable of several interpretations but is obviously a play on the sun in the arms. The sun, while apparently setting in the west, never, in fact, decreases in its radiance, and so was a simile of the Empire's glory which encircled the world. Possibly, therefore, one might render the motto as 'Brilliance without setting' – a characteristic to be shared by the province.

3 M.A. Ormsby, *British Columbia: A History* (Vancouver, Macmillan 1958) pp. 16 and 26, and E.O.S. Scholefield, *British Columbia from the Earliest Times to the Present* 1 (Montreal, S.J. Clarke 1914) pp. 139-43

4 For a discussion on the Spanish arms and seals relevant to their presence in what is now British Columbia, see appendix C.

5 For what is probably the definitive study of the 'Nootka difficulty' see W.R. Manning, in *Annual Report of the American Historical Association for the year 1904* (Washington 1905).

6 E.O. Essig, 'The Russian Settlement at Ross,' *California Historical Society Quarterly* 12 (September 1933) pp. 191-216. This colony lasted until 1841.

7 D.O. Johansen, *Empire of the Columbia* (New York, Harper & Row 1967) (2nd ed.) p. 116

8 Ibid. p. 117

9 This charter appears in *Alaska Boundary Tribunal Proceedings* (Washington 1904) 2, pp. 25-8.

10 For a discussion on the Russian arms and seals relevant to their claims in what is now British Columbia, see appendix C.

11 Scholefield, *British Columbia,* p. 429

12 The original treaty (15 June 1846, ratification 19 June 1846) is preserved at the PRO: SP 108 and F 094. The Great Seal of the United States, in a metal skippet attached to the document, is in excellent order.

13 *Charters, Statutes, Orders in Council Relating to the Hudson's Bay Company* (London, Hudson's Bay Company 1963) p. 221

14 Ibid. p. 127 ff.: An Act to provide for the Government of British Columbia (2 August 1858) 21 and 22 Vic., c. 99

15 Ibid. p. 131 ff.: An Act for the Union of the Colony of Vancouver Island and the Colony of British Columbia (6 August 1866) 29 and 30 Vic., c. 67; and ibid. p. 223 ff.: An Indenture dated 3 April 1867 between the Hudson's Bay Company and The Queen surrendering Vancouver Island to Her Majesty.

16 Act of the Privy Council (Imperial), 16 May 1871, to be effective from 20 July 1871

17 Tonnochy: no. 268, defaced

18 When impressed, on the right and left respectively

19 On an impression both parts of the legend would start at the left centre; see PABC: MSS: proclamation of James Douglas, CB, Governor and Commander in Chief of Colony of Vancouver Island, 2 April 1861; seal impressed over green wafer at upper left of document.

20 Tonnochy: no. 268

21 Order by the Lieutenant Governor in Council, 18 August 1871, notified in *The Government Gazette* (British Columbia) 10, p. 2, 2 September 1871

22 The seal was usually impressed over white paper and a wafer of red wax onto a paper document, or over vellum and a similar wax wafer onto a vellum document.

23 PABC: MSS: proclamation of Frederick Seymour, Governor and Commander in Chief of Her Majesty's Colony of British Columbia and its Dependencies, dated 17 November 1866 (bringing about the union between the colonies of British Columbia and of Vancouver Island)

24 CA, WCS: 72.9

25 Ibid. 72.11

26 No. 390

27 40 Vic., c. 3: an act respecting the great seals of the provinces of Canada, other than that of Ontario and Quebec (assented to 28 April 1877)

28 In accordance with British Columbia order in council no. 268 of 19 July 1895, which included the following statement: 'On a memorandum from the Honourable the Provincial Secretary pointing out that the Province has no authorised Great Seal and Arms, and that by Section 136 of the "British North America Act" the Lieutenant Governor in Council of a Province is empowered to specify the Arms which may be adopted ...' – which in fact is not so. To this erroneous statement we can trace, in great measure, the whole unhappy and unnecessary saga of British Columbia's armorial problems.

29 An impression of this seal is attached to British Columbia order in council no. 390, dated 16 September 1896

30 According to a memorandum 'Re: The Great Seal of the Province of British

Columbia' prepared by the Provincial Library and forwarded to the author by the
Assistant Provincial Librarian, 7 January 1960

31 CA: Gts. 78.200 dated 2 November 1908: *Chequey ermine and sable, on a fesse gules,
a bull's head caboshed argent, pied of the second between two garbs or.* For an account of his
family see Sir Bernard Burke, *History of the Colonial Gentry,* 1891 and 1895 (reprint
London, Heraldry Society 1970) 2, p. 414 ff.

32 CA, WCS: 69.12

33 PABC microfilm: correspondence relative to the provincial coat of arms: Joseph
Pope to Premier Richard McBride, 5 August 1904

34 British Columbia order in council no. 271 dated 11 May 1904. This order referred
to order in council no. 390, dated 18 September 1896, which concerned the great
seal deputed of the province and its design (which was *per accidens* heraldic) as seals
came within provincial competence in accordance with the federal statute of 1877
(40 Vic., c. 3). It is significant that order in council no. 271 of 1904 did not refer to
order in council no. 268, dated 19 July 1895, which cited as its basis section 136 of
the British North America Act, 1867. This section confines itself to 'Great Seals'
and never once in it do the words or phrases arms, crest(s), supporters, ensigns
armorial, armorial ensigns, armorial bearings, or motto(s) occur. Order no. 268 of
1895 described an heraldic design, modified and subsequently included in the
great seal deputed of the province in accordance with order no. 390, as arms,
crest, supporters and motto.

35 CA: 14 Garter, f. 401: Joseph Pope, Under Secretary of State of Canada, to Ambrose Lee, Bluemantle Pursuivant of Arms, 6 February 1905

36 Probably inspired by the suggestion (of Canon Beanlands?) that a coronet be
placed over all, somewhat as a fess enarched; see CA: 14 Garter, f. 396, copy of
letter from Frederick J. Fulton, Provincial Secretary of British Columbia, to
Joseph Pope, Under Secretary of State of Canada, 24 December 1904.

37 PAC: External Affairs file no. 90, 'Secretary of State file 64/1905': Ambrose Lee,
York Herald of Arms, to Joseph Pope, Under Secretary of State of Canada, 22
December 1905

38 CA: 14 Garter, f. 418: Joseph Pope, Under Secretary of State of Canada, to Ambrose Lee, York Herald of Arms, 22 January 1906

39 Ibid. f. 413: same to same, 8 December 1905

40 CA: 14 Garter, f. 410: Keith William Murray, Portcullis Pursuivant of Arms, to
Ambrose Lee, Bluemantle Pursuivant of Arms, 9 August 1905

41 It will be appreciated that at this time, the early 1900s, Newfoundland was not yet
a province of Canada, and that it was not until 1929 that the ancient arms and
supporters of Nova Scotia were restored.

42 When in the normal course of events the papers of the departments of governments are deposited in the provincial archives, it may well be that they will amplify
the sequence of events leading up to the assigning of arms by royal warrant in
1906. One would expect the papers of the provincial secretary to be the most
rewarding from this point of view.

43 CA: 14 Garter (folder at front): Sir Richard McBride, Agent General for British
Columbia, to Sir Alfred Scott-Gatty, KCVO, Garter Principal King of Arms, 18 May
1916

44 From time to time, in justification of the continued use of the royal crest as the provincial crest, reference is made to Canon Beanlands's hint that as the Imperial Privy Council had found in favour of the province in *Jura Regia,* so it followed that the provincial authorities could take this crest as that for the province (Beanlands to Provincial Secretary of British Columbia, 27 July 1907, in memorandum in footnote 30 above). The case to which the canon refers is the case of the Attorney General of British Columbia and the Attorney General of Canada (1889), 14 App. Cas. 295. This case referred to mineral rights and had nothing to do with armorial bearings; it was a case subject to common law, whereas arms come under the laws of arms, which are civil law. The worthy canon, adept in heraldic design, ill served the province by bringing forward such a complete *non sequitur.* In the same letter Canon Beanlands also told the Provincial Secretary that 'The Royal Lion was not assumed as a Crest' for the Province, with the result that one is completely at a loss to follow his argument.

45 No. 482

46 I am indebted to L. J. Wallace, Deputy Provincial Secretary, for the text of this oath, and for many other kindnesses in connection with the preparation of this chapter.

47 Specific authority for this has not been located, so far, but without doubt it is implied in the order of the Queen in council, 7 August 1869, and the Canadian order in council, 28 February 1870, concerning *inter alia,* a flag for each of the Lieutenant Governors of Ontario, Quebec, Nova Scotia, and New Brunswick. Lord Kimberley, Secretary of State for the Colonies, to Sir John Young, Bt., Governor General of Canada, 16 July 1870 (Canada no. 191) indicates approval of the final design.

48 CA: I 75.7

CHAPTER 12

Manitoba

What we now know as Manitoba was originally part of that vast domain ruled over by the Hudson's Bay Company from its incorporation by King Charles II in 1670. The arms and seals of that company will be discussed later, in chapter 15 on the Territories – the Northwest and the Yukon.

ASSINIBOIA, RED RIVER SETTLEMENT

The first subdivision of this enormous area came about in 1811 with the sale by the Hudson's Bay Company of 116,000 square miles in the valleys of the Red River and the Assiniboine to Lord Selkirk, a Scottish landowner who planned to establish there a refuge for his compatriot Highlanders.[1] Appropriately, this area became known as the District of Assiniboia, which contained the Red River Settlement.

Following their reconveyance to the Hudson's Bay Company in 1836,[2] while no arms of public authority appear to have been assigned for the area, nevertheless specific seals for official purposes were in fact made. Such a one is the round seal, measuring 1½ inches (38 millimetres) in diameter, the brass die and counter die of which are preserved in the Provincial Archives of Manitoba [12.1].[3] The centre is inscribed GOVERNOR (on the top line) OF (on the next line and) ASSINIBOIA (on the bottom line). The edge consists of a simple strap and buckle design which is inscribed, starting at the lower left and going round to the lower right, RED RIVER SETTLEMENT. This seal was intended to be impressed directly onto the surface of the paper.

In the Archives of the Hudson's Bay Company and also those of Manitoba are to be found wax (shellac) impressions of another official seal of the Governor of Assiniboia

12.1 *Male brass die of the seal of the Governor of Assiniboia, Red River Settlement* PAM *(see note 3)*

12.2 *Official seal of the Governor of Assiniboia, Lieutenant Colonel W.B. Caldwell, 1848-55* PAM *(see note 4)*

which dates from the governorship of Lt. Col. William Bletterman Caldwell, from 1848 to 1855. Oval in shape, greater in width than in height, it consists of a shield of the royal arms of the period surrounded by the Garter. This is ensigned by the crown and supported by the lion and unicorn which stand upon the motto scroll bearing the royal motto. Placed about the scroll are roses, thistles, and shamrocks. The treatment is, naturally, Victorian and strongly reminiscent of the armorial upper part of the Newfoundland pattern of the first deputed great seals of that reign, discussed in chapter 5. Beneath the motto scroll runs the legend ASSINIBOIA. The seal measures 3 1/16 inches (78 millimetres) at its widest and 15/16 inch (24 millimetres) at its narrowest. An example of this seal is attached to letters of administration issued by the Governor on 20 September 1853 [12.2].[4]

RIEL'S 'PROVISIONAL GOVERNMENT'

Proceeding in chronological order we come next to the attempt of Louis Riel and his followers between 1869 and 1870 to establish what they termed a provisional government[5] in the Red River Country with Fort Garry (Winnipeg) as its headquarters. While even the most ardent supporters of this regime could never claim that it was the heir to a constitutional devolution of government, nevertheless its bitterest opponents would be the first to point out that it did exercise *de facto* power for an appreciable period of time. It behoves us, therefore, to enquire whether or not any symbols of authority were used by Riel's 'provisional government.' Neither shields of arms nor seals appear to have been used, but we know from contemporary evidence that they used a banner or flag which flew over Fort Garry.

This made its first appearance on Friday, 10 December 1869. The damp and foggy weather did not prevent 'great firing and éclat over it,'[6] by the supporters of the cause. With that good humour which relieved many a tense moment in this rebellion, they responded to '3 cheers for the Provisional Government' with '3 groans for Mulligan,' the local Chief Constable!'[7]

For several months this flag continued to fly over Fort Garry, but by April 1870, Riel himself caused the Union Flag or Jack to be run up and share the honours, saying that if anyone wanted the 'provisional government's' flag hoisted it could be 'done so under the British one as under the protection of it.'[8] Riel's flag even presided over 'a large number of people assembled to celebrate the Queen's birthday. Races were run about three miles from town and general good feeling existed.'[9] Such are vignettes of the conflicting situations during these all-too-unnecessary troubles.

For day-to-day accounts of the hoisting of the 'provisional government's' flag,[10] its various sizes,[11] and even whether it went up and down the pole easily,[12] we are indebted to that eye witness, Alexander Begg, whose diary, known to us as the Red River Journal, has become a basic document for the study of the local scene at this time. We know nothing of the actual design of the flag, since, although Begg at one point in his journal drew its shape, and the text implies that he intended to show its design, the outline is all that he provided.[13] That it was longer in the fly than in the hoist is all of which we are certain. Either his artistic ability forsook him or, more likely, he was called away from making his entries and forgot to fill in the details later. Alas, we shall probably never now know exactly how this flag was comprised, as descriptions and illustrations all differ.[14] However, the general weight of testimony is that it consisted of a white background upon which were placed fleurs-de-lis and shamrock.[15]

In a sense, the cause, or probably it would be more accurate to say the occasion, for this strange rebellion, if that is really the term, was the lack of effective government in the area, whether ultimately company, imperial, or federal; during this period authority over Rupert's Land was surrendered by the Hudson's Bay Company back into the hands of the Crown, which then conveyed it to the jurisdiction of the Canadian government.[16] We need not concern ourselves further here with this extremely complex aspect of history. It must suffice to say that once the Canadian government had asserted her authority within the troubled Red River country, and Riel's 'provisional government' had ceased to function, the new Province of Manitoba was created by virtue of the Manitoba Act of 1870.[17] By this the Red River country was combined with other parts of Rupert's Land to form Manitoba, which came into being on 15 July of that year and was thus the first province to join the new Dominion.[18]

MANITOBA
ENSIGNS ARMORIAL AND SEALS

At a Privy Council meeting held at Ottawa on 2 August 1870, the design of the great seal deputed of the new province was decided upon [12.3]. Various sections of the Manitoba Act required a seal although none, in fact, provided for its creation.[19] The seal was to comprise a shield upon which a buffalo stood with its head towards the viewer with the Cross of St George placed along the top of the escutcheon and in the centre of this cross a royal crown; round the edge of the seal the legend called for was THE GREAT SEAL OF THE PROVINCE OF MANITOBA. From the constitutional point of view, thus far so good – at least, that is how the Prime Minister, Sir John A. Macdonald, interpreted section 136 of the British North America Act, and its implications, views he set out in a memorandum submitted to the Governor General, Sir John Young, Bt., about a year before, in June 1869.[20]

However, when one considers the actual wording of the order in council the source of future difficulties can be noted: 'said Seal shall be composed of Vert, a Buffalo, Guardante proper. On a Chief Argent a St. George's Cross – Gules with the Royal Crown in centre.'[21] Taken as they stand these words could be interpreted as an attempt by the Governor General, upon the advice of the Privy Council, to create arms. However, such an act was beyond his jurisdiction and competence as the constitution of the country then stood. Yet again, the order in council required that the new province have a deputed great seal which would be, from the technical point of view, almost impossible to accomplish unless it was envisaged that an artist was to paint up each impression made by the seal with the fairly complicated colours called for, as the order is not content to describe the design of the seal but blazons it as well; in other words, it requires that it be in certain colours.

My personal view is that there was no intention on the part of the Governor General in Council to attempt an act for which they were not empowered as the constitution then stood: it need hardly be said that the Privy Council of Canada was well versed in its legal powers and, it should be noted, not once in the text of the order is the word 'arms' used. Conversely, it was not intended that each impression of the seal of Manitoba should be rendered in full colour, and it was not in practice. Rather the explanation may well be that a drafting clerk, zealous yet unskilled in armory and with no appreciation of the technicalities of seal die-making, let alone sealing, decided to put the description of the Great Seal Deputed of Manitoba into heraldic language. Yet by doing so, especially in view of the designs of the deputed great seals of the other provinces of the Dominion,[22] which did contain the arms assigned for each by royal warrant, the order in council of 1870 concerning Manitoba would, to a person not adept in these matters, appear to assign not only a seal but also arms for that province. So indeed it was interpreted, as witness, among other examples, the carving and emblazoning of these 'arms' in the Parliamentary Library at Ottawa.

How this solecism slipped through the council meeting will probably never be fully explained. While Macdonald took a particular interest in the constitutional significance of deputed great seals, and had definite opinions as to the procedure by which they should come into being, as we have already seen, nevertheless he had, apparently, neither interest in nor knowledge of heraldry as such, let alone the laws of arms. It will be recalled that he never put his own armorial position *en règle*. On the other hand, Young was so interested in this subject that in May 1871, within nine months of the Privy Council meeting which decided upon the design of the great seal for Manitoba, he had obtained from Ulster King of Arms a patent altering his crest so as to include three gold maple leaves in commemoration of his vice-regality.[23] In view of the time that it took for

12.3 *Great Seal Deputed of Manitoba, 1870-1903*   12.4 *Great Seal Deputed of Manitoba since 1903*
PAM *(see note 21)*   *Author's collection*

letters to pass at that period between Government House, Ottawa, and the Ulster
Office, Dublin Castle, and remembering that Heralds are not wont to rush their fences
in these matters, it is very possible that the Governor General was discussing this change
of crest with Ulster King of Arms at the very same period as the Manitoba seal design
was settled at the council table. The possibilities are intriguing to say the least, even if the
final solution of this conundrum seems to be no nearer.

We must, however, pass back to the province under discussion. While Manitoba had a
deputed great seal since 1870 – the die was despatched from Ottawa to Fort Garry (by
way of St Paul, Minnesota) on 29 August of that year [24] – it was not for another
thirty-five years that arms were finally assigned for the province. In 1903 the provincial
authorities made the first move towards placing Manitoba's armorial position *en règle*. [25]
The result was that the Gordian knot caused by the ambiguity of the wording of the
order in council of 1870 was finally cut by King Edward VII on 10 May 1905, when by a
warrant under his hand and seal he assigned for Manitoba the following arms: *vert, on a
rock a buffalo statant proper on a chief argent, the cross of St George*. [26] [plate 18.1]

The inspiration for this design arose, obviously, from the 1870 great seal deputed of
the province. For all but two centuries, the Hudson's Bay Company had exercised
viceregal jurisdiction over the area out of which Manitoba was carved. The principal
charge of the company's arms is the red Cross of St George, and so it was appropriate
that this should form part of the arms for the province. The buffalo, which is the major
charge of the provincial arms, was the most singular of the several fauna of the area.
While the buffalo has long existed as a charge in heraldry, especially in Central Euro-

pean armory, the use of the entire animal is unusual.[27] More often the head alone is found, as in the arms of the Polish Herb (clan) known as Pomian: *or, the head of a buffalo caboshed sable, transfixed by a sword in bend proper.*[28] Many, if not most, of the horns found in crests of Continental origin are those of the buffalo, as in the case of the crest of the Earl Mountbatten of Burma.[29] Certainly, in the heraldry of British North America the entire buffalo in the arms of Manitoba is, to my knowledge, unique.

SEALS

Great Seal Deputed of Manitoba

The great seal of the province following 1870 has already been discussed earlier in this chapter. The authority for the present Great Seal Deputed of the Province of Manitoba follows from the provincial order-in-council of 10 December 1903, which provided 'that the Great Seal consist of a seal, colored gold, two-and-three quarter inches [70 millimetres] in diameter, bearing an impression of the Coat-of-Arms encircled by the words "The Great Seal of the Province of Manitoba."'[30] [12.4] The date of the order was, apparently, in anticipation of the final assignment of arms for the province by royal warrant, which took place, as pointed out earlier in this chapter, in 1905.

This seal, which is physically kept in the custody of the Provincial Secretary, is impressed onto the surface of the document it attests.

Privy seal of the Lieutenant Governor

The Lieutenant Governor of Manitoba has a privy seal which consists of a broad-based shield of arms of Manitoba, as assigned in 1905, surrounded by a circle of pellets which forms the inner limit of the legend band [12.5]. The legend, starting at the lower left of the seal, reads THE LIEUTENANT GOVERNOR OF MANITOBA ·. A rope design forms the outer edge of the seal, the diameter of which is 2⅕ inches (56 millimetres).

Manitoba is similar to Newfoundland in having a privy seal containing a non-personal design – in each case the arms of the province – rather than incorporating the personal arms of the Lieutenant Governor. The latter never appears to have been the custom in Manitoba.

This privy seal is used to authenticate documents sent to embassies of other countries as well as certificates of Notaries Public, Justices of the Peace, Commissioners of Oaths, and the like.

FLAGS

Flag of the Lieutenant Governor

The official flag of the Lieutenant Governor of Manitoba consists of a Union Flag or Jack in the centre of which is a white disc, or plate. Upon this is placed the shield of arms of the province, while round the edge of the plate is arranged a wreath of green maple leaves [plate 22.4].[31]

12.5 Privy seal of the
Lieutenant Governor of Manitoba
Author's collection

Provincial flag

The provincial flag of Manitoba consists of the Red Ensign with a shield of the arms for the province in the fly, in the proportions of two by length and one by width [plate 24.1]. This flag stems from the personal assent of Her Majesty The Queen in conjunction with an Act of the Provincial Legislature.[32] Since the flag was to incorporate parts of the royal armorial ensigns, namely the Union Badge in the canton or upper left-hand corner to the viewer, laid down by order in council dated 5 November 1800, and the Red Ensign, laid down by royal proclamation dated 1 January 1801, it was first necessary that the personal assent of Her Majesty to such an incorporation of royal ensigns be sought through the Governor General, prior to the royal assent being given by the Lieutenant Governor to the Bill of the Provincial Legislature. This having been received from Her Majesty,[33] the flag came into official use on and after 12 May 1966.

To John A. Bovey, Provincial Archivist of Manitoba, I am especially grateful, not only for all the assistance he has given me in connection with this chapter, but also for having read it in manuscript. Mrs E.C. Avery, Secretary to the Lieutenant Governor of Manitoba, has also been most helpful.

NOTES

1 *Charters, Statutes, Orders in Council Relating to the Hudson's Bay Company* (London, Hudson's Bay Company 1963) p. 229 ff.: indenture granting Red River Colony to Thomas, Earl of Selkirk, dated 12 June 1811

2 Ibid. p. 231 ff.

3 PAM: Red River Settlement, Council of Assiniboia, governor's seal

4 HBC: B235/2/3, f. 588: letters of administration issued by W.B. Caldwell, Governor of Assiniboia, to Louise McLeod (widow) in the estate of Jean Baptiste Larocque, deceased, 20 September 1853; and see also PAM: Red River Settlement, Council of Assiniboia, governor's seal (impression)

5 See oath of the president given in G.F.G. Stanley, *Louis Riel* (Toronto, The Ryerson Press 1964) p. 129.

6 W.L. Morton, ed., 'Alexander Begg's Red River Journal and Other Papers Relative to the Red River Resistance of 1869-1870,' *The Publications of the Champlain Society* 34, (Toronto 1956) p. 225

7 Ibid. pp. 443-4

8 Ibid. p. 360 (20 April 1870)

9 Ibid. p. 375 (24 May 1870)

10 Ibid. p. 225 ff.

11 Ibid. p. 297

12 Ibid. p. 365

13 Ibid. p. 225

14 For example, Capt. G.L. Huyshe, *The Red River Expedition*, (London and New York, Macmillan & Co. 1871) p. 14; Messrs Elliott and Brokovski, *Preliminary Investigation and Trial of Ambrose D. Lepine for the murder of Thomas Scott, Being a full report of the proceedings in this case before the Magistrates' Court and the several Courts of Queen's Bench in the Province of Manitoba, 1874* (Montreal, Burland Desbarats Lithographic Coy.) frontispiece. Louis Schmidt, secretary of the first provisional government, added a buffalo to the charges; see Morton, 'Begg's Red River Journal,' p. 467.

15 Morton, 'Begg's Red River Journal,' pp. 75, 225 (n. 2), 443, and 467; and also Donald A. Smith's report to the federal government, 1870, in W.L. Morton, ed., *Manitoba: The Birth of a Province,* Manitoba Record Society Publications 1 (Altona, Manitoba, D.W. Freeman & Sons 1965) p. 31

16 By order in council, 23 June 1870, consequent upon Rupert's Land Act, 1868, 31-32 Vic., c. 105, 1868; for the text of each see *Charters ... Relating to the Hudson's Bay Company,* p. 171 ff., and p. 135 ff.

17 See E.H. Oliver, ed., *The Canadian North-West: Its Development and Legislative Records: Minutes of the Councils of the Red River Colony and the Northern Department of Rupert's Land* 2 (Ottawa, Government Printing Bureau 1914-15) p. 964 ff., for text of the Manitoba Act, 1870, 33 Vic., c. 3 (Canada), An Act to amend and continue the Act Thirty-two and Thirty-three Victoria, Chapter three, and to establish and provide for the government of the Province of Manitoba.

18 PAC: RG 7, G18, vol. 23(2), despatch 165, Granville to Young

19 Oliver, *Canadian North-West,* p. 966 (sections 10 and 11 of the act) and p. 967 (section 16)

20 PRO: CO 42/676 ff. 322-327r: memorandum by Sir John A. Macdonald concerning the dominion and provincial great seals, 25 June 1869

21 PAC: RG 6, C1, vol. 15, file 344: copy of order in council, 2 August 1870, in Canada, *Sessional Papers,* 1871, no. 20, p. 106; and for an impression of this seal see PAM: certificate dated 22 June 1875 appointing John Gunn a commissioner to take affidavits. The diameter of this seal is 2 1/16 inches (53 millimetres).

22 The usual situation which obtained in Nova Scotia at this period concerning its great seal has been touched upon in chapter 7.

23 Conrad M.J.F. Swan (Rouge Dragon Pursuivant of Arms), 'The Beaver and the Maple Leaf in Heraldry,' *The Coat of Arms* 10 (July 1968) p. 101

24 Canada, *Sessional Papers,* 1871, no. 20, p. 106: Under Secretary of State for the Provinces to the Honble A.G. Archibald, Lieutenant Governor of Manitoba, 29 August 1870

25 Province of Manitoba order-in-council no. 8880, dated 10 December 1903

26 CA: I 74.220

27 Possibly the only others are the original arms of the Lords, later Princes, of Auersperg of Bohemia: *gules a bison passant or;* see *Grosses und allgemeines Siebmacher: Der Mährische Adel* 4, book 10 (Nuremberg 1899). I am indebted to M. Adolf F.J. Karlovsky for drawing this to my attention.

28 See Simon Konarski, *Armorial de la noblesse polonaise titrée* (Paris 1958) pp. 225 and 241

29 *Out of a coronet or, two horns barry of ten argent and gules, issuing from each three linden leaves vert, and from the outer side of each horn four branches barwise having three like leaves pendent therefrom also vert* (for Hesse) (CA: Peers IX.95 and I 76.241)

30 Province of Manitoba order-in-council no. 8880, dated 10 December 1903

31 Specific authority for this has not been located, so far, but without doubt it is implied in the order of the Queen in council, 7 August 1869, and the Canadian order in council, 28 February 1870, concerning *inter alia,* a flag for each of the Lieutenant Governors of Ontario, Quebec, Nova Scotia, and New Brunswick. Lord Kimberley, Secretary of State for the Colonies, to Sir John Young, Bt., Governor General of Canada, 16 July 1870 (Canada no. 191) indicates approval of the final design; see PRO: CO 43/157.

32 Manitoba Act

33 CA: I 83.59

CHAPTER 13

Saskatchewan

ENSIGNS ARMORIAL

On 1 September 1905, a further province, formed, in part or whole, from the Districts of Athabaska, Assiniboia, and Saskatchewan, entered the Dominion and was called Saskatchewan.

The authorities of the new province must have moved quickly over arms, for within three weeks, Joseph Pope, Under Secretary of State, was able to forward a suggested design from Ottawa to Ambrose Lee, Bluemantle Pursuivant of Arms, in London. Pope considered it very appropriate,[1] and Lee foresaw no technical difficulties,[2] with the result that, by a royal warrant dated 25 August 1906, King Edward VII assigned arms for the province of Saskatchewan, based on the original design by the Canadian armorist E.M. Chadwick,[3] as follows: *vert, three garbs in fess or, on a chief of the last a lion passant guardant gules.*[4] [plate 18.2]

Agriculture, the principal occupation, industry, and source of wealth of the area, especially at that period, is represented by the combination of three gold wheat sheaves against a green background. The chief, or broad band across the top of the shield, bears a lion passant guardant from the royal arms. As the major part of the arms is vert, the tinctures of the chief have been transposed so as to comply with the requirements of the best heraldry, and so avoid having a gules or red chief next to a vert or green field.[5] The result is an excellent example of the best in modern armory; indeed it is timeless in form. The combination of a lion passant guardant with three wheat sheaves is truly royal, bringing together charges from the arms of the sovereign and of the heir apparent who, as Prince of Wales, is also Earl of Chester – the arms of which earldom consist of three sheaves of wheat.

SEALS

Great seals deputed of Saskatchewan

Section 11 of the Saskatchewan Act authorizes the Lieutenant Governor to prescribe the form of the great seal of the province and to take it into use. Accordingly, during the first week of the existence of the province the Lieutenant Governor issued an order in council dated 5 September 1905 whereby his own privy seal was to be the great seal deputed of the province. Obviously this was an *ad interim* arrangement until something more permanent could be decided upon and implemented.[6] The well-established precedent for the use of privy seals by officers administering a government in the course of their official duties has already been discussed in chapter 2. This situation lasted for some fourteen months during which the royal warrant granting arms for Saskatchewan was issued and, presumably, a new deputed great seal made, for on 26 November 1906, a further order in council was issued whereby

the Privy Seal of His Honour the Lieutenant Governor as the Great Seal of the Province, be cancelled on the first day of December proxime, and that on, from and after the said first day of December, upon all occasions that may be required, a Common Seal, to be called the Great Seal of the Province of Saskatchewan, which said Seal shall be composed of the Arms granted to the Province with the legend or inscription 'The Great Seal of the Province of Saskatchewan,' shall be used.

The design of the seal has been the same ever since [13.1].[7] A broadly based shield of somewhat Tudor design contains the arms of Saskatchewan with the field or background to the wheat sheaves hatched for green; the remainder of the charges, however, do not appear to be so treated. The legend is contained within two concentric circles of rope-like pattern and reads, starting at the centre base, THE GREAT SEAL OF THE PROVINCE OF SASKATCHEWAN, with a small mullet or five-pointed star to mark the end of the legend. The seal is $2^{7}/_{10}$ inches (69 millimetres) in diameter and is usually impressed over a red wafer onto the surface of the letters patent, commissions, or other documents which pass under it. The Provincial Secretary is the official keeper of the Great Seal Deputed of Saskatchewan.[8]

The decision of the Executive Council in 1906 to have a basically simple deputed great seal, so that it would fulfil its functional purpose of identification, could not have been more sound. Indeed, their conception was drawn from one of the best periods of armorial seals, in which one finds even royal seals comprising simply a shield of arms surrounded with a legend, such as, for example, the privy seal of Edward 1 of 1290.[9] Alas, the Saskatchewan authorities were not served by an engraver capable of realizing their conception in sigillographic form with distinction and elegance. The actual seal bears all the characteristics of the commerical stationers – that band of men who, unwittingly, have probably done more harm to heraldry and to seals than any other group. The result was, almost inevitably, pedestrian in the extreme. However, fortu-

13.1 Great Seal Deputed of Saskatchewan since 1906
Author's collection

nately even seals are known to wear out with use or at least lose their original definition, and so have to be renewed from time to time. Doubtless on such an occasion something worthy of the 1906 decision could be executed.

Privy seal of the Lieutenant Governor

The use of the privy seal of His Honour A.E. Forget, Lieutenant Governor of Saskatchewan, as the temporary great seal of the province between 5 September 1905 and 1 December 1906 has been referred to earlier in this chapter. Unfortunately, no examples of this privy seal have so far come to light.

Apart from this known instance, it does not seem to have been the custom, nor is it today the custom, for the Lieutenant Governor of the province to pass official or semi-official documents under his privy seal. [10]

FLAGS

Flag of the Lieutenant Governor

Unlike almost all other Canadian provinces, Saskatchewan appears to have no official flag for the Lieutenant Governor. When he attends a function, the general custom is for the Canadian flag, the Saskatchewan flag, and the Union Flag or Jack to be flown. [11]

Should an official flag for the Lieutenant Governor be desired, then it would doubtless be covered by the intention implied in the order of the Queen in Council of 7

August 1869 and the Canadian order in council of 28 February following concerning viceregal flags.[12]

Provincial flag

On 22 September 1969, a provincial flag for Saskatchewan was dedicated in the Legislative Chamber at Regina. A blazon of this flag is *per fess vert and or, in the canton a shield of the arms for Saskatchewan and in the fly a prairie lily palewise slipped and leaved proper* [plate 24.2]. This flag was the subject of a proclamation some ten days before in which it was declared that the 'background of green and gold [is] symbolic of the northern forested areas of the province and of the southern grain field areas ... [with] ... in the fly the provincial floral emblem'.[13]

In writing this chapter I am grateful for the assistance received from L.J. Beaudry, Deputy Provincial Secretary of Saskatchewan; D.H. Bocking, Assistant Provincial Archivist; Kathleen R. McKenzie, Secretary to the Lieutenant Governor; Major D.G. Scott Calder, ED, Serjeant-at-Arms of the Legislative Assembly; and in particular to Allan R. Turner, when Provincial Archivist, not only for reading the chapter in manuscript but also for his unfailing kindness throughout its preparation.

NOTES

1 CA: 14 Garter, f. 257: Joseph Pope, Under Secretary of State, to Ambrose Lee, Bluemantle Pursuivant of Arms, 20 September 1905

2 PAC: in Pope additional material from External Affairs, file no. 89, 'Secretary of State file 58/1904': Ambrose Lee, Bluemantle Pursuivant of Arms, to Joseph Pope, Under Secretary of State, 3 October 1905

3 He made his suggestions as earlyy as April 1905; see CA: 14 Garter, f. 280.

4 CA: I 75.34

5 According to the usages of British heraldry, it would have been permissible to have a red chief, but the arrangement settled upon is considered preferable.

6 See order in council (Saskatchewan) 26 November 1906

7 The oldest document impressed with this seal in the possession of the Saskatchewan Archives Board is dated 1908; see AS: Records of the Provincial Secretary, Proclamations, 1903-8, no. 5: proclamation convening the Legislative Assembly to meet on 2 April 1908 dated 7 March 1908.

8 *Revised Statutes of Saskatchewan* 1965, c. 33.3(b)

9 BM Catalogue 709 cited in C.H. Hunter Blair, 'Armorials on English Seals from the Twelfth to the Sixteenth Centuries,' *Archaeologia* 89, p. 8 and plate 8(h)

10 I am indebted to Kathleen R. McKenzie, Secretary to the Lieutenant Governor of Saskatchewan, who has confirmed the present-day practice.

11 Kathleen R. McKenzie to Conrad Swan, York Herald of Arms, 6 November 1969

12 PRO: CO 43/157: Lord Kimberley, Colonial Secretary, to Sir John Young, Bt., Governor General, 16 July 1870 (Canada no. 191) indicating approval of the final design

13 This flag has not yet been recorded in Her Majesty's College of Arms.

CHAPTER 14

Alberta

ENSIGNS ARMORIAL

In 1905 the Province of Alberta was formed out of part of the District of Athabaska and the District of Alberta, together with the western portions of the Districts of Saskatchewan and Assiniboia. The new province was named in honour of Queen Victoria's fourth daughter, Princess Louise Caroline Alberta, wife of the Marquess of Lorne, Governor General of Canada from 1878 to 1883.

Fairly soon after the creation of the new province, the matter of arms was under consideration, and by January 1906 Joseph Pope, Under Secretary of State of Canada, was in correspondence with Ambrose Lee, York Herald of Arms, on behalf of the provincial authorities.[1] On 30 May 1907, arms were duly assigned by royal warrant as follows: *azure, in front of a range of snow mountains proper a range of hills vert, in base a wheat field surmounted by a prairie both also proper, on a chief argent a St George's cross.*[2] [plate 20.1]

As in Manitoba, the Hudson's Bay Company had for almost two centuries exercised viceregal powers over a large part of that area out of which the new province of Alberta was formed and so it is appropriate that the principal charge of the arms of that company, the Cross of St George, is placed in chief on a broad band running across the upper part of the shield. The stark simplicity of this essentially armorial charge, which goes back to the mediaeval beginnings of heraldry in the twelfth century, emphasizes the singular interest of the remainder of the arms. Although twentieth-century in origin, they belong by inspiration to that genre of heraldry which is pictorial rather than armorial, and which was at its height, in British heraldry at least, at the turn of the eighteenth and nineteenth centuries. The classic example is surely the Nile Augmentation of Honour to the arms of Admiral Lord Nelson which comprise a panoramic representation of the *waves of the sea from which a palm-tree issuant between a disabled ship on the dexter and a ruinous battery on the sinister all proper.* [3] At about the same time we find this approach in French armory and then later in the American state arms, such as those for New York and Maine, Nebraska and Montana, to name but four. Independence was achieved by Columbia, Ecuador, and Bolivia during the early popularity of this type of heraldry, which helps to explain why the arms for these countries also are of the same kind. That this type of official heraldry lingered on well into the nineteenth century, in certain areas at least, is attested by the semi-panoramic arms of the Orange Free State, for example. At the present moment we witness a resurgence of this approach with the devices or badges of most Iron Curtain countries. The national or state emblem, device, or badge for Rumania was established in accordance with the 1948 Constitution and modified by that of 1965, and is a splendid example of this type of approach. Almost impossible to blazon, the badge consists of a complicated forest and mountain scene, with in the left foreground an oil derrick; over this rises the sun with golden rays towards a red star; all within a wreath of wheat ears and stalks tied at the bottom with a ribbon of the national colours bearing the words REPUBLICA ROMANIA SOCIALISTA.

This situation attests to the fact that heraldry is tied to no one country or form of constitution but is of international and universal application. Even the various trends, good and bad, in this art and science are no respecters of barriers of whatever kind. Indeed, it seems that a nadir in heraldic practice seems always to be present in one area or other of the world at any given moment even if, mercifully, the converse is frequently true also.

It might well be asked, why do armorists in general and heralds in particular object to this panoramic type of heraldry? The answer would be that the basic purpose, the very *raison d'être,* of armory is identification. Accordingly, in order to fulfil its functional purpose an armorial design must be capable of immediate recognition, whether displayed on some large flag flying from a tall building or very much reduced onto writing paper heading, a seal, or the like. It has been found during the eight hundred odd years of the use of arms that if an armorial design uses charges which are identifiable in silhouette, and not dependent upon internal configurations for recognition, then those arms will fulfil their basic purpose of identification, whether displayed large or small. Panoramic scenes depend upon internal configurations and so reduce the potential utility of those arms upon which they occur.

In view of this, and recalling that Alberta's arms were assigned when the resurgence of heraldry inspired by pristine practice was well under way, one is intrigued to know how such a situation could come about. The answer is a warning to us all.

The general background to the matter of provincial arms helps one to understand the situation more fully. By 1906, due to the untiring efforts of Joseph Pope, Under Secretary of State of Canada, every province had put its armorial position *en règle* with the exception of Saskatchewan and Alberta which had just come into being. Indeed, Pope had been working for almost ten years to this end,[4] and no little tact, diplomacy, and firmness had been required of this indefatigable armorist. He and his great collaborator at the College of Arms, Ambrose Lee, then York Herald of Arms, had between them

14.1 Great Seal Deputed of Alberta
Author's collection

performed a Herculean task. By early 1906, Saskatchewan's armorial affairs were moving smoothly to a successful conclusion, agreeable to both the local authorities and the heralds.

Not so, however, for Alberta. Apparently, from the beginning, the provincial government had wanted something pictorial, and as early as 2 January 1906, York felt he must counsel against such arms and made some alternative suggestions accordingly.[5] Six months passed, winter turned to spring and spring to summer, and there was still hesitation over a design on the part of the province.[6] Late that autumn (1906), when the arms of Saskatchewan had been settled, Pope observed 'our Provinces are now all provided with that commodity except Alberta, from which I think you [York] will hear shortly.'[7] Yet winter came and was almost gone before the Under Secretary of State could send to York, in March 1907, a further design. One can almost hear the sigh of weary disassociation with which Pope described it, simply, as 'what the local authorities desire.'[8] The two could hardly have been in closer agreement. York replied:

Although the design is of the poorest class of heraldry, I can see no positive objection ... [providing] ... the 'blazon' can satisfactorily be settled, to its being granted. Unfortunately in all such cases *we* get the discredit of the poor design, and not the real authors thereof!'[9]

And so it was, for within two months, on 30 May 1907, a royal warrant granted and assigned as the arms for Alberta the design desired above all else by the authorities of the province.

Having said that, it is only just to add that these arms are probably among the best of

14.2 Flag of the Lieutenant Governor of Alberta
Author's collection

their kind. In the hands of a skilful heraldic artist they can be rendered to a considerably stylized degree.

SEALS

Great Seal Deputed of Alberta

Kept in the custody of the Provincial Secretary,[10] and apparently the same as the one first brought into use on 2 December 1907,[11] the Great Seal Deputed of Alberta is circular in shape and measures 2⁹/₁₀ inches (74 millimetres) in diameter [14.1]. A some-what Tudor-shaped shield of the provincial arms occupies the centre. Round the edge of the seal, between two concentric circles of rope-like design, is inscribed the legend, starting just to the left of the centre base, THE SEAL OF THE PROVINCE OF ALBERTA, with, as the stop, a mullet, or five-pointed star, between three decorative parallel lines, the centre one of which extends to the left and right further than the other two. The seal is usually impressed onto the surface of the document over a gold paper wafer.

The rare combination of an armorial shield with a seal of this colour brings to mind immediately the Golden Bulla of Henry VIII, preserved at the Public Record Office in London. The Great Seal Deputed of the Province of Alberta ranks, therefore, as one of the few examples of a golden seal of public authority in the history of these administrative instruments of the Crown.[12]

What has been said of the general design of the Great Seal Deputed of Saskatchewan applies, I feel, *mutatis mutandis,* to that of Alberta.

Privy seal of the Lieutenant Governor

It does not appear ever to have been the custom for the Lieutenant Governor of Alberta to use a privy seal *ex officio*. [13]

FLAGS

Flag of the Lieutenant Governor

The official flag of the Lieutenant Governor of Alberta [14.2] is of the customary design for most of the Queen's provincial representatives; that is to say, it consists of a Union Flag in the centre of which is placed a white disc, which in turn is charged with a shield of the arms for the province surrounded by a wreath of green maple leaves. [14]

Provincial flag

The provincial flag is blue in colour and rectangular in shape, being longer in the fly than in the hoist [plate 24.3]. In the centre is placed a shield of the arms for Alberta.

The flag was the subject of a provincial order in council on 17 January 1967 [15] and of a provincial statute on 1 June following. [16] It thus first came into use during Canadian Centennial Year.

I am grateful for the kindness of P.B. Howard, Deputy Provincial Secretary of Alberta; Captain G.A. Johnson, Secretary to the Lieutenant Governor; W.H. MacDonald, Clerk of the Legislative Assembly, and especially for all the help provided by A.D. Ridge, Provincial Archivist, who also read the chapter in the course of its preparation.

NOTES

1 PAC: in Pope additional material from External Affairs, file no. 90, 'Secretary of State file 64/1905': Ambrose Lee, York Herald of Arms, to Joseph Pope, Under Secretary of State, 2 January 1906

2 CA: I 75.127. So far crest and supporters have not been assigned for this province.

3 CA: Gts. 20.262

4 CA: 14 Garter, f. 300: Joseph Pope, Under Secretary of State, to Ambrose Lee, York Herald of Arms, 9 March 1907

5 CA: ibid. 294: Ambrose Lee, York Herald of Arms, to Joseph Pope, Under Secretary of State, 2 January 1906. The designs do not appear to have survived.

6 Ibid. 295: Joseph Pope, Under Secretary of State, to Ambrose Lee, York Herald of Arms, 4 July 1906

7 Ibid. 275: same to same, 17 October 1906

8 Ibid. 300: same to same, 9 March 1907

9 PAC: in Pope additional material from External Affairs, file 90 'Secretary of State file 64/1905': Ambrose Lee, York Herald of Arms, to Joseph Pope, Under Secretary of State, 22 March 1907

10 The Provincial Secretary's Act, *Revised Statutes of Alberta,* 1955, c. 25, s. 4

11 Provincial order-in-council, OC 624/07. So far no evidence has come to my notice of the use of an interim great seal between the foundation of the province in 1905 and this order in council.

12 Manitoba is the other Canadian province where such a seal is required.

13 I am indebted to Capt G.A. Johnston, Secretary to the Lieutenant Governor of Alberta, who has confirmed this fact.

14 The authority for this is doubtless implied in the order of the Queen in council, 7 August 1869, and the Canadian order in council, 28 February 1870.

15 No. 75

16 This flag has yet to be recorded in Her Majesty's College of Arms.

CHAPTER 15

The Territories

HUDSON'S BAY COMPANY

On 2 May 1670, King Charles II issued a charter under the Great Seal of the Realm in which he constituted as a body corporate his cousin, Prince Rupert of the Rhine, and certain of his associates under the name of the 'Governor and Company of Adventurers of England trading into Hudsons Bay.'[1] Thus came into being one of the most successful and long-lived of those many proprietory English companies which in the seventeenth century stretched from the Arctic Circle to the Carolinas, and to whom we owe the development in great part of so much of North America. Of all these companies only this corporation, soon to be commonly known as the Hudson's Bay Company, has continued, and riding the course of history, has already celebrated the tercentenary of its foundation.

By the royal charter of 1670, the Hudson's Bay Company was invested with certain territories which

said land [was to] bee from henceforth reckoned and reputed one of our Plantacions or Colonyes in America called *Ruperts Land* ... the said Governor and Company for the tyme being and theire successors [to be] the true and absolute Lordes and Proprietors of the same Territory.'[2]

They were empowered to make war, to build forts, and to maintain battleships.[3] Accordingly, for the next two hundred years the Hudson's Bay Company exercised its viceregal powers over Rupert's Land and an ever-increasing area to the north and west[4] which, at its greatest extent, stretched from Hudson Bay to the Pacific. Out of this and other territories, part of Ontario has been carved, as well as Manitoba, Saskatchewan,

15.1 *Seal of the Hudson's Bay Company, 1683*
HBC (see note 8)

Alberta, British Columbia, and the Yukon Territory, leaving what is now known as the Northwest Territories which, in a sense, can thus be regarded as the lineal heir of the company.

From an early date in its history, certainly from 1678,[5] the Company expressed its existence and authority in armorial form. As befitted those who held their lands 'as of our Manor of East Greenwich in our County of Kent in free and common Soccage ... paying yearely to us our heires and Successors for the same two Elkes and two Black beavers,'[6] not to mention the company's primary initial interest, several fur-bearing animals were included in the design; four beavers arranged about a St George's Cross for arms; a seated fox on a cap of maintenance as crest, and two elks – or moose, often confused – for supporters.

In 1680 the committee of the company ordered a 'Little Seale of the Armes of the Company ... for the sealing of our Letters'[7] and three years later an oval silver seal with an ivory knocker is referred to in the minutes of 25 July.[8] This bore the shield of arms, supporters, motto, and crest consisting of a fox seated on a cap of maintenance. The diameter of the seal at its vertical widest is 9/10 inch (23 millimetres) and at its horizontal narrowest 4/5 inch (21 millimetres) [15.1].

Later, seals for specific officers were evolved – one notes, for example, a seal for the Governor in Chief of about 1837 or earlier [15.2]. This shows the armorial bearings described above, with the cross hatched as gold. The seal is oval in shape, longest from top to bottom. The legend reads, starting at the upper left of the seal, GOVERNOR IN CHIEF, and starting again at the lower left and running down round the base of the seal, OF RUPERTS LAND. The diameter of this seal at its widest is 1 1/5 inches (30 millimetres)

15.2 *Seal of the Governor in Chief of Rupert's Land, c. 1837* HBC *(see note 9)*

15.3 *Seal of the Governor and Company, 1852* HBC *(see note 10)*

and at its narrowest 1 1/16 inches (28 millimetres).[9]

When exercising their viceregal powers, the Governor and Company applied their seal to the document – as, for example, when ordering W.B. Caldwell, Governor of the Territory of Assiniboia, to receive the oaths of certain persons as justices of the peace in his district in 'our Territory of Rupert's Land' on 19 November 1852. The circular seal used for this purpose [15.3] contained the complete armorial achievement described above; there is no legend. It is impressed directly onto the document using a paper-covered wafer of wax. The diameter of the seal is 1 1/2 inches (38 millimetres).[10]

The use of armorial seals was well established throughout the entire period of rule by the Hudson's Bay Company. However, at the beginning of the present century it was discovered that no record of an official grant appeared to exist in either the College of Arms or the archives of the company. The embarrassing presumption was that for over two hundred years ensigns armorial had been used without due authority. Faced with this predicament, the Governor and Company immediately sought to rectify the situation and place their armorial entitlement beyond all possible doubt. This they achieved through letters patent dated 26 September 1921, which were issued by the Kings of Arms for the following armorial bearings:

Arms: *argent, a cross gules, between four beavers sable*
Crest: *upon a cap of maintenance gules, turned up ermine, a fox sejant proper*
Supporters: *on either side an elk proper*
Motto: PRO PELLE CUTEM [11] (For a skin a skin)[12] [plate 6]

15.4 *Seal Deputed of the North West Territories*
AS *(see note 13)*

15.5 *Seal Deputed of the Northwest Territories*
Author's collection

THE NORTHWEST TERRITORIES
ENSIGNS ARMORIAL, SEAL, AND FLAG

After the surrender by the company of Rupert's Land back into the hands of the Crown in 1870, and the transfer of this area and the North Western Territory to the new Dominion of Canada, we note its first diminution by the creation of the Province of Manitoba in 1870. The remainder was called the North West Territories. No arms were assigned specifically for these territories but a seal of public authority [15.4] was duly brought into being and used in the customary manner for the authentication of proclamations,[13] civil commissions,[14] and the like. This seal was 2³/₁₀ inches (59 millimetres) in diameter and was impressed, usually over a red paper wafer, onto the surface of the document concerned. The royal arms of general purpose post-1837 are placed on an oval shield, which in turn is surrounded by the Garter and ensigned by the crown. The supporters are the lion and the unicorn. On a scroll suspended from a 'gas bracket' of the Victorian period is the motto DIEU ET MON DROIT. Round the edge, between a double-beaded design, runs the legend, beginning at the bottom of the seal, THE SEAL OF THE NORTH WEST TERRITORIES ·.

This design appears to derive in the main from the deliberations of the Secretary of State for the Provinces and his Under Secretary in the last months of 1869. It was suggested that the model should be the seal as then in use in Ontario and that, like it, the seal for the North West Territories should be provisional.[15] If this is the seal for the engraving of which the Auditor General was billed to the extent of $15 in December of that year,[16] one can only conclude that the work must have been well done, as the seal was in use for the next thirty-three years at least.[17] It seems probable that this is the seal for which the press had been ordered by the end of August 1870, and which Ottawa promised to despatch for use, by way of St Paul, Minnesota, as soon as it was ready.[18]

With the creation of Saskatchewan, Alberta, and the Yukon Territory, and the increased areas of Manitoba, Quebec, and Ontario, the size of the North West Territories was reduced to its present dimensions (its name now being Northwest Territories). As a result, Ottawa assumed direct control of administration, with the result that such seals as were infrequently required in connection with the territories up to 1956 were those of the federal authority.

However, the years following World War II saw an awakening interest in this area and a gradual devolution once again of authority from Ottawa. One expression of this process was the decision of the federal government to request that Her Majesty The Queen assign specific armorial bearings for the Northwest Territories.[19] This was duly accomplished in 1956 as follows:

Arms: *per bend wavy gules and vert billety or, in sinister chief the mask of an arctic fox argent, on a chief indented also argent, a barrulet wavy azure*
Crest: *on a wreath argent and gules, a compass rose proper between two narwhals haurient and addorsed or*[20] [plate 21.1]

The diagonal division of the shield represents the treeline. The green to the left recalls the Mackenzie Valley while the red on the other side stands for the tundra. Billets of gold and the mask of a white fox symbolize important bases of northern wealth – minerals and furs. The broad white band across the upper part of the shield, with its lower indented edge, stands for an ice-field. The wavy blue line through the band recalls the Northwest Passage. Upon a wreath of the colours of the territories, white and red, is placed the crest. The location of the Magnetic North Pole in the territories is recalled by a compass rose, which in turn is guarded by two gold narwhals erect and facing outwards.

Seals deputed of the Northwest Territories

The historic seals used in connection with the Northwest Territories have already been discussed earlier in this chapter. It simply remains, therefore, to make mention of the present deputed seal of this area [15.5]. The shield of arms and crest as assigned in 1956 form the central design and are contained within a diameter of 1 1/2 inches (38 millimetres). The encircling band of 3/8 inch (10 millimetres) width bears the legend THE SEAL OF THE NORTHWEST TERRITORIES. This seal was authorized by a federal order in council which came into effect on 15 December 1956.[21]

Territorial flag

The flag of the Northwest Territories [plate 24.5] consists of the shield of arms of the territories placed on a pale argent or vertical broad white band on an azure background. This flag, the proportions of which are four long by two broad, was approved by the Council of the Northwest Territories on 31 January 1969,[22] and was the subject of an ordinance by the 44th Session of the Council, being assented to by the Commissioner on 18 February 1971.[23]

THE YUKON TERRITORY
ENSIGNS ARMORIAL, SEAL, AND FLAGS

The Yukon Territory is part of the original North Western Territory which was leased to the Hudson's Bay Company in 1821, and so came under its direct governance until, along with Rupert's Land, it passed to the new Dominion of Canada in 1870. For the next quarter of a century it formed an undifferentiated part of the North West Territories until it was organized into the Yukon District. Three years later, in 1898, it was raised to its present status as a territory,

Accordingly, what has been said earlier in this chapter with regard to the use of arms and seals by the Hudson's Bay Company in connection with their governmental administration applies to the Yukon Territory, especially between 1821 and 1870. The subsequent use of official seals by the authorities of the North West Territories, which included what is now the Yukon Territory, has also been discussed.

Between the erection of the territory in 1898 and 1956 a profusion of devices made their appearance in connection with this area. The writing paper headings of various government departments and agencies reflect these well. The royal arms of general purpose are, appropriately enough, to be found on letters from the Department of the Interior, Mining Lands and Yukon Branch, written from Ottawa in 1917,[24] and from the Yukon Territorial Government, Office of the Territorial Agent, License and Tax Collector, written from Whitehorse in 1925.[25] Possibly of even greater interest, and certainly more singular, is the appearance of a shield of arms bearing several of the provincial arms quarterly, ensigned by a royal crown, with the lion and unicorn supporters and motto as from the royal arms of general purpose. This was in use on the writing paper of the Commissioner's Office, Yukon Territory, Dawson, in 1923.[26] This, it will be noted, was two years after armorial ensigns particular to Canada had been proclaimed by King George v in 1921. However, by 1925 one finds these arms of Canada on the heading of the paper of the office of the Gold Commissioner of the Yukon Territory, for use from Dawson.[27] In view of the immediate federal responsibility for the territory this was most appropriate. However, in the same year, but on a letter written three months after the previous one, a shield of arms bearing the arms of Ontario, Quebec, Nova Scotia and New Brunswick, as laid down by the royal warrant of 1868 for the seal of Canada, is to be found at the heading of paper from the same Gold Commissioner's Office[28] – possibly a commendable economy on the part of a civil servant using up old stock.

Thus, no arms or seals particular to the Yukon Territory were officially assigned either upon the creation of the territory or for many years thereafter.[29] Indeed, it was not until the middle of this century that the federal authorities sought to rectify this anomaly. Accordingly, in 1956 Her Majesty The Queen assigned the following armorial bearings for the Yukon Territory:

15.6 Seal of the Yukon Territory
Author's collection

Arms: *azure, on a pallet wavy argent, a like pallet of the field, issuant from base two piles reversed gules, edged also argent, each charged with two bezants in pale, on a chief argent, a cross gules, surmounted of a roundel vair*
Crest: *on a wreath or and gules, a malamute standing on a mount of snow proper*[30] [plate 21.2]

The wavy blue and white line in the centre of the shield represents the Yukon River, from which the territory takes its name, and also the other rivers of the area in which the discovery of placer gold led to the Klondike Gold Rush. The mountainous nature of the territory, as well as its mineral resources, are alluded to by the two symbolic mountains and the gold discs. The St George's cross on the broad upper band, or heraldic chief, refers to the early exploration and development carried out, in the main, by Englishmen. The roundel of heraldic fur at the centre of the cross refers to the fur trade. The malamute dog of the crest has played an important part in the early history of the Yukon Territory. It is noted for its courage, loyalty, and stamina.

Seal deputed of the Yukon Territory

The historic seals applicable to the Yukon Territory have already been discussed earlier in this chapter in connection with the Northwest Territories. It therefore but remains to describe the present Seal Deputed of the Yukon Territory [15.6]. In the centre are the shield of arms and crest as assigned in 1956, which in turn are surrounded by a circle of pellets. The legend reads, starting at the lower left, THE SEAL OF THE YUKON TERRITORY . The outer edge of the seal consists of a rope design. The diameter is $2^1/_{10}$ inches (53 millimetres).

Territorial flag

By an ordinance of the Council of the Yukon Territory of 1967, a flag for the territory was formally adopted.[31]

A blazon of the flag would be: *per pale vert and azure, on a pale argent, the shield of arms and the crest of the Yukon Territory with in base a wreath of* Epilobium angustifolium *proper* [plate 24.6]. That is to say, there are three vertical stripes, green, white, and blue, with the green nearest the mast. On the central white panel, whose width is 1 ½ times that of each of the other two, is placed a fully coloured representation of the shield of arms and crest of the territory. Beneath the shield are placed in cross two stalks of the territorial floral emblem, *Epilobium angustifolium,* popularly known as fireweed.

The design, proportions, and tones of colours are specified in the schedule to the flag ordinance.[32] However, while the verbal description of the schedule calls only for 'the Yukon crest,' which, if taken literally, signifies simply the malamute on a mount of snow all placed upon a crest wreath or and gules (gold and red), nevertheless from the illustration provided in the schedule it is obvious that the intention was to include both the crest and the shield of arms of the territory.[33]

I wish to record my gratitude to the following who have helped in connection with this chapter: F.G. Smith, QC, Chief Magistrate, Northwest Territories, and H.J. Taylor, Territorial Secretary, Government of the Yukon Territory, who despite many official duties have never failed to respond to a request for assistance from me; the Right Reverend Paul Piché, OMI, Bishop of Mackenzie; E.J. Boxer, Secretary, NWT Historical Advisory Board; Gail Robinson, Secretary, NWT Historical Standing Committee; and Lt. Cmdr. Alan B. Beddoe, OC, OBE, OSTJ, RCN (Rtd.), who designed the arms of the two territories, and whose interest in and lifelong devotion to armory in Canada will always be remembered.

NOTES

1 *Charters, Statutes, Orders in Council Relating to the Hudson's Bay Company* (London, Hudson's Bay Company 1963) p. 4

2 Ibid. pp. 11-12

3 Ibid. p. 18

4 For example, the grant of 1821

5 HBC: A 15/1, f. 13, entry in Grand Journal dated 28 May 1678 concerning the payment of 18 shillings to Thomas Phipps for a 'small Seale with the Companyes Armes.' This and the other quotations from the archives of the Hudson's Bay Company given in this chapter are published by permission of the Hudson's Bay Company. See also E.E. Rich, *The History of the Hudson's Bay Company, 1670-1870*, vol. 1, 1670-1763 (The Hudson's Bay Record Society 1958) p. 50. The tinctures have, however, varied from time to time; see Ramsey Traquair, 'The Coat of Arms,' *The Beaver* (June 1945) p. 43 ff.

6 *Charters ... Relating to the Hudson's Bay Company*, p. 12

7 HBC: A 1/2, f. 25, entry in minutes book dated 27 May 1680

8 Ibid. f. 115d, entry in minutes book dated 25 July 1683

9 HBC: where, in addition to this seal, others are preserved which come within roughly the same category, such as, for exaple, the two oval seals of about 1810 or 1821 which have the same arms, crest, supporters, and motto as the Governor in Chief's seal, but are inscribed round the edge, starting at roughly centre left and going down round the bottom of the seal, GOVERNOR OF THE SOUTHERN [NORTHERN, as the case may be] FACTORY and starting once again at the upper left and going over the top of the seal, OF RUPERTS LAND (vertical and longest diameter 1 1/5 inches [30 millimetres], horizontal and narrowest diameter 1 1/10 inches [28 millimetres]).

10 HBC: E16/4, f. 5: Governor and Comany to W.B. Caldwell, Governor of the District of Assiniboia, 19 November 1852

11 CA: Gts. 89.125

12 Possibly an adaptation of Book of Job 2:4 – *Pellem pro pelle.* In the motto one might consider the sentiment *pro pelle* (for the skins or pelts of animals [we venture our]) *cutem* (skins [of a man]). Yet again, it may be an adaptation (misquotation?) from Juvenal, *Satire* 10.192: *pro cute pellem,* 'Hide in place of skin,' which for the Hudson's Bay Company could be interpreted as 'hides exchanged for human skin,' 'hides purchased at the price of human skin.' The deliberate (accidental?) inversion on the motto *pro pelle cutem* means no more than '(we give) human skin in exchange for hides.'

13 AS: proclamation dated 23 March 1903 by the Lieutenant Governor summoning the meeting of the Legislative Assembly of the North-West Territories on 16 April 1903

14 HBC: A 33/5, f. 143: commission dated 19 August 1889 issued by the Lieutenant Governor of the North-West Territories appointing David Hepburn Russell to be a commissioner of oaths

15 PAC: RG 6, C1, vol. 10A, file 996: Under Secretary of State for the Provinces suggests a provisional seal for the North West Territories to be modelled on that of Ontario,

30 September 1869; Secretary of State for the Provinces recommends this suggestion and adds the legend, 18 November 1869.

16 PAC: RG 6, C2, vol. 2, pp. 245-6, 22 December 1869

17 It appears that the seal of the North West Territories which came into use eventually was in fact a *second* seal, in view of the fact that on 30 June 1870 the Secretary of State for the Provinces asked William McDougal to return the great seal 'intended' to be used in the North West Territories, and that on 9 July 1870 William McDougal wrote to the Secretary of State for the Provinces returning the seal and saying that it had never been within two hundred miles of the North West Territories! See PAC: RG 6, C1, vol. 10A, file 996. Or, of course, it may have been re-issued.

18 Canada, *Sessional Papers,* 1871, no. 20, p. 106: G. Powell for Under Secretary of State for the Provinces to the Honble A.G. Archibald, Lieutenant Governor of Manitoba, 29 August 1870

19 In about 1922 some 'arms' supposedly for the Northwest Territories made their appearance and were put forward with some persistence, but never officially. They were: *gules, four garbs or, on a chief chequay of three rows argent and azure, a polar bear passant proper.* The provenance of this curious phenomenon has never been fully explained. Comdr. Alan Beddoe has suggested that the American armorist, Howard M. Chapin, who took an interest in Canadian heraldry at about this time, may have been responsible.

20 CA: Misc. Enrol. 1.225. The Secretary of State of Canada addressed his request to Her Majesty on 17 February 1956.

21 Order in council (PC 1956-1778) dated 29 November 1956

22 The design was by Robert Bessant of Margaret, Manitoba.

23 Chapter F-6 of the *Revised Ordinance of the Northwest Territories* 1974. The flag has yet, however, to be recorded at Her Majesty's College of Arms.

24 PAC: Yukon Territorial Records 1917-25

25 Ibid.

26 Ibid.

27 Ibid.

28 Ibid.

29 A phenomenon similar to that experienced by the Northwest Territories – see footnote 19 above – occurred in connection with the Yukon Territory at about the same time; the blazon of the 'arms' supposedly of the latter being: *azure, issuant from base three piles reversed gules, edged argent, each charged with three bezants in pale, on a chief indented or, a lion passant guardant gules.*

30 CA: Misc. Enrol. 1.224 where 'malamute' is rendered as 'husky dog.'

31 *Ordinances of the Yukon Territory* 1967 (second session) chapter 3: an ordinance to adopt a flag for the Yukon Territory (assented to 1 December 1967)

32 Ibid: green (503-115), blue (502-204), red (509-103) as in *Standard Paint Colours,* part 1 (1-GP-12C, 1965) Canadian Government Specification Board

33 This flag has yet to be recorded at Her Majesty's College of Arms.

APPENDIXES

APPENDIX A

Royal style and titles

This appendix contains the royal style and titles on the grands sceaux, great seals of the realm, great seals of Canada, and deputed great seals referred to in this work, with extended forms and translations. The style and titles are given below in full, but on the actual seals (which are illustrated in the figures referred to in each case) those parts within brackets do not appear. Variations of legend and motto are dealt with in the appropriate chapters.

FRANCIS I [2.1]

FRA[N]CISCVS · DEI · GRATIA · FRANCORVM · REX · PRIMVS · Francis I, by the Grace of God, King of the French

HENRY IV [2.2]

HENRICVS QUARTUS DEI GRATIA FRANCORUM REX Henry IV, by the Grace of God, King of the French

LOUIS XIII [2.3]

LOUIS XIII PAR LA GRACE D[E] DIEV ROY D[E] FRANCE ET D[E] NAVARRE Louis XIII, by the Grace God, King of France and of Navarre

LOUIS XIV [2.4]

LOVIS XIIII · PAR · LA · GRACE · DE · DIEV · ROY · DE · FRANCE · ET · DE · NAVARRE ·
Louis XIV, by the Grace of God, King of France and of Navarre

LOUIS XV [2.5]

LOVIS · XV · PAR · LA · GRACE · DE · DIEV · ROY · DE · FRANCE · ET · DE · NAVARRE ·
Louis XV, by the Grace of God, King of France and of Navarre

HENRY VII [2.6]

HENRICUS · DEI · GR[ATI]A · REX · ANGLIE · & · FRANCIE · & · DOMINUS ·
HIBERNIE · Henry, by the Grace of God, King of England and France and Lord of
Ireland

JAMES VI AND I [2.7]

IACOBVS · D[EI] · G[RATIA] · MAG[NAE] · BRIT[ANNIAE] · FRAN[CIAE] · ET ·
HIB[ERNIAE] · REX · James, by the Grace of God, King of Great Britain, France and
Ireland

CHARLES II [2.8 and 2.9]

CAROLVS · II · DEI · GRA[TIA] · MAG[NAE] · BRITAN[NIAE] · FRAN[CIAE] · ET ·
HIB[ERNIAE] · REX · FID[EI] · DEFENSOR · Charles II, by the Grace of God, King of
Great Britain, France and Ireland, Defender of the Faith

ANNE [2.10]

ANNA · DEI · GRATIA · MAGNAE · BRITANNIAE · FRANCIAE · ET · HIBERNIAE ·
REGINA · FIDEI · DEFENSOR · ETC Anne, by the Grace of God, Queen of Great
Britain, France and Ireland, Defender of the Faith, etc.

GEORGE II [7.2]

GEORGIUS II · D[EI] · G[RATIA] · MAG[NAE] · BRI[TANNIAE] · FR[ANCIAE] · ET ·
HIB[ERNIAE] · REX · F[IDEI] · D[EFENSOR] · BRUN[SVICENSIS] · ET ·
LUN[EBURGENSIS] · DUX · S[ACRI] · R[OMANI] · I[MPERII] · AR[CHI-] ·
THES[AURARIUS] · ET · PR[INCEPS] · EL[ECTOR] · George II, by the Grace of God,
King of Great Britain, France and Ireland, Defender of the Faith, Duke of Brunswick
and Luneburg, Arch-Treasurer of the Holy Roman Empire, Prince Elector

GEORGE III

From accession, 1760, until Union with Ireland, 1 January 1801 [8.1]

GEORGIUS · III · D[EI] · G[RATIA] · MAG[NAE] · BRI[TANNIAE] · FR[ANCIAE] · ET · HIB[ERNIAE] · REX · F[IDEI] · D[EFENSOR] · BRUN[SVICENSIS] · ET · LUN[EBURGENSIS] · DUX · S[ACRI] · R[OMANI] · I[MPERII] · AR[CHI-] · THES[AURARIUS] · ET · EL[ECTOR] · George III, by the Grace of God, King of Great Britain, France, and Ireland, Defender of the Faith, Duke of Brunswick and Luneburg, Arch-Treasurer of the Holy Roman Empire, and [Prince] Elector

On the George III seal for Cape Breton Island [7.9] the inscription of the royal titles is as above with the variation of F[RANCIAE] and the addition at the end of inscription of PR[INCEPS] before ELEC[TOR].

On the George III seal for Quebec [6.7] the inscription of the royal titles is as in 8.1 with the exception that at the end it reads ET · PR[INCEPS] · EL[ECTOR] · .

From 1 January 1801 until his death, 1820 [9.2]

GEORGIUS TERTIUS · DEI · GRATIA · BRITANNIARUM REX · FIDEI DEFENSOR · George III, by the Grace of God, King of the Britains, Defender of the Faith

GEORGE IV [7.10]

GEORGIUS · QUARTUS · DEI · GRATIA · BRITANNIARUM · REX · FIDEI · DEFENSOR · George IV, by the Grace of God, King of the Britains, Defender of the Faith

WILLIAM IV [7.5 and 9.4]

GULIELMUS IV D[EI] · G[RATIA] · BRITANNIAR[UM] · REX · F[IDEI] · D[EFENSOR] · William IV by the Grace of God, King of the Britains, Defender of the Faith

VICTORIA [11.1]

VICTORIA DEI GRATIA BRITANNIAR[UM] REG[INA] F[IDEI] D[EFENSOR] Victoria by the Grace of God, Queen of the Britains, Defender of the Faith

On the seal for the Province of Canada [10.8] the inscription was: VICTORIA D[EI] · G[RATIA] · BRITANNIARUM REGINA FID[EI] · DEF[ENSOR] ·

On the temporary Great Seal Deputed of Canada (1867-9) [4.1] the inscription was: VICTORIA D[EI] · G[RATIA] · BRIT[ANNIARUM]* · REG[INA] · F[IDEI] · D[EFENSOR] ·

On the Great Seal Deputed of Canada [4.2] the inscription was: VICTORIA DEI GRATIA BRITANNIAR[UM] REGINA F[IDEI] · D[EFENSOR] ·

* BRITT on seal

EDWARD VII [4.3]

EDWARDVS VII · D[EI] · G[RATIA] · BRIT[ANNIARVM]* · ET TERRARVM TRANSMAR[INARVM] · QVAE IN DIT[IONE] · SVNT BRIT[ANNICA] · REX F[IDEI] · D[EFENSOR] · IND[IAE] · IMP[ERATOR] · Edward VII, by the Grace of God, King of the Britains and of the Lands beyond the Seas which are in the British dominion, Defender of the Faith, Emperor of India

GEORGE V [4.4]

GEORGIVS V D[EI] · G[RATIA] · BRIT[ANNIARVM]* · ET TERRARVM TRANSMAR[INARVM] · QVAE IN DIT[IONE] · SVNT BRIT[ANNICA] · REX F[IDEI] · D[EFENSOR] · IND[IAE] · IMP[ERATOR] · George V, by the Grace of God, King of the Britains and of the Lands beyond the Seas which are in the British dominion, Defender of the Faith, Emperor of India

EDWARD VIII

(None taken into use)

GEORGE VI [4.5]

GEORGIUS · VI · D[EI] · G[RATIA] · MAG[NAE] · BRIT[ANNIAE] · HIB[ERNIAE] · ET · TERR[ARUM] · TRANSMAR[INARUM] · QUAE ·IN · DIT[IONE] · SUNT · BRIT[ANNICA] · REX · F[IDEI] · D[EFENSOR] · IND[IAE] · IMP[ERATOR] · George VI, by the Grace of God, King of Great Britain and Ireland and of the Lands beyond the Seas which are in the British dominion, Defender of the Faith, Emperor of India

On the George VI Great Seal for Newfoundland [5.8] the inscription was: GEORGIVS VI · DEI · GRATIA · MAG[NAE] · BR[ITANNIAE] · HIB[ERNAE] · ET TERR[ARVM] · TRANSMAR[INARVM] · QVAE IN DIT[IONE] · SVNT BRIT[ANNICA] · REX · FIDEI · DEFENSOR · IND[IAE] · IMP[ERATOR] ·

ELIZABETH II [4.6]

REINE · DU · CANADA · ELIZABETH · II · QUEEN · OF · CANADA ·

* BRITT on seal

APPENDIX B

Privy seals of the Governors General of Canada

The majority of the examples illustrated below are preserved at the Public Archives of Canada (Department of Paintings, Drawings, and Prints), Ottawa.

FIGURE B1

Steel female die (without legend) of the privy seal of Charles Stanley (Monck) Viscount Monck of Ballytrammon, co. Wexford etc., Governor General 1867-8. Diameter 1½″ (38mm)

Arms: *gules, a chevron between three lions' heads erased argent.* The shield is ensigned by the coronet of a Viscount.
Crest: *on a wreath argent and gules, a dragon passant wings elevated sable*
Supporters: *dexter, a dragon wings elevated argent, langued gules, holding over the dexter shoulder a laurel branch fructed proper; sinister, a lion argent, langued gules, holding over the sinister shoulder a laurel branch fructed proper*
Motto: FORTITER FIDELITER FELICITER (Boldly, faithfully, successfully)[1]

FIGURE B2

Impression of the privy seal (without legend) of Sir John Young, Bt., GCB,[2] GCMG[3] (Baron Lisgar of Lisgar and Baillieborough, co. Cavan from 2 November 1870), Governor General 1868-72. Diameter 1½″ (38mm)

B1

PAC: PDP

B2

PAC: PDP

Arms: *argent three piles sable, each charged with a trefoil slipped or, on a chief sable, three annulets or, and in canton the augmentation of a baronet being an inescutcheon argent, a sinister hand erect couped at the wrist and appaumé gules.* The shield on the seal is encircled by the collar of a GCB, and from the sinister depends the badge of a GCMG.

Crest: *on a wreath argent and sable, a demi-lion rampant gules, charged on the shoulder with a trefoil slipped or, holding in the dexter paw* (not visible on this impression) *a sword erect proper,* which, after 18 May 1871 by a grant of Ulster King of Arms, was changed to *a sprig of three maple leaves all proper.* The document shown here is dated 1869.

Motto: PRUDENTIA (Prudence)[4]

FIGURE B3

Lead impression of the privy seal of Sir Frederick (Hamilton-Temple-Blackwood) Earl of Dufferin, co. Down, Viscount Clandeboye, of Clandeboye in the same County, and a Baronet, KP[5], etc. Governor General 1872-8. Diameter 3⅛″ (79mm)

Arms: *quarterly, 1 and 4, azure, a fess or, in chief a crescent argent, between two mullets or, and in base a mascle argent* (Blackwood); *2nd quarterly, 1 and 4, or, an eagle displayed sable, 2 and 3, argent, two bars sable, each charged with three martlets or* (Temple); *3rd gules, three cinquefoils pierced ermine, on a chief or, a lion passant gules* (Hamilton)[6] *overall the augmentation of a baronet, an inescutcheon argent, a sinister hand erect couped at the wrist and appaumé gules.* The shield on the seal is surrounded by the collar of a KP and ensigned by the coronet of an Earl.

B3

PAC: PDP

B4

PAO: S4756

Supporters: *dexter, a lion gules, armed and langued azure, gorged with a collar [vere a tressure flory counter-flory or]; sinister, an heraldic tyger [ermine], gorged with a tressure flory [vere flory counter-flory gules]*

Motto: STRAIGHT FORWARD[7]

FIGURE B4

Impression of privy seal (without legend) of preceding. Armorial bearings as for preceding except that in addition to the collar of a KP and the badge of that order depending to the dexter, the badge of a GCB depends to the sinister.[8] Diameter 1³/4″ x 1¹/4″ (45mm x 32mm)

FIGURE B5

Lead impression of the privy seal of Sir John Douglas Sutherland Campbell (by courtesy Marquess of Lorne as son and heir to the 8th Duke of Argyll, then still living), KT,[9] GCMG, Governor General 1878-83. Diameter 3¹/4″ (82mm)

Arms: *quarterly, 1 and 4, gyronny of eight or and sable* (Campbell); *2 and 3, argent, a galley or lymphad sable, sails furled, flag and pennons flying and oars in action proper* (Lordship of Lorne) overall a label of three points or.[10] The coronet ensigning the shield is that of a Marquess.

B5

PAC: PDP

B6

PAC: PDP

Crest: *on a wreath or and sable, a boar's head fessewise erased or, armed argent*
Supporters: *on either side a lion guardant gules*
Motto: NE OBLIVISCARIS (Forget not) [11]

FIGURE B6

Lead impression of the privy seal of Sir Henry Charles Keith (Petty-Fitzmaurice), Marquess of Lansdowne, co. Somerset, GCMG, etc., Governor General 1883-8. Diameter 3¼" (82 mm)

Arms: *quarterly, 1 and 4, ermine, on a bend azure, a magnetic needle pointing to a polar star or* (Petty); *2 and 3, argent, a saltire gules, a chief ermine* (Fitzmaurice). The coronet of a Marquess ensigns the shield on the seal.
Crests: *1 / on a wreath of the colours argent and azure, a beehive beset with bees diversely volant proper; 2 / on a wreath of the colours argent and gules, a centaur drawing a bow and arrow proper the part from the waist argent*
Supporters: *on either side a Pegasus ermine bridled crined winged and unguled or, each charged on the shoulder with a fleur-de-lis azure*
Motto: VIRTUTE NON VERBIS (By courage, not words) [12]

FIGURE B7

Lead impression of the privy seal of Sir Frederick Arthur (Stanley) Baron Stanley of

B7

PAC: PDP

B8

PAC: PDP

Preston, co. Pal. Lancaster, GCB, Governor General 1888-93. Diameter 3¹/₁₆″ (78mm)

Arms: *argent, on a bend azure, three stags' heads caboshed or, a crescent azure, for difference.*
The coronet of a Baron ensigns the shield on the seal.
Crest: *on a chapeau gules, turned up ermine, an eagle wings extended or, preying on an infant in
its cradle proper swaddled gules, the cradle laced or*
Supporters: *dexter, a griffin wings elevated and sinister, a stag each or, and ducally gorged with a
line reflexed over the back and charged on the shoulder with a crescent azure*
Motto: SANS CHANGER (Without changing)[13]

FIGURE B8

Lead impression of the privy seal of Sir John Campbell Hamilton (Gordon) Earl of
Aberdeen, Baronet of Nova Scotia, GCMG, etc., Governor General 1893-8. Diameter
3¹/₈″ (79mm)

Arms: *azure three boars' heads couped or, armed proper langued gules, within a tressure flowered
and counterflowered interchangeably with thistles, roses and fleurs-de-lis or.* The coronet of an
Earl ensigns the shield on the seal.
Crest: *issuing from a torse azure or and gules, two arms holding a bow and arrow straight upward
in a shooting posture and at full draught all proper (mantled gules, doubled ermine)*
Supporters: *dexter, a doctor of divinity and sinister, a doctor of law each vested and adorned with
his peculiar habit and ornaments proper*
Mottoes: FORTUNA SEQUATUR · NE NIMIUM (Let fortune follow. No excess)[14]

B9

PAC: PDP

B10

PAC: PDP

B11

PAC: PDP

B12

PAC: PDP

FIGURE B9

Lead impression of the privy seal of Sir Gilbert John (Elliot-Murray-Kynynmound) Earl of Minto, co. Roxburgh, Baronet of Nova Scotia, GCMG, etc. Governor General 1898-1904. Diameter 3⅛" (79mm)

Arms: Several serious errors have occurred in the engraving of this seal. In the first instance the quarters in the grand quarters have been reversed. Other discrepancies will be noted in the course of the following blazon: *1 and 4, grand quarters, quarterly 1 and 4, argent, a hunting horn sable, stringed gules, in dexter chief point a crescent also gules* (not shown), *on a chief wavy azure* (not shown), *three mullets argent* (Murray of Melgund); *2 and 3, azure, a chevron argent, between three fleurs-de-lis or* (Kynynmound of the Ilk); *2 and 3, grand quarters gules, on a bend engrailed* (not so shown) *or, a baton azure, within a bordure vair* (shown here as something approximating *an orle of cubes*) (Elliot of Minto); *overall a chief of augmentation argent, with a moor's head couped in profile proper* being the Arms of Corsica in commemoration of the first Earl's services as Viceroy of that kingdom. The coronet of an Earl ensigns the shield on the seal.
Crest: *on a wreath argent and azure, issuant from clouds a dexter arm embowed throwing a dart all proper and in an escrol over the same this motto* NON EGET ARCU *(mantled gules, doubled ermine)*
Motto: SUAVITER ET FORTITER (Mildly but firmly)[15]

FIGURE B10

Lead impression of the privy seal of Sir Albert Henry George (Grey) Earl Grey, Viscount Howick, co. Northumberland, Baronet, GCMG, etc. Governor General 1904-11. Diameter 3⅛" (79mm)

Arms: *quarterly, 1 and 4, gules, a lion rampant within a bordure engrailed argent [in the dexter chief point a mullet or]; 2 and 3, barry of six argent and azure, on a bend gules, a bezant in dexter chief; overall the augmentation of a Baronet, an inescutcheon argent, a sinister hand erect couped at the wrist and appaumé gules.* The coronet of an Earl ensigns the shield on the seal.
Crest: *on a wreath argent and gules, a scaling ladder or, hooked and pointed azure*
Supporters: *dexter, a lion guardant purpure, ducally crowned or; sinister, a tiger guardant proper*
Motto: DE BON VOULOIR SERVIR LE ROY (With good will serve the king)[16]

FIGURE B11

Lead impression of the privy seal of HRH Prince Arthur William Patrick Albert, Duke of Connaught and of Strathearn, KG,[17] etc., Governor General 1911-16. Diameter 3⅛" (79mm)

Arms: *the royal arms of general purpose (post-1837) with an inescutcheon of Saxony and differenced with a label of three points argent, with 1st and 3rd charged with a fleur-de-lis azure, the 2nd charged with a cross gules.* The shield on the seal is surrounded by the Garter and ensigned by the coronet of a son of the Sovereign.

Crest: *standing on the coronet of a son of the Sovereign a lion guardant or, wearing a like coronet charged on the shoulder with a label as in the arms*

Supporters: *dexter, a royal lion charged on the shoulder with a label as on the arms and wearing the coronet of a son of the Sovereign; sinister, a royal unicorn charged on the shoulder with a label as on the arms* [18]

FIGURE B12

Bronze counter seal of the privy seal of Sir Victor Christian William (Cavendish) Duke of Devonshire, KG, etc., Governor General 1916-21. Diameter 3³/₁₆″ (81mm)

Arms: *sable, three bucks' heads caboshed argent.* The shield on the seal is surrounded by the Garter and ensigned by the coronet of a Duke. [19]

FIGURE B13

Steel counter seal of the privy seal of Sir Julian Hedworth George (Byng) Baron Byng of Vimy, of Thorpe-le-Soken, co. Essex, GCB, etc., Governor General 1921-6. Diameter 3³/₁₆″ (81mm)

Arms: *quarterly sable and argent in the first quarter a lion rampant also argent, overall in bend sinister a representation of the colours of the 31st Regiment. A crescent gules for difference.* The shield of the seal is surrounded by the motto riband and laurel wreath of a GCB (military) from which depends the appropriate badge; the shield is also ensigned by the coronet of a Baron. [20]

FIGURE B14

Steel counter seal of the privy seal of Sir Freeman (Freeman-Thomas) Viscount Willingdon, of Rattan, co. Sussex, GCSI,[21] etc., Governor General 1926-31. Diameter 3¹/₄″ (82mm)

Arms: *quarterly 1 and 4, argent, three lions rampant gules, a chief azure* (Thomas), *2 and 3, ermine, two pallets in pale azure, overall three fusils conjoined in fess or* (Freeman). The shield on the seal is surrounded by the motto riband and collar of a GCSI; the badge of a GCIE[22] depends to the dexter and the badge of a GBE[23] to the sinister. The coronet of a Viscount ensigns the shield.

Crest: *1 / on a wreath argent and gules, a demi-lion rampant gules, charged on the shoulder with an ermine spot argent* (Thomas); *2 / issuant out of an antique crown azure, a boar's head proper* (Freeman)

Supporters: *on either side a freeman armed cap à pie in English armour of the seventeenth century proper*

Motto: HONESTY IS THE BEST POLICY [24]

B13
PAC: PDP

B14
PAC: PDP

B15

PAC: PDP

B16

PAC: PDP

FIGURE B15

Steel counter seal of the privy seal of Sir Vere Brabazon (Ponsonby) Earl of Bessborough, GCMG, etc., Governor General 1931-35. Diameter 3¹/₄″ (82mm)

Arms: *gules, a chevron between three combs argent.* The shield on the seal is surrounded by
the motto riband of a GCMG, and from this depends the badge of that order. The coronet
of an Earl ensigns the shield.
Crest: *out of a ducal coronet azure, three arrows one in pale two in saltire points downwards
entwined by a snake proper. Mantled gules, doubled argent.*
Supporters: *on either side a lion reguardant proper standing on a grassy mount also proper*
Motto: PRO REGE, LEGE, GREGE (For the king, the law, and the people)[25]

FIGURE B16

Steel counter seal of the privy seal of Sir John (Buchan) Baron Tweedsmuir of Elsfield,
co. Oxford, GCMG, Governor General 1935-40. Diameter 3¹/₄″ (82mm)

Arms: *azure, a fess between three lions' heads erased argent.* The shield on the seal is ensigned
by the coronet of a Baron.
Crest: *on a wreath argent and azure, a sun flower proper and in an escrol over the crest this motto,*
NON INFERIORA SECUTUS (Not following meaner things). (*Mantled gules, doubled ermine
but not shown on the seal.*)

B17

PAC: PDP

B18

PAC: PDP

Supporters: *on a compartment, dexter, a stag proper attired or, collared gules; sinister, a falcon proper, jessed belled and beaked or, armed and collared gules* [26]

FIGURE B17

Steel counter seal of the privy seal of Sir Alexander Augustus Frederick William Alfred George (Cambridge) Earl of Athlone, KG, etc., Governor General 1940-46. Diameter 3⁵/₁₆″ (84mm)

Arms: *quarterly, 1 and 4, grand quarters, the royal arms of general purpose as borne by George III, 1801-16 (without the electoral bonnet), differenced by a label of three points the centre point charged with St George's cross and each of the other points with two hearts in pale gules; 2 and 3, grand quarters, or, three stag attires fesswise in pale the points of each attire to the sinister sable, impaling or, three lions passant in pale sable, langued gules, the dexter forepaws also gules, overall an inescutcheon paly bendy sinister sable and or, in the centre of the grand quarters a crescent sable, for difference.* The shield on the seal is surrounded by the Garter and ensigned by the coronet of an Earl.

Crest: *on a wreath or and sable, a dog's head and neck paly bendy sinister sable and or, langued gules, a crescent argent, for difference*

Supporters: *dexter, a lion sable, the dexter forepaw gules; sinister, a stag proper each charged with a crescent argent, for difference; upon a compartment comprising a grassy mount proper*

Motto: FEARLESS AND FAITHFUL [27]

FIGURE B18

Steel counter seal of the privy seal of Sir Harold Rupert Leofric George (Alexander) Viscount Alexander of Tunis, of Errigal, co. Donegal, GCB, etc., Governor General 1946-52. Diameter $3^{5}/_{16}''$ (84mm)

Arms: *per pale argent and sable, a chevron and in base a crescent all countercharged on a canton azure, a harp or, stringed argent.* The shield on the seal is surrounded by the collar of a GCB (military) from which depends in the centre the appropriate badge of that order and, similarly, to the dexter the badges of a GCMG and a Companion of the DSO; then to the sinister those of a CSI and a holder of the MC.
Crest: *upon a wreath argent and sable, an arm in armour embowed the hand holding a sword all proper*
Supporters: *dexter, a piper of the Irish Guards holding under the interior arm a bagpipe; sinister, a sepoy of the 3 /2nd Punjabi Regiment holding in the exterior hand a rifle all proper and charged on the shoulder with an escutcheon barry nebuly of six argent and azure, and standing on a compartment comprising a grassy mount proper*
Motto: PER MARE PER TERRAS PER ASTRA (By sea, by land, by the stars)[28]

FIGURE B19

Bronze counter seal of the privy seal of the Right Honble Vincent Massey, CH,[29] etc., Governor General 1952-9. Diameter $3^{1}/_{4}''$ (82mm)

B21

Arms: *argent, on a chevron between three lozenges sable, each charged with a fleur-de-lis also argent as many stags' heads erased or.*[30] The badge of a Companion of Honour depends from beneath the shield, which in turn is placed upon an eight-pointed Maltese cross of a Bailiff Grand Cross of the Most Venerable Order of the Hospital of St John of Jerusalem.

Crest: *issuant out of an Eastern crown or, a bull's head sable, armed or, and charged on the neck with a lozenge argent, thereon a fleur-de-lis also sable. (Mantled sable, lined argent)*

Motto: DUM TERAR PROSUM (I am useful as long as demands are being made upon me)[31]

FIGURE B20

Fibreglass counter seal (without legend) of General the Right Honble Georges Philias Vanier, DSO,[32] MC,[33] etc., Governor General 1959-67. Diameter 3″ (76mm)

Arms: *or, on a chevron paly azure and gules, two swords chevronwise points inward gold, in chief an oak tree couped proper between a fleur-de-lis also azure, and a trefoil slipped vert, and in base a representation of the gate of the Citadel of Quebec flying thereon the flag of the Governor General of Canada*

Crest: *on a wreath or, azure and gules, a representation of the tower and steeple of the Church of St Catherine at Honfleur in France all gold*

Motto: FIAT VOLUNTAS DEI (May the will of God be done)[34]

B22

B23

FIGURE B21

Original design by Geoffrey Mussett, Herald-Painter of the College of Arms, prepared under the direction of the author, then Rouge Dragon Pursuivant of Arms, for the privy seals of the Right Honble Daniel Roland Michener, cc,[35] etc., Governor General 1967-74. The matrices are hard white plastic (male) and steel (female). Diameter 2³/₄″ (70mm)

Arms: *azure four bendlets interlaced in saltire between in chief a representation of the royal crown and in base a fleur-de-lis or.* Depended from beneath the shield are, to the dexter, the badge of a Companion of the Order of Canada and, to the sinister, that of a Knight of Justice of the Most Venerable Order of the Hospital of St John of Jerusalem.
Crest: *on a wreath of the colours, or and azure, in front of a demi-lion or, supporting a representation of the Mace of the House of Commons of Canada proper a plate charged with a maple leaf gules*
Supporters: *dexter, a deer gules, attired and unguled or, charged on the shoulder with a plate thereon a rose gules, barbed and seeded proper; sinister, a deer argent, also attired and unguled or, charged on the shoulder with a torteau thereon a square buckle argent*[36]
Motto: LIBRE ET ORDONNÉ (Free and orderly)[37]

B24

FIGURE B22

Impression of the privy seal of Roland Michener as Governor General. Diameter 2³/₄″ (70mm)

FIGURE B23

Impression of the privy seal (without legend) of Roland Michener as Governor General. Diameter 2¹/₈″ (54mm)

FIGURE B24

Impression of the interim privy seal for use by a Governor General until he has one engraved bearing his own arms, legend, and the like. At the time of writing such a seal was in use by His Excellency the Right Honble Jules Léger, Governor General since 1974. The design consists of the Arms of Canada ensigned by the royal crown. The inscription reads, from lower left, · GOVERNOR GENERAL · GOUVERNEUR GENERAL · with in base the word CANADA, which legend is contained on the inner edge by a circle of pellets, and on the outer by a rope design. Diameter 2³/₄″ (70mm)

NOTES

1 UKA: Peers Peds. 186.69/6.327

2 Knight Grand Cross of the Most Honourable Order of the Bath

3 Knight Grand Cross of the Most Distinguished Order of St Michael and St George

4 UKA: D.133/13.81; G.231/37.24. For further details concerning Lord Lisgar's maple leaf crest, see Conrad M.J.F. Swan (Rouge Dragon Pursuivant of Arms), 'The Beaver and the Maple Leaf in Heraldry' *The Coat of Arms* 10 (July 1969) p. 101 and *Heraldry: Ulster and North American Connections,* (Ulster-Scot Historical Foundation, Belfast 1972) p. 16.

5 Knight of the Most Illustrious Order of St Patrick

6 UKA: G.257

7 UKA: F.430

8 PAO: S4756, MSS, Macaulay Papers 1873: commission to J.K. Macaulay to be a major in the militia, 9 April 1873

9 Knight of the Most Ancient and Most Noble Order of the Thistle

10 I am indebted to His present Grace for information on this detail.

11 CLL: the armorial bearings of this ducal house are recorded in the Public Register of all Arms and Bearings in Scotland I, f. 50.

12 Garter Stall Plate in St George's Chapel, Windsor Castle

13 CA: Gts. 64.217

14 CLL: Public Register ... Scotland, I, f. 78. For a somewhat better rendering of these armorial bearings (although uneven in execution) see CRC: reverse of Lord Aberdeen's Governor General's medal by Allan Wyon.

15 Ibid. 18, f. 43. For a somewhat better, though not completely accurate, rendering of these armorial bearings, see CRC: reverse of Lord Minto's Governor General's medal by Allan Wyon.

16 CA: Peers VII.53

17 Knight Companion of the Most Noble Order of the Garter

18 Garter Stall Plate, St George's Chapel, Windsor Castle. There is an interesting coloured carving of these armorial bearings on the back of the throne for the Governor General's lady in the Senate Chamber at Ottawa.

19 CA: Peers VIII.203

20 Ibid. 111

21 Knight Grand Commander of the Most Exalted Order of the Star of India

22 Knight Grand Commander of the Most Eminent Order of the Indian Empire

23 Knight Grand Cross of the Most Excellent Order of the British Empire

24 CA: Norfolk 29.110

25 CA: Peers IX.6239. For a particularly fine emblazonment of these armorial bearings by A. Scott Caster, RCA, see the Dominion Drama Award, 1933.

26 CLL: Public Register ... Scotland, 31, f. 60

27 CA: I 76.166

28 CA: Gts. 109.86. For a bilingual armorial certificate by York Herald of Arms, for Lord Alexander's armorial bearings as Prior of the Priory of Canada of the Most Venerable Order of the Hospital of St John of Jerusalem see the exemplification preserved at St John's House, Ottawa.

29 Companion of Honour

30 On 11 December 1963 an honourable augmentation to the armorial bearings of Mr Massey was made by HM The Queen and comprised *a canton azure, charged with the crest of Canada, videlicet, on a wreath argent and gules, a lion passant guardant or, royally crowned proper holding in its dexter forepaw a maple leaf gules.*

31 CA: Gts. 94.64. For a bilingual armorial certificate similar to that for Lord Alexander (see note 28 above) see the exemplification preserved at St John's House, Ottawa.

32 Companion of the Distinguished Service Order

33 Military Cross

34 CA: Gts. 123.248. For an armorial bilingual certificate similar to that for Lord Alexander (see note 28 above) see the exemplification preserved at St John's House, Ottawa.

35 Companion of the Order of Canada

36 For a discussion of these supporters and their significance in Canadian heraldry see Conrad Swan (York Herald of Arms), 'Precursive Grant,' *Heraldry in Canada* 3 (June 1969) pp. 2-4.

37 CA: 131.191. For a bilingual armorial certificate similar to that for Lord Alexander (see note 28 above) see the exemplification preserved at St John's House, Ottawa.

Arms and seals of Spain and of Russia

We have already noted in chapter 12 how Spain in the late eighteenth century and Russia in the early years of the nineteenth century extended their authority into what we now know as British Columbia. The purpose of this appendix is to describe the armorial and sigillographic expressions of the authority of those two powers when exercised in that area.

SPAIN
ENSIGNS ARMORIAL

Charles IV (1788-1808) was King of Spain at the time of the Nootka settlement by his subjects. His arms of dominion and sovereignty were as follows: *quarterly, 1 and 4, gules, a castle or* (Castile); *2 and 3, argent, a lion rampant gules* (sometimes represented as *purpure*) *crowned or* (Leon), *enté en point argent, a pomegranate gules, seeded and slipped proper* (Granada). In this form the arms date from 1217, when Ferdinand III, King of Leon *jure patris*, succeeded to Castile *jure matris*. As his mother's dominions were the more ancient of the two, her ensigns were marshalled before those of his father. The silver division in base charged with a pomegranate for Granada was added later. The pun involved in each of these arms is obvious, including the pomegranate — *pomum granatum*, the apple of Granada.

Over the arms just described there is frequently placed an inescutcheon of *France Modern*. These were introduced to the Arms of Spain when the grandson of Louis XIV of France succeeded to the Spanish throne as Philip V in 1713 [plate 7].

At times the arms described above are added as an inescutcheon to a considerable number of quarterings, as follows:

1/ (first row) *or, four pallets gules* (Arragon)
2/ *per saltire, the chief and base paly or and gules, the flanks argent, charged with an eagle displayed sable* (Sicily)
3/ *gules, a fesse argent* (Austria)
4/ *azure, semy of fleurs-de-lis or, a bordure compony argent and gules* (Burgundy)
5/ (second row on dexter side of inescutcheon) *or, six fleurs-de-lis 3, 2, and 1 azure* (Parma)
6/ (on sinister side of inescutcheon) *or, five balls gules, in chief another azure, charged with three fleurs-de-lis* (Tuscany)
7/ (third row) *bendy or and azure, a bordure gules* (Burgundy, ancient)
8/ *or, a lion rampant sable* (Flanders)
9/ *argent, an eagle displayed gules, crowned the Sachsen or* (Tyrol)
10/ *sable, a lion rampant or* (Brabant)

It will be appreciated that almost all of these quarterings came to be added to the Spanish Armorial Achievement with the advent of the Hapsburgs to the throne of Spain.

A royal crown consisting of four pearl-encrusted complete arches (one wholly and three partly visible in representations) ensigns the arms, which are as often as not displayed on an oval cartouche. The principal order of Spain, the Golden Fleece, frequently surrounds the arms. The headship of this order, founded in 1429 by Philip the Good, Duke of Burgundy, passed to the Hapsburgs and was brought to Spain by them. The collar of the order consists of a repeated device of two steels striking upon a flint, causing sparks to flash out on either side. From the centre of the collar depends the badge, which consists of the Golden Fleece.

SEAL

The Great Seal of Charles IV [C1], effective during the greater part of the Spanish occupation of Nootka, was taken into use in 1790. It was double-sided, with a profile effigy bust of the king on the obverse. He is shown, facing the viewer's right, wearing a wig of the period with uniform coat, breast-plate, gorget, sash, and badge of the Order of the Golden Fleece suspended from his neck by a riband. The composition is finished off in a customary manner of the period with his cloak and mantle folded round the lower part of the effigy. Starting at the left, near the king's upper arm, and following the upper circumference, the legend reads: CAROLUS · IV · D · G · HISPANIARUM · REX · (Charles IV, by the Grace of God, King of the Spains). A plain circular edging completes this side of the seal.

The reverse shows the totality of quarters described above, arranged on an oval shield and hatched, in part. The shield is ensigned by a royal crown consisting of pearl-encrusted arches (one wholly visible and three partly so) which rise to a small orb and

C1 Obverse and reverse of the Great Seal of Charles IV of Spain
AHN (see note 1)

cross where the arches meet. The latter rise from strawberry leaves mounted on a jewelled circlet; between the strawberry leaves are pearls on short spikes. On either side of the crown are ribands. The shield is surrounded by the collar of the Order of the Golden Fleece, from which depends the badge of that order. The whole design is contained within a moulded frame which constitutes the outer edge of the seal. The diameter is $3^7/16$ inches (88 millimetres).[1]

Of the seals used by Charles IV of Spain, one of particular interest in the history of British Columbia is his privy seal [c2] applied to the convention dated 28 October 1790 between Great Britain and Spain, whereby he agreed to withdraw his subjects from Nootka.[2] This impression is on wax applied directly to the document. The design consists of the complete scheme of quarterings and inescutcheons as on the great seal described above. The main shield is oval and ensigned by a royal crown, as before; however, on this privy seal, in addition to the collar of the Order of the Golden Fleece, those of two further unidentified orders also surround the oval shield. The inscription round the edge of the seal is obscured except for the word REX at the upper left. It probably read CAROLUS IV · D · G · HISPANIARUM · · REX, as on the privy seal, impressed through paper, used for ratifying the treaty between Great Britain and Spain dated 25 May 1793.[3] The diameter of the privy seal on the 1790 convention is 1 inch (25 millimetres).

No seals particular to the Nootka Settlement as such have been located so far.

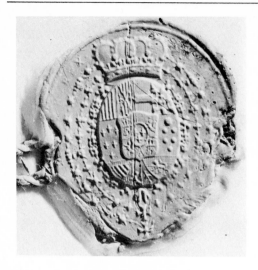

C2 Privy seal of Charles V of Spain
PRO (see note 2) Crown copyright

C3 Great Seal of Alexander I of Russia, 1801-25
PRO (see note 5) Crown copyright

RUSSIA
ENSIGNS ARMORIAL

Under Tsar Alexander I (1801-25), Russia asserted her sovereignty from Alaska down the coast of what we now know as British Columbia to the northern tip of Vancouver Island.

The armorial expression of this authority [plate 8] is displayed on and about a double-headed black eagle supporter with red beaks, legs, and claws. The shield on the breast of the eagle is known in heraldry by the word *Moscow,* and may be blazoned: *gules, the mounted effigy of St George slaying the dragon all proper.* In some representations this design faces to the dexter and in others to the sinister.

We find this shield developing at the turn of the fourteenth and fifteenth centuries, on the seal of the Grand Duke of Moscow, Basil III (1389-1425). Within half a century the conception of Moscow as the third Rome, as the successor of Byzantium, had developed; this is reflected in the appearance of the imperial ensigns of Byzantium – the double-headed eagle – amid those of the Grand Dukes of Moscow who were soon to be Caesars or Tsars of all the Russias.

By the time of Boris Godunov (1598-1606), the armorial bearings of the Tsars reached their basic form, save for the seventeenth-century additions of the orb and sceptre in the eagle's talons.

The crowns on the heads of the eagle and that ensigning the complete achievement are of a form peculiar to Russia. This type of crown and those of the bishops of the Greek and allied rites have a common ancestor in the crowns of the Emperors of

Byzantium which came to Russia from Constantinople upon its evangelization in the tenth century following the conversion of St Vladimir, Prince of Kiev.

The collar about the necks of the eagle and falling down beneath the shield of *Moscow* is that of the Order of St Andrew founded by Peter the Great in 1698. The badge of the order, which depends from the collar, consists of the double-headed and crowned eagle upon the breast of which is an effigy of St Andrew being martyred on a blue cross; at the extremity of the four arms are inscribed the letters SAPR (Sanctus Andreas Patronus Russiae). The collar consists of a series of double-headed eagles each bearing a shield of *Moscow* on its breast, a blue St Andrew's cross charged on red rays, also inscribed SAPR, and a military trophy, placed in alternate series.

Sometimes on the wings of the supporter eagle shields of arms of various parts of the Tsar's dominions are displayed. On the dexter wing are placed:

1/ *argent, a dragon sable, winged gules, crowned or* (Kazan)
2/ *gules, an eagle displayed argent, crowned or* (Poland)
3/ *or, a double-headed eagle displayed sable, charged on its breast with a shield: azure, a cross triple-traversed within a bordure or* (Tauria)
4/ *tierced in pairle: i azure, a representation of St Michael the Archangel vested and winged proper, about his head a nimbus or, his dexter hand holding a sword erect wavy and on his sinister arm a shield all proper* (Kiev): *ii argent, between two bears rampant respectant sable, upon a throne the back of which terminates in a candelabra of three branches each holding a candle enflamed a sceptre and a cross in saltire all proper, a terrace in base azure, charged with two fish naiant respectant in fesse also argent* (Novgorod): *iii gules, a lion rampant guardant or, crowned supporting a cross botonny argent* (Vladimir)

On the sinister wing are placed:

1/ *azure, in chief a Russian imperial crown in base a scimitar fessways proper* (Astrakan)
2/ *ermine, two arrows in saltire and a bow in fess gules, overall two martins (or sables) counter rampant supporting a Russian imperial crown all proper* (Siberia)
3/ quarterly: Kabarda, Ineria, Kurtalinia, and Armenia, enté en point Cirassia, overall Georgia, or else (in small reproductions) Georgia alone, *videlicet, or, a representation of St George proper mounted on a horse sable, slaying a dragon also sable, winged vert*
4/ *gules, semy of roses argent, a lion rampant crowned or, brandishing a sword in the dexter paw and in the sinister the scabbard proper* (Finland).[4]

SEAL

The Great Seal of Alexander I [c3] was single-sided. The design consists of the imperial double-headed eagle bearing on its breast a shield of *Moscow* in which St George and his mount face to the sinister. About the neck of the eagle supporter and down on either side and below the shield is placed the collar of the Order of St Andrew. A sceptre and orb are held by the eagle's dexter and sinister talons respectively. The whole composition is ensigned by an imperial Russian crown, and the heads of the eagle are similarly crowned.

On a band which surrounds this design are placed six shields of arms. Starting at the upper right, they are those of Vladimir, Kazan, and Siberia; and starting at the upper

C4 Seal of the Russian American Company
HBC (see note 6)

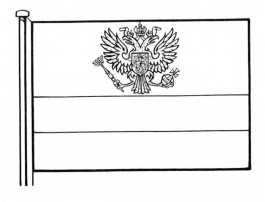

C5 Flag of the Russian American Company

left they are Kiev, Novgorod, and Astrakan — all of which are blazoned above in the description of the complete achievement of the imperial arms. Those of Vladimir, Kiev, and Novgorod are ensigned by royal crowns of a Western European design (two complete arches); the remainder are ensigned by antique crowns. Intertwined among these shields of arms is a delicate garland of flowers, which may be roses.

The legend is engraved on a riband which follows the circumference. Starting at the upper right it reads АЛЕКСАНДРЪ · I · БОЖИЕЮМИЛОСТIЮИМПЕРАТОРЪ · И САМОДЕРЖЕЦЪ · ВСЕРОССIИСКИИ · (in transliteration: ALEKSANDR I BOZHIEYU MILOSTIYU IMPERATOR I SAMODERZHETS VSEROSSIYSKIY; that is to say, ALEXANDER I BY GOD'S GRACE ALL-RUSSIAN EMPEROR AND AUTOCRAT). A rope design forms the outer edge of the seal, whose diameter is $5^3/_{10}$ inches (134 millimetres).[5]

The Russian American Company

The Russian American Company of St Petersburg, to describe it by its full name, was established in 1799 by the imperial government as a private company with exclusive commercial trading rights in what we now know as Alaska, and as a foundation for the administration of Russia's North American colonial possessions. While there were differences, there were many similarities between it and the Hudson's Bay Company.

SEAL

The Russian American Company does not appear to have had arms, but it has an official seal [c4]. This consisted of the double-headed eagle upon the breast of which is charged a shield of *Moscow* (hatched in part and with St George facing to the sinister). The collar of the Order of St Andrew is placed around the necks of the eagle and hangs down on either side and beneath the shield. Each head of the eagle is crowned, and the whole device is ensigned with the imperial Russian crown. In the eagle's talons the sceptre and orb are held in the usual manner.

In the exergue is an inscription which in transliteration runs: ROSSIYS · AMERIKANS · KOMPANII PECHAT (Seal of the Russian American Company). The legend, starting at the upper right, reads, in transliteration, POD VYS · EGO IMPERATORS · VELICHES · POKROVITELSTVO (Under the Patronage of His Supreme Imperial Majesty). A simple circle of rope forms the outer edge of the seal, which was applied onto wax placed directly onto the surface of the document. The diameter is $1^1/_{10}$ inches (28 millimetres).[6]

FLAG

The flag of the Russian American Company [c5] was as follows: *per fess argent, and the base per fess azure and gules, in chief a double-headed eagle sable, imperially crowned and ensigned by an imperial crown proper charged on the breast with a shield of* Moscow *the dexter talon holding a sceptre and the sinister an orb or.*[7]

In connection with the preparation of this appendix I am particularly indebted to G.H. Bolsover, OBE, PhD, Director, School of Slavonic and East European Studies, University of London, for his assistance.

NOTES

1 AHN: Sección de Sigilografía − Sello num. 690 − Arm° 3. Caja 48, num. 8 and see *Catalogo de Menendez Pidal* 48/8, no. 407, p. 406.

2 PRO: FO 94/284 (part I)

3 PRO: FO 94/248 (part 2)

4 For further details on the Arms of Imperial Russia see Yelena Ivanovna Kamentseva and Nikolay Vladimirovich Ustzugov, *Русская сфрагистика и гералдика* (Russian Sigillography and Heraldry) (Moscow, State Publishing House 'Higher Education' 1963).

5 PRO: FO 94/222: treaty between Great Britain and Russia, 6/18 July 1812

6 HBC: F29/2, f. 218: seal attached to agreement between the Russian American Company and the Hudson's Bay Company, 22 March 1849

7 M.A. le Gras, *Album des pavillons, guidons, flammes de toutes les puissances maritimes* (Paris, Auguste Bry 1858) p. 59

GLOSSARY OF HERALDIC TERMS

References in parenthesis are to figures in which examples of the terms defined may be found.

ABBREVIATIONS

A arms
C crest
GQ grand quarter

Q quarter(s)
S supporter

ACCOLLÉ side by side – especially of two shields
ACHIEVEMENT the totality of armorial bearings, used in contradistinction to its several parts – arms, crest, helm, mantling, motto, and supporters
ADDORSED back to back
AFFRONTÉ a beast or object placed so as to show its full front to the viewer
ANNULET a ring (B2, A)
ANTIQUE CROWN a coronet from which rise an indefinite number of pyramidal rays – also called an eastern crown (B14, C)

APPAUMÉ of an open hand or gauntlet when showing the palm (B2, A)
ARGENT silver
ARMED concerning claws, horns, talons, and teeth of birds, beasts, and monsters
ARMS strictly speaking applies only to the charges, the design borne on a shield; often freely used when referring to the complete armorial achievement
ATTIRED bearing antlers (B21, S)
ATTIRES antlers of a stag (B17, Q 2 & 3)
AUGMENTATION an honourable addition to armorial insignia (B2, A)
AZURE blue

BAR a narrow horizontal ordinary narrower than a fess (B3, GQ 2, Q 2 & 3)

BARBED having the leaf-like sepals which appear between the petals of the heraldic rose (B21, S)

BARRY division of the field into an even number of horizontal pieces (B10, Q 2 & 3)

BARRY NEBULY an ornamental line reminiscent of stylized clouds used for the division of arms (B18, S)

BARRULET a narrow bar

BARWISE of charges placed horizontally and one above the other

BATON a charge comprising two diagonal lines from dexter chief to sinister base cut short at the ends and not extending to the edge of the shield (B9, Q 2 & 3)

BEND an ordinary formed by two diagonal lines from dexter chief to sinister base (B7, A)

BEND SINISTER, IN following the line of a bend (running from sinister chief to dexter base) (B13, A)

BENDLET the diminutive of the bend

BEZANT a gold roundel (i.e. circular object) supposed to have been derived from Byzantine coins (B10, Q 2 & 3)

BILLET an upright, oblong figure

BILLETY a field semy of Billets (plate 7.1)

BORDURE a band surrounding a shield or division thereof at its outer edge (B10, Q 1 & 4)

CABOSHED of an animal's head affronté, cut off and showing no part of the neck (B12, A)

CANTON a rectangle in dexter chief less than a quarter of the shield (B2, A)

CAP OF MAINTENANCE a cap of crimson velvet lined and turned up ermine, frequently forming the base of the crest (plate 6, C)

CHAPEAU see cap of maintenance (B7, C)

CHARGE any object or figure placed on an heraldic shield or comprising part of an armorial composition

CHEVRON an heraldic ordinary (B1, A)

CHEVRONEL term for two or more chevrons borne on a shield

CHEVRONWISE charges placed so as to follow the line of a chevron (B20, A)

CHIEF an ordinary formed by a horizontal line so as to contain the uppermost part of a shield (B2, A)

CINQUEFOIL a stylized floral form having five petals (B3, Q 3)

COMB a utensil for arranging hair, usually shown in armory as having a double edge (B15, A)

COMPONY a single row of chequers

COUNTERCHANGE reciprocal exchange of tincture for charges when placed on a party of varied field (B18, A)

COMPARTMENT area below the shield (B16)

COUPED cut, cut short evenly (B8, A; B2, A; B9, A)

COURANT running

CRESCENT a charge in the form of a stylized crescent moon (B3, Q 1 & 4)

CREST a device mounted on the helm (not a synonym for arms)

CRINED describing the colour of hair or mane

CROSS OF ST ANDREW a silver or white saltire, or diagonal cross, on a blue field or background

CROSS OF ST GEORGE a plain red cross extending to the edges of a shield the field or background of which is silver or white

CROSS OF ST PATRICK a red saltire, or diagonal cross, on a silver or white field or background

CROSS PATY having the limbs splayed and with straight ends

CROWN see antique crown, mural crown, naval crown

DEMI halved (the upper or front half) (B21, C)

DEXTER right-hand side of shield from the point of view of the person behind it, and so the left-hand side to the viewer

DIFFERENCE to add to or vary pre-existing arms so as to achieve distinctiveness for one reason or another

DISPLAYED with the wings expanded (B3, GQ 2, Q 1 & 4)

DOUBLED lined with a particular tincture, of mantling

DUCAL CORONET a coronet of four strawberry leaves (three visible), not to be confused with the coronet of a duke (B15, C)

DUCALLY CROWNED crowned with the preceding (B10, S)

DUCALLY GORGED see gorged

EASTERN CROWN see antique crown

ELECTORAL BONNET a cap of crimson velvet with a gold tassel in the centre of its crown, turned up ermine, to be seen ensigning the inescutcheon of Hanover in the royal arms of general purpose, 1801-16 (plate 12)

ELEVATED raised, of wings of birds, etc. (B1, S)

EMBOWED bent, curved (B9, C)

ENGLAND the royal arms of England from the reign of Richard I (1189-99): *gules, three lions passant guardant in pale or* (plate 9)

ENGRAILED of ornamental line dividing a shield into parts or outlining a figure on a shield, comprising repeated semi-circles with points outwards (B10, Q 1 & 4)

ENSIGNED having insignia, e.g. a crown or coronet placed above it (B1)

ENTÉ EN POINT a chevronlike division at the base of a shield (for Granada in plate 7)

ERASED torn off and leaving a ragged edge (B1, A)

ERMINE fur with black tails on white (B6, Q 2 & 3)

ERMINE SPOT tail of an ermine used as a charge (B14, C)

ESCROL a ribbon or scroll, especially for bearing a motto

EXTENDED stretched out (B7, C)

FESS an ordinary comprising a broad band placed horizontally across a shield and occupying about one third of the total area (B16, A)

FESS, IN occupying the position of a fess

FESSEWISE horizontal (B17, Q 2 & 3)

FIELD the background or surface of a shield and the like upon which the armorial design is shown

FLORY COUNTER-FLORY decorated with fleurs-de-lis on each side

FRANCE MODERN the royal arms of France from c.1375: *azure, three fleurs-de-lis or* (3.1)

FRUCTED bearing fruit (B1, S)

FUSIL a diamond-shaped figure narrow in its minor axis (B14, Q 2 & 3)

GALLEY an ancient ship for both sailing and rowing, shown with one mast unless otherwise blazoned (B5, Q 2 & 3)

GARB a sheaf of cereal/grain

GORGED encircled round the neck or throat (B3, S)

GORGED, DUCALLY the neck or throat encircled by a ducal coronet (q.v.) (B7, S)

GRAND QUARTER see quarters, grand

GRIFFIN an heraldic monster comprising head, breast, wings, and forelegs like those of an eagle with the hindquarters and tail of a lion; also having ears (B7, S)

GUARDANT of a beast with its head turned so as to face the viewer (B11, C)

GULES red

GYRONNY of a shield, divided into a number of triangular pieces radiating from the middle point (B5, Q 1 & 4)

HANOVER the royal and electoral arms of Hanover (3.12, Q 4)

HATCHED with tinctures indicated by means of lines at different angles, dots, and plain surface

HAURIENT of a fish, placed vertically with head upwards

HELM protective metal armour for head and neck to the crown of which the crest (q.v.) is secured

HERALDIC TYGER *see* tyger, heraldic

IMPALING of two Coats of Arms marshalled on one shield on either side of a central vertical line (3.11, Q 1 & 4)

INDENTED of ornamental line dividing a shield into parts or outlining a figure on a shield, comprising a series of small triangular peaks

INESCUTCHEON a small shield

IRELAND the royal arms of Ireland: *azure, a harp or, stringed argent* (plate 10, Q 3)

ISSUANT proceeding out or from

JESSED with thongs attached to the legs, of a falcon

LABEL a riband or narrow band from which depend usually three or five ribands (B5, A)

LANGUED concerning the colour of the tongue of a creature (B1, S)

LIVERIES frequently the principal metal and colour of the arms which are taken to be the colours of the person or authority concerned; in particular instances, however, livery colours can be otherwise

LOZENGE a diamond-shaped figure (B19, A)

LYMPHAD *see* galley

MANTLING a piece of material which hangs from the helm

MARTLET an heraldic swallow-bird represented as having feather tufts at the ends of its legs but no feet (B3, GQ 2 & 3)

MASCLE a voided lozenge (B3, Q 1 & 4)

MOSCOW the imperial arms of Russia from the reign of Basil III (1389-1425), Grand Duke of Moscow: *gules, the mounted effigy of St George slaying the dragon all proper* (plate 8)

MULLET five-pointed star (B3, Q 1 & 4)

MURAL CROWN a crown in the form of an embattled wall

NAIANT swimming

NAVAL CROWN a circlet upon which are mounted alternately the stems and sails of ships

OR gold

ORDINARY one of the earliest forms of heraldic device; geometric shapes such as the chevron, chief, pale, fess, bend, plain cross throughout, etc.

PALE an ordinary formed by two vertical lines containing the central part of a shield

PALE, CANADIAN a pale occupying about one half (rather than the more usual one third) of the total width of the design (plate 22.1)

PALE, IN of a number of objects as occupying the position of a pale, as in the arms of England (plate 9, Q 2 & 3)

PALE, PER the division of a shield or charge by a central vertical line and with different tinctures on either side (B18, A)

PALL a figure resembling the letter Y

PALLET two or more narrow vertical stripes (B14, Q 2 & 3)

PALY a design comprising an equal number of vertical stripes or pallets coloured alternately (B20, A)

PALY BENDY SINISTER divided paly and bendy sinister (B17, Q 2 & 3)

PASSANT walking, of a beast (B3, Q 3)

PEGASUS a winged horse (B6, S)

PHEON barbed head of an arrow engrailed on the inner side of the barbs (9.7)

PIERCED with a round hole in the centre showing the field or some other tincture (B3, Q 3)

PILE a wedge-shaped figure which(unless otherwise blazoned) issues from the chief (B2, A)

PLATE a silver roundel (B21, C)

PROPER in natural or normal colours

PURFLED bordered, guarded, or lined with fur; if applied to armour, it signifies garnished, usually with gold

PURPURE purple

QUARTERLY the subdivision of a shield into four or more divisions

QUARTERS four or more subdivisions of a shield

QUARTERS, GRAND a quarter which is itself quartered

RAMPANT of a beast, with one hind paw on the ground, and the other three raised, the tail erect with the beast looking to its front (B13, A)

REGUARDANT of a charge, with the head turned so as to look backwards over the shoulder (B15, S)

ROUNDEL a flat, circular object

ROYAL LION (supporter) a differenced version of the dexter supporter of the royal arms of general purpose from 1603 (B11, S)

ROYAL UNICORN (supporter) a differenced version of the sinister supporter of the royal arms of general purpose from 1603 (B11, S)

SABLE black

SALTIRE a diagonal cross in the form of an X (B6, Q 2 & 3)

SALTIRE, IN assuming the form of a saltire (B15, C)

SALTIRE, PER following the line of a saltire

SAXONY the royal arms of Saxony: *barry often or and sable, a crown of rue in bend vert* (B11, A)

SCOTLAND the royal arms of Scotland: *or, a lion rampant within a double tressure flory counter-flory gules* (plate 5, Q 1 & 4)

SEEDED of flowers, bearing seed vessels (B21, S)

SEJANT seated

SEMY strewn with any charge, as in 'semy-de-lis,' strewn with fleurs-de-lis

SINISTER left-hand side of shield from the point of view of person behind it, and so the right-hand side to the viewer

SLIPPED of a flower, leaf, or twig when it has the stem by which it was attached to parent stem or plant

STATANT of a beast, standing, e.g. of a lion having all four paws on the ground and facing to the dexter unless otherwise stated

SUPPORTERS figures on either side of a shield supporting or guarding it

SURMOUNTED of a charge, having another charge placed over it

TIERCED divided into three parts, e.g. 'tierced in fess,' as in the arms of Canada (plate 14)

TIERCED IN PAIRLE parted per pall (q.v.)

TIERCED IN PAIRLE REVERSED parted per pall (q.v.) reversed (plate 13.1, inescutcheon)

TINCTURES the two metals (or and argent), seven colours (azure, gules, sable, vert, purpure, tenné [orange], murrey or sanguine [reddish purple]), and two furs of the ermine and vair patterns

TORSE a crest wreath represented as a twisted ribbon of two tinctures (unless otherwise specified) placed at the point where the crest is joined to the helm

TORTEAU a red roundel (B21, S)

TREFOIL a stylized leaf with three lobes, usually slipped (B2, A)

TRESSURE a narrow band inset from the edge of the shield, usually double (B8, A)

TRICK a method of indicating the tinctures by means of abbreviations, as, for example: a. or ar. (argent); b. (i.e. blue) or rarely, az. (this can be confused with ar. [argent]); g. or gu. (gules); o. or often written in full (or); v. or vt. (vert); purp. (purpure); ppr. (proper); s. or sa. (sable) (7.1; 10.1)

TYGER, HERALDIC an heraldic monster having the body, limbs, mane, and tail of a lion, and the head of a wolf, but with the upper jaw terminating in a frontal horn (B3, S)

UNDY wavy (q.v.)

UNGULED of an animal having hoofs (B21, S)

UNICORN heraldic creature with the head and body of a horse, one long horn projecting from the forehead, cloven hoofs, a lion's tail, tufted hocks, and a beard

VAIR an heraldic fur with white and blue (unless otherwise specified) pieces which represent the belly and back skins of the grey squirrel

VERT green

VESTED clothed

VOLANT flying

WAVY undulating, of a line dividing a shield into parts or outlining a figure placed on a shield

WREATH (crest) see torse

CREDITS

3.12, 13   Royal Ontario Museum, Toronto

3.15, 16   By courtesy of the Gentleman Usher of the Black Rod, The Senate of Canada

3.14, 17   By permission of the Speaker of the Legislative Assembly, New Brunswick; photographs by the New Brunswick Information Service

4.2; 5.4; 6.7 (obv.), 11, 12, 14; 7.6, 7; 8.5; 9.6; 10.7, 8   Reproduced by permission of the British Library

4.3, 4, 5; 5.6, 7, 8; 6.7 (rev.), 8; 7.3 (obv.), 8, 9, 10; 8.1; 10.2 (obv.); C2, 3   Crown copyright, reproduced with the permission of the Controller of Her Majesty's Stationery Office

4.6   Illustration included by kind permission of the Deputy Minister of Consumer and Corporate Affairs and Deputy Registrar General of Canada; photograph by courtesy of the National Film Board

5.1   College of Arms, London

5.2   Courtesy of the Newfoundland Provincial Archives

5.3, 5; 6.13; 9.5; 10.9; 11.1 (a)   By courtesy of the Trustees of the British Museum

6.2   Les Archives des Ursulines de Québec

6.3, 4, 5, 6, 9, 16, 17, 18   Archives nationales du Québec, collection Initiale

6.10 (obv.); 7.4 (obv.); 8.3, 4; 9.2 (obv.); 10.4 (obv.), 5 (obv.); 11.1 (b)   Fuller Collection, University of London Library

8.2   Government of Prince Edward Island

9.1, 3, 4, 7, 8   Reproduced by permission of the Provincial Archives of New Brunswick

9.2 (rev.)   Reproduced with permission from the Legislative Library of New Brunswick

10.2 (rev.), 3, 4 (rev.), 5 (rev.), 6, 11, 12, 13, 14; B4   Public Archives of Ontario

11.2   Provincial Archives of British Columbia

12.1, 2, 3   Provincial Archives of Manitoba

15.1, 2, 3; C4   Hudson's Bay Company

15.4   Archives of Saskatchewan

B21-23   By kind permission of the Right Honble Roland Michener, CC

B24   By kind permission of His Excellency the Governor General

C1   Archivo Histórico Nacional de Madrid

INDEX

Bold figures refer to illustrations (page or plate number).

This book
was designed by
WILLIAM RUETER
with the assistance of
ANTHONY CHIUMENTO
and was printed by
University of Toronto Press
and bound by
The Bryant Press
Limited